TRENDING TOWARD
#JUSTICE

Also by Kenneth Jost

The Harvard Strike
(co-authored with Lawrence E. Eichel,
Robert D. Luskin, and Richard M. Neustadt

Supreme Court Yearbook
(annual series)

The Supreme Court A to Z
(5th ed., 2012)

The New York Times on the Supreme Court

TRENDING TOWARD
#JUSTICE

December 2015

To Jeff Trammell

With liberty & justice for all.

Kenneth Jost

KENNETH JOST

To James
Still special
After all these years

"Look at the facts of the world. You see a continual and progressive triumph of the right. I do not pretend to understand the moral universe, the arc is a long one, and my eye reaches but little ways. I cannot calculate the curve and complete the figure by the experience of sight; I can divine it by conscience. But from what I see I am sure it bends towards justice."

—Theodore Parker (abolitionist minister), 1857

"The arc of the moral universe is long, but it bends toward justice."

—Martin Luther King, Jr., various occasions

Contents

#Preface

The German military theorist Carl von Clausewitz famously observed that war is "the continuation of politics by other means." In the 21st century United States, law has been the continuation of politics by other means, perhaps more so than at any previous time in American history.

Major political disputes over such issues as the president's authority as commander in chief, the separation of powers between Congress and the president, and civil rights for gays and lesbians have all come to a head not in legislative bodies, but in courts.

Courts have long played an outsized role in the United States. As early as the 1830s, the French visitor Alexis de Tocqueville aptly observed, "There is hardly a political question in the United States that does not sooner or later turn into a judicial one."

The conflicts of the early 21st century differ to some extent in the degree to which legal arguments divide cleanly along partisan lines between the two major political parties. It was not always this way. When I came of age in the 1960s, Republicans and Democrats could be found on both sides of the decade's two major issues: the Vietnam War and the civil rights revolution.

In Washington for the past 25 years, I have watched partisan lines sharpen on major issues not only among politicians but also among judges. The Supreme Court perhaps set the tone for the 21st century by deciding the presidential election of 2000 along starkly partisan lines.

In *Bush v. Gore*, five Republican-appointed justices awarded the presidency to Republican nominee George W. Bush. The ruling cut off a recount in the pivotal state of Florida that could have – we will never know – ended with a victory for Democrat Al Gore. The dissenters were two Democratic appointees and two Republican-appointed justices who had evolved on the bench into moderate liberals.

In office, Bush won bipartisan approval for his response to al Qaeda's September 11, 2001, terrorist attacks on the United States. But he squandered his political capital by trampling on the Constitution and international law in the name of an ostentatiously proclaimed "War on Terror." Democrats helped stoke growing criticism of the administration's policies of targeting Muslim Americans and immigrants at home and holding suspected foreign terrorists offshore at the U.S. naval base at Guantánamo Bay, Cuba.

Bush had bipartisan though not unanimous support at the start of the Iraq War in March 2003. Partisan divisions increased, however, as it became clear that the administration had executed a preconceived plan to take on Saddam Hussein on the basis of misread intelligence and misleading arguments.

By 2003, the administration's counterterrorism policies were also being litigated in court. In a succession of decisions, the Supreme Court rejected the administration's efforts to avoid judicial review of its treatment of suspected U.S. citizen or foreign terrorists despite the court's Republican-appointed majority.

With Democrat Barack Obama in the White House, the parties' views of presidential and federal powers shifted. Obama staked his legacy on enacting legislation to increase access to health care. Republicans did all they could to block the Affordable Care Act in Congress; once it was enacted, Republicans went straight to court to challenge what they derisively labeled "Obamacare."

With the Bush-appointed chief justice John G. Roberts Jr. casting the pivotal vote, the Supreme Court narrowly upheld the law's major provisions in June 2012. The other eight justices divided precisely along party lines with four Republican appointees voting to strike down the entire law and four Democratic appointees voting to uphold the major provisions.

Republicans and conservative advocacy and interest groups brought additional legal challenges that remained pending more than two years later. Obama's opponents also continued to accuse the administration of abusing its powers by making regulatory tweaks along the way.

Meanwhile, the two parties also divided on two major civil rights issues: racial justice for African Americans and Latinos and marriage rights for gays and lesbians. Republicans and Democrats began diverging on race-related issues as early as the 1970s, but the dividing lines became very sharp by the early 2000s.

At the Supreme Court, Justice Sandra Day O'Connor, a Republican appointee, joined with liberal justices in 2003 in a decision that reaffirmed the limited use of racial preferences in public universities' admissions policies to achieve campus diversity. But Bush's appointment of conservative justice Samuel A. Alito Jr. seemed to tilt the balance toward greater skepticism of racial preferences.

As for gay rights, Democrats gradually came to embrace LGBT equality beginning in the 1990s. The slow evolution culminated in President Obama's decision to endorse marriage rights for same-sex couples in May 2012 as he prepared to stand for re-election.

At their national conventions, the two parties adopted platforms with diametrically opposed positions. Democrats favored marriage rights for gay and lesbian couples; Republicans favored what they called "traditional marriage"—one man, one woman. Obama won; at the same time, gay marriage supporters won four statewide referenda on the issue, their first ballot-box victories after more than two dozen defeats.

Republicans have continued to oppose marriage equality even as federal and state courts have shifted. The shift began with the Supreme Court's decision in 2013 to strike down the so-called Defense of Marriage Act (DOMA), which barred federal marriage-based benefits to same-sex couples even if legally wed in their state.

With all but complete unanimity, courts read Justice Anthony M. Kennedy's opinion in *United States v. Windsor* as precedent for striking down the state-enacted marriage bans for same-sex couples. The state cases were being teed up for the high court to hear in its 2014 term and to decide by June 2015.

The Supreme Court confirmation process also became intensely political in the 21st century. All four 21st century justices won confirmation on divided votes: Roberts, Alito, and Obama's two appointees: Sonia Sotomayor and Elena Kagan. Political fights over lower court judgeships indicate that Supreme Court nominations are likely to continue as political battlegrounds for the foreseeable future.

Legal purists may shake their heads over the politicization of the courts, but similar partisan disputes go back as far as John Adams and Thomas Jefferson. In the United States of the 21st century, politics does not stop at the courthouse door – if it ever did. Still, the arc of the law in the United States has trended toward justice, however fitfully and unevenly. Those advances have been hard-won, but with courage and resolve among Americans of conscience and good will there will be more to come.

#Prologue

My career in journalism dates back to my school days in my home town of Nashville, Tennessee. I was editor of my junior high school newspaper, The Bailey Bombardier, *and for two years editor of* The Paw Print, *the student newspaper at what was then Peabody Demonstration School (now, University School of Nashville). As editor, I wrote a column calling for racial integration at the school; the administration spiked the editorial, but later allowed it to be printed after I had written a separate column criticizing the censorship.*

In college, I was a reporter, producer, managing editor, and news director of the student radio station WHRB. Among other assignments, I was the studio anchor for WHRB's coverage of the student strike in spring 1969. When police arrested all but one of the station's reporters who had been covering the radicals' seizure of University Hall, I was left mostly on my own to inform the Cambridge community of the tumultuous events. Recalling that experience, I am always sympathetic when broadcast anchors have to fill with nothing new to report.

From college, I went back to Nashville as a reporter at what was then called The Nashville Tennessean *(now, simply* The Tennessean*). After six years there, most of the time as reporter and columnist on the court beat, I took a sabbatical from journalism to work as legislative assistant and press secretary to Al Gore, a college classmate and a colleague from the* Tennessean *newsroom. While working on Capitol Hill, I took the opportunity to attend Georgetown Law School at night, but with the intention of returning to journalism in due course.*

My opportunity to return to journalism came in the form of an offer to be editor of The Los Angeles Daily Journal, *a daily law newspaper with a young staff in need of a strong newsroom leader. I worked hard to improve the newspaper and bring out the best in the newsroom staff and succeeded, but at the expense of inflicting my overzealousness on many reporters and editors who deserved better. Luckily for me, some of them can still recall those years fondly and gratefully.*

Always eager to return to the East Coast, I moved back to Washington and transitioned in 1988 to what was first a string and later a full-time job with Congressional Quarterly. *Eventually, I became a staff writer and later associate editor at* CQ Researcher, *CQ's weekly issue backgrounder service: 24-page reports on major topics in the news. In 1992 I was also invited to take over* Supreme Court Yearbook *when the annual series' first author, Joan Biskupic, left CQ for* The Washington Post. *I combined those two roles for 21 years until 2013 when CQ Press abolished my full-time position at* CQ Researcher, *along with two others, for budget reasons. I now continue as a contributing writer for* CQ Researcher *and as author of* Supreme Court Yearbook.

While at CQ, I wrote a monthly column for CQ Weekly *for five years. When the column was discontinued, for budget reasons, I began my own blog,* Jost on Justice, *and used it as a platform for classic, newspaper-style weekend columns. What follows in this book are some that I especially liked and that I hope will still have some relevance after passage of time. To begin, here are my tributes to two of my journalist heroes who profoundly influenced my career: Anthony Lewis, the* New York Times *columnist, and John Seigenthaler, my editor at the* Tennessean.

A Passionate Voice for Justice

(*Jost on Justice*, April 22, 2013)

Fifty years ago, the U.S. Supreme Court was something of a backwater beat. The regular press corps was so small — half a dozen newspaper and wire service reporters — that they sat between counsel table and the bench, able to stare straight up at the nine justices. Protocol was so relaxed that reporters could use typewriters to take notes.

Things are much different today. The regular press corps is larger: about 30 people have "permanent" press credentials. The press gallery has been moved off to the side of the court's bench, with some seats inside the courtroom, others in cubicles just outside, and obstructed-view hallway seats for an overflow crowd that can number more than 100 for arguments in a major case.

Protocol and security are also tighter. Reporters can bring pen and paper only. In an era of ubiquitous cell phones and BlackBerrys, reporters are admonished strictly to leave all electronic devices in the downstairs press room.

Beyond the visible differences in the arrangements for news media, the coverage of the Supreme Court also has changed dramatically. There is more coverage by more news organizations on more platforms: newspapers and magazines, radio and television, and the web. And the coverage is both more detailed and more insightful, with careful attention to making stories legally precise as well as fully accessible to general audiences.

No single individual deserves more credit for this transformation than Anthony Lewis, who died last month (March 25) two days shy of his 86th birthday after an award-winning journalistic career that spanned six decades. Lewis held the Supreme Court beat for *The New York Times* for less than a decade, 1955-1964, but he established a new standard for coverage by which Supreme Court reporters have been judged ever since.

The *Times*'s obituary, written by Adam Liptak, Lewis's successor four-times-removed, aptly conveys the debt that readers and viewers of Supreme Court coverage today owe to Lewis. Before Lewis, Supreme Court coverage was apt to consist of "pedestrian recitations" of decisions with little by way of context or legal reasoning. The "thorough knowledge" of the court that Lewis gained during a year of study at Harvard Law School as a Nieman fellow changed that. Lewis's articles, Liptak writes, "were virtual tutorials about currents in legal thinking, written with ease and sweep and an ability to render complex matters accessible."

Like countless others, this writer first read Lewis's work — while a teenager — in *Gideon's Trumpet*, Lewis's masterful and celebratory account of the Supreme Court's 1962 decision that required the government to provide lawyers to indigent defendants in criminal cases. By the time the book was published, in 1964, Lewis had already won his two Pulitzer prizes. The first, in 1955, was for stories helping to clear a Navy employee wrongly accused of disloyalty during the McCarthy era. The second, in 1963, was for his coverage of the Supreme Court, especially of its epochal decisions on reapportionment and redistricting.

Lewis left the Supreme Court beat in 1964, but he did not leave behind his knowledge of law or his passion for justice. After a few years in the London bureau, Lewis started a 32-year career in 1969 as a *Times* columnist under the rotating titles "At Home Abroad" or "Abroad at Home."

Whether writing about events in the United States or in foreign countries, Lewis constantly returned to stories of people who had been wronged by misuse of law or cast aside by virtue of its neglect. In a tribute in *The New York Review* (May 9), Georgetown law professor and immigrant rights' advocate David Cole recalled Lewis's recurrent columns on the harsh strictures of immigration law and immigration court decisions.

The tributes to Lewis that began with his death continued in Washington last week [April 18] as the Constitution Project bestowed on him and three others its constitutional champions award for their work on *Gideon* and its legacy. Accepting the award on his behalf, his widow, Margaret Marshall, the former chief justice of the Massachusetts Supreme Judicial Court, recalled Lewis's devotion to the U.S. Constitution.

"Tony loved the Constitution of the United States," Marshall said. "He lived the Constitution. He taught the Constitution. He believed in the Constitution. He wrote about the Constitution over and over and over and over." In Lewis's view, Marshall continued, the greatness of the United States — what conservatives might call "American exceptionalism" — "lies in our willingness to accept the Constitution, as interpreted by judges, as law."

Lewis retired the column on December 15, 2001. With the 9/11 attacks fresh in mind, Lewis reaffirmed his belief in the rule of law. "Without the foundation of law, this vast country could never have survived as one, could never have absorbed streams of immigrants from myriad cultures," Lewis wrote. "With one terrible exception, the Civil War, law and the Constitution have kept America whole and free."

Lewis cautioned, however, that the rule of law is not self-executing. "Freedom under law is hard work," he concluded. "If rulers cannot be trusted with arbitrary power, it is up to citizens to raise their voices at injustice." Lewis raised his voice at injustice, eloquently and passionately, over more than half a century of turbulent times at home and abroad. His voice is now silenced, but his legacy lives on in the work of those — like myself — whom he educated and inspired.

A Search for Justice
(Jost on Justice, July 20, 2014)

John Seigenthaler put me behind bars barely a year after I started working for him as a reporter at was then called *The Nashville Tennessean.* It was not the kind of assignment I had anticipated when I started out in journalism in my hometown after graduating from Harvard in 1970. But after one day in the Nashville-Davidson County jail and three days in the county workhouse, I turned out a creditable series detailing the somewhat squalid conditions in the two facilities.

Seigenthaler, who died earlier this month [July 11] at age 86 after a storied career as editor and publisher at what is now simply *The Tennessean,* loved the undercover reporter technique of getting at hard-to-get stories. A few years earlier, he had sent John Hemphill, later an editor at *The New York Times,* to do the jail and workhouse story. Other undercover stories he assigned included exposes of conditions in nursing homes (Nat Caldwell, a Pulitzer Prize winner), the state's major mental hospital (Frank Sutherland, later editor in Nashville himself), and, most daringly, the Ku Klux Klan – infiltrated for nearly a year by Jerry Thompson, a good old boy who could pass as a redneck racist despite a heart of gold.

Modern day journalism ethicists disapprove of the undercover technique; deception, they say, is incompatible with the truth-telling mission of the true journalism. But Seig—as he was known to his staff and countless friends— was a newspaperman of the old school. As a cub reporter in the early 1950s, he earned his stripes by talking a would-be suicide off what was then the Shelby Street Bridge (now renamed the Seigenthaler Bridge in his honor). He won a National Headliner award for his story of tracking down a business executive and his wife who had faked their deaths to collect insurance money.

Later, Seig uncovered corruption in Teamsters union locals in Tennessee, stories that led to the impeachment of a bribe-taking state court judge and eventually to the jury tampering trial of Teamsters president James Hoffa. The Teamsters stories brought him to the attention of the young Robert F. Kennedy, then counsel to a Senate investigating committee. Seig edited RFK's book *The Enemy Within*, cementing a relationship that put him inside the Kennedy circle for life and took him to Washington to work for Kennedy at the Justice Department for a year.

As Kennedy's right-hand man, Seigenthaler was dispatched to Montgomery, Ala., in May 1961 to try to protect the group of Freedom Riders traveling from Nashville to Alabama to claim their rights to desegregated interstate transportation. A white mob blocked the buses and beat many of the riders; one in the crowd used a lead pipe to smash Seigenthaler's skull. He lay unconscious at the scene for 45 minutes, according to the accounts, and spent 10 days in a hospital.

Seigenthaler was remembered in the *Tennessean*'s obituary as "a fierce advocate for racial equality"—and so he was, but not from birth. He grew up unaware of the racial segregation that the family's black maid lived with when she left their home.

After becoming editor of the *Tennessean* in 1962, however, Seigenthaler put the paper's news and editorial columns behind the civil rights revolution. He hired the first black reporter in the newsroom, W. A. (Bill) Reed. As religion editor, Reed's assignments included the weekly Monday story "A Reporter Goes to Church." When the influential pastor of one of the city's biggest churches objected to being covered by a black reporter, Seigenthaler told him that Bill was the paper's religion reporter. Period.

Less visibly but just as sincerely, Seig later became a strong supporter of LGBT equality. Without fanfare, he supported and protected gay reporters in the newsrooms of the '70s and '80s from any unenlightened attitudes from inside or outside the newspaper. After he retired, he funded the National Lesbian and Gay Journalism Association's awards for radio and TV coverage of LGBT issues. And in 2004 he was the moderator of what was described as Nashville's first public forum on LGBT issues, cosponsored by the Human Rights Campaign and American Civil Liberties Union.

After putting me on the court beat in fall 1971, Seigenthaler gave me valuable pointers and backed me up whenever I needed it in my often critical coverage of the bar and the judiciary. Forty years later, I am still covering the courts, and I still share the disappointment that Seigenthaler often voiced that the bench and bar so often fail to deliver justice, especially to racial and ethnic minorities and the poor.

Not long after my jail story, Seigenthaler co-authored the book *A Search for Justice* with three of the newspaper's reporters: Hemphill, Frank Ritter, and Jim Squires. The book was based on the reporters' coverage of the trials of assassins James Earl Ray and Sirhan Sirhan and of Clay Shaw, the New Orleans district attorney turned JFK-assassination conspiracy theorist. Seig's opening chapter is a blistering criticism of the criminal justice system.

My copy includes this inscription: "For Ken —I gave him a look at 'justice' early— and he gave me a look at injustice. With regards for his willingness to search, John Seigenthaler." The search goes on, John. *Requiescat in pace.*

–30–

1

#Justices

"The judicial power of the United States shall be vested in one Supreme Court and in such inferior courts as the Congress shall from time to time ordain and establish." (U.S. Constitution, Art. III, sec. 1.) The Constitution does not specify the number of justices, nor any qualifications for the position except for nomination by the president and confirmation by the Senate. Surprisingly, justices need not be lawyers, although all of them to date have been. Through history, 112 people have served as a Supreme Court justice. (Unlike Grover Cleveland, Charles Evans Hughes is counted only once for his separate tenures: 1910-1916 and 1930-1941.)

As I began writing Supreme Court Yearbook, *the court was about to begin a record-setting 11 years from 1994 to 2005 with no changes in membership – the longest stretch without a new justice since 1811-1823, when the court had only seven members. But there was rapid turnover in the early years of the 21ˢᵗ century with the appointment of a new chief justice, John G. Roberts Jr., and three associate justices within the span of six years. Two of the new members were chosen by a Republican president, George W. Bush, and two by a Democrat, Barack Obama. Here are profiles of The Nine, along with the three living retired justices.*

#HailtotheChief

"No one could have come to the position of chief justice of the United States with a better legal resume than John G. Roberts Jr." That's how I began Supreme Court Yearbook 2005-2006 *to chronicle Roberts's confirmation and his first term in the court's center seat. Roberts had been a star student at a private high school and then at Harvard College. From there, he advanced through Harvard Law School and a Supreme Court clerkship to influential legal jobs in the White House and the solicitor general's office in the 1980s and early 1990s. Over the next decade, he earned a reputation as a premier Supreme Court litigator with a top Washington law firm before finally taking a seat in 2003 on the federal appeals court for the District of Columbia. President Bush initially nominated Roberts for the seat of retiring associate justice Sandra Day O'Connor and then, with the death of Chief Justice William H. Rehnquist on Sept. 3, 2005, chose him instead to lead the court. Here are some of my columns on Roberts, from his initial nomination and confirmation through the first nine terms of the Roberts Court.*

Roberts' Real Views Are ...
(*CQ Weekly,* Aug. 15, 2005)

Will the real John G. Roberts Jr. be revealed when the Senate Judiciary Committee reviews his nomination to the Supreme Court next month? Will it be the young, bull-in-china-shop Reaganaut who scorned the right to privacy and worked to limit civil rights enforcement? Or will it be the age-wizened advocate of judicial humility, who promises to respect legal precedent, lightly criticizes judicial activism but also defends the courts' role in protecting individual rights?

Supporters of the nomination are busy promoting the second picture. They are selling Roberts as a lawyer's lawyer and a judge's judge — careful, conscientious and confirmably non-ideological.

Opponents and skeptics fear the first is the true picture. They think Roberts at age 50 may remain what he appears to have been in his 20s:

A committed conservative with no use for Supreme Court decisions protecting civil rights for minorities and reproductive freedom for women.

His many admirers, who range across the ideological spectrum, argue that Roberts would not ride roughshod over the high court's decision-making of the past 30 years. Still, Roberts is the only person who can directly answer that question — and senators are right to place the burden of proof on him, not on those who are not yet convinced.

Democrats will explore the issue by pressing Roberts for his views on the role of precedent and the legal principle of *"stare decisis"* — Latin for "let the decision stand." They will be looking for an assurance as strong as Roberts gave when he was up for confirmation to the federal appeals court two years ago.

When asked then about *Roe v. Wade,* Roberts called the landmark 1973 abortion-rights decision "binding precedent" and said he had no personal views that would prevent him from following it while on the D.C. Circuit Court of Appeals. As Attorney General Alberto R. Gonzales has pointed out, however, a Supreme Court justice "is not obliged to follow precedent if you believe it's wrong."

A half-century's practice proves the point. The high court has expressly overturned about 120 of its prior rulings since 1954. And the rate has been about the same under three very different chief justices: Earl Warren, Warren E. Burger, and William H. Rehnquist.

The liberal Warren Court overturned precedents to outlaw racial segregation and enforce constitutional rights for criminal defendants. The Burger Court had a pick-and-choose policy — creating new precedents at times to expand constitutional rights and at other times to narrow them.

Under Rehnquist, the court has worked to discard old rulings that limited government aid to religious education and allowed private suits against state governments for violating federal laws. But the conservative Rehnquist Court also set aside precedent with its decisions in the past three years to bar execution of juvenile or mentally retarded offenders and invalidate state laws banning gay sex.

"Precedent is very important in any legal system," says Burt Neuborne, a professor at New York University Law School and former national legal director of the American Civil Liberties Union. "But one of the most important things for a Supreme Court justice is to recognize that in some situations precedent has to change."

Against this background, Roberts' bow to precedent in his new Judiciary Committee questionnaire is hardly illuminating. He blandly writes that precedent "plays an important role in promoting the stability of the legal system" and says judges should recognize they operate "within a system of rules developed over the years."

Roberts showed less obeisance to precedent in the memos he wrote in the Reagan Justice Department. Then, he derided *Roe* as "unprincipled jurisprudence" and criticized the court's decisions recognizing a right of privacy. Writing in 1981, Roberts speculated about the possibility of overturning a high court decision barely two years earlier allowing private employers to use racial quotas in hiring.

Later, at Justice and as associate White House counsel, Roberts endorsed legislation that would have prohibited federal courts from ordering school busing. No less a conservative than Theodore B. Olson — then an assistant attorney general and later President George Bush's first solicitor general — successfully blocked administration support for the measure by arguing that the bill was unconstitutional.

In his two years on the D.C. Circuit, Roberts has been a careful legal craftsman. And Neuborne and a conservative counterpart, Pepperdine Law School Professor Douglas Kmiec, are among those who think the nominee's present-day respect for precedent is genuine. Kmiec, who knew Roberts from his own days in the Reagan Justice Department, says Roberts may be open to arguments for overriding precedent, "but I don't think that's where he starts."

In his questionnaire, Roberts said judges should practice "self-restraint" and rule with "a degree of institutional and personal modesty and humility." With a lifetime seat on a closely divided Supreme Court at stake, senators need to ask Roberts to elaborate on how he would translate that broadly phrased principle into practice.

Evolution, Black Robe Style
(*CQ Weekly*, Sept. 26, 2005)

While he was an associate Justice in the 1970s, William H. Rehnquist dissented from all of the Supreme Court's decisions establishing constitutional rules against sex discrimination. He questioned the constitutional basis for the *Miranda* decision on police interrogation and took every opportunity to narrow the scope of the ruling.

In his last few years on the bench, however, Chief Justice Rehnquist upheld Congress' right to pass broad legislation aimed at eliminating sex-based "overgeneralizations" in the workplace. And, defying a congressional statute, he reaffirmed the *Miranda v. Arizona*'s judicially crafted right to remain silent, saying the practice had become "part of our national culture."

Times change. Laws change. Justices change. And, so, Rehnquist had changed. . . . In court watchers' terms, he had "evolved."

For the past two months, expert observers, interest groups, senators and the public have been trying to decide whether Rehnquist's designated successor has evolved from the true-believing Reaganaut of the 1980s into a judicial non-ideologue.

With the confirmation by the Senate of John G. Roberts Jr. as chief justice now only days away, the question is still pending. Liberals fear and conservatives seem to believe that the answer is no — or at least not much. And the evidence from Roberts' own words — in 17 hours of questioning before the Senate Judiciary Committee — is circumstantial and ambiguous.

• Exhibit No. 1: Roberts' acceptance of a constitutional right to privacy, which he now finds in specific provisions of the Bill of Rights and in the "liberty component" protected by the Due Process Clause. But Roberts carefully avoided personally endorsing the most controversial applications of the doctrine to abortion rights, gay sex or the "right to die." Legal conservatives liked what they did not hear.

• Exhibit No 2: Roberts' rejection of key conservative doctrines of constitutional interpretation, including the "original intent" approach of Justices Antonin Scalia and Clarence Thomas. The Constitution should be interpreted according to present-day circumstances, Roberts said, and the Framers' broad phrasings need to be interpreted broadly. "We need to take them at their word," he said. Liberals liked what they thought they heard.

• Exhibit No 3: Roberts' self-identification as a "modest" judge, with no "agenda," no "platform," only a devotion to judicial restraint and the rule of law. He cited first among his judicial heroes federal appeals court judge Henry J. Friendly, for whom Roberts clerked. Roberts recalled that Friendly greatly enjoyed newspaper editorialists' inability to pigeonhole him as liberal or conservative. Conservatives and liberals liked what they heard — but undoubtedly heard different things.

• Exhibit No. 4: Roberts' limited distancing of himself from the conservative positions taken as a Justice Department and White House lawyer in the 1980s and 1990s. Repeatedly, Roberts stressed the difference between his role then as an advocate for administration policies and his present and presumed future roles on the federal bench. But despite persistent questioning by Democratic senators, Roberts specifically disavowed only one position: his toying with the idea of limiting federal judges' lifetime tenure. Conservatives smiled at what they heard; liberals frowned.

The list goes on, to no firm conclusion. Liberals liked Roberts' obeisance to precedent, while conservatives heard a road map for overturning some of their least favorites. Conservatives applauded his opposition to using international law to interpret the Constitution, while liberals took heart from his statement that the president is not above the law.

In one significant clue, Roberts voiced his strongest admiration among Supreme Court justices not for Rehnquist — for whom he also clerked — but for Robert H. Jackson, the very model of judicial evolution. As Franklin D. Roosevelt's attorney general, Jackson was an unabashed advocate of executive power. But as Supreme Court justice, Jackson wrote what became the leading judicial opinion to limit expansive use of presidential power in wartime.

Conservative advocacy groups view judicial evolution with no less disapproval than religious fundamentalists reserve for biological evolution. What happens, they ask, to supposed conservatives such as Sandra Day O'Connor, Anthony M. Kennedy, and David H. Souter when they reach the Supreme Court?

Conservatives take comfort when they hear Thomas quoted as saying behind closed doors not long after his confirmation, "I'm not evolving." They're hoping that Roberts will do likewise.

Like Darwinian evolution, however, judicial evolution is a fact. The process is unpredictable; the direction and timing as difficult to forecast as the issues Roberts will face over what could be the next three decades. But Roberts will evolve, one way or another, and his many strengths — intellect, character, and personal charm — may enable him to bring a closely divided court along with him.

Supreme Confidence

(*CQ Weekly*, June 19, 2006)

Babe Ruth had a famous reply in 1931 when asked to explain how he could justify being paid $5,000 more than President Herbert Hoover: "I had a better year than he did."

By that standard, John G. Roberts Jr. deserves to double his annual salary of $212,100 as the chief justice of the United States — because he's certainly had a better year than the $400,000-a-year president of the United States who appointed him.

George W. Bush's poll numbers have been sagging now for months, but Roberts is basking in warm praise from his colleagues and generally positive assessments from others, including some who opposed his confirmation nine months ago. "There's no question that he's taken over very firmly and very effectively the reins of being chief justice," says Elliot Mincberg, legal director of the liberal group People For the American Way, which led the unsuccessful fight to get the Senate to reject Roberts' nomination.

Mincberg reserves judgments on the court's ideological direction, but conservatives and disinterested court watchers sing Roberts' praises with no qualifications. "He has a solid A," says Douglas Kmiec, a conservative constitutional law expert at Pepperdine Law School.

Tellingly, Roberts is drawing kudos for modesty and judicial restraint — the ideals he stressed in his remarks during the Judiciary

Committee's confirmation hearing last September. Far from sharpening the court's ideological divisions, as many conservative interest groups were hoping, Roberts has steered the court toward narrower decisions and a surprisingly high percentage of unanimous opinions.

In that sense, Roberts represents the antithesis of Bush's repeated promises to pick justices for the Supreme Court in the mold of hard-line conservatives Antonin Scalia and Clarence Thomas. Roberts has taken conservative stances in most of the court's closely divided cases. But his opinions, including two lengthy dissents, have none of Scalia's signature scorn for opposing views. And Roberts shows no inclination to copy Thomas in wanting to reconsider established precedents.

Admittedly, more divisions are likely to emerge during the next two weeks as the court wraps up its final 19 cases for the term before recessing for the summer. For that reason court watchers caution that it's premature to be grading Roberts. That's all the more true because — as the youngest chief justice in 200 years — Roberts' tenure will be measured not in months or years, but in decades.

It's even earlier to start evaluating Bush's other appointee, Samuel A. Alito Jr., who took the bench in February. His first two opinions were unanimous decisions favoring criminal defendants written in workmanlike fashion. But in one, he made a passing reference to legislative history that prompted Scalia to repeat his unbending opposition to any consideration of legislative debate to help resolve issues of statutory construction. Roberts joined Alito's opinion — thus underscoring that Scalia is all alone in that view.

From all appearances, Roberts has quickly won the confidence of his eight colleagues, all but one of whom came to the Supreme Court with more judicial experience than Roberts' two years on the D.C. Circuit Court of Appeals. Justice Stephen G. Breyer has publicly complimented Roberts for allowing more debate in the justices' private conferences. At the same time, George Washington University law professor Orin Kerr suggests that Roberts appears to be persuading the other justices to follow him in his publicly announced preference for unanimity whenever possible.

Both on and off the bench, Roberts has shown a friendly, down-to-earth style without any of the self-importance that his predecessor,

William H. Rehnquist, occasionally displayed by dressing down stumbling attorneys during arguments and adding those famous gold stripes to his judicial robes. "He does a very good job of self-deprecating humor," Mincberg notes. As reported by Bloomberg News, Roberts even uses Washington's subway system.

With such high praise for his performance so far, the question naturally arises whether any of Roberts' past opponents are having second thoughts. Mincberg says no. He notes that Roberts and Alito helped form the 5-4 majority in the court's May 30 decision narrowing free-speech protections for public employees. And he worries that along with Scalia and Thomas, the four will continue to form a solid conservative bloc on a range of civil liberties issues. That puts all the more focus on Justice Anthony M. Kennedy, who continues to disappoint conservatives on some issues — such as his two June 12 opinions favoring challenges by death row inmates.

The court has already teed up some high-profile issues for the term that begins in October, including abortion and racial diversity in public schools. But Roberts deftly defused some tough issues early in this term. Maybe his luck will hold.

In any event, for now Roberts' many admirers might be forgiven for thinking of him instead of Bush the next time they hear the Marine band strike up "Hail to the Chief."

Riding Roughshod Over Precedent
(*Jost on Justice*, Sept. 19, 2010)

It has been five years this month since Judge John G. Roberts Jr. went before the Senate Judiciary Committee seeking confirmation to be chief justice of the United States. Roberts won senators over with his legal knowledge, smooth demeanor, and personal charm. He also promised, if confirmed, to respect precedent, forswear any "agenda," strive for fewer divided rulings, and decide cases like an idealized umpire — calling balls and strikes according to a strike zone defined by others, not by him.

The chief justice, of course, is not subject to reconfirmation. But if he were called on to answer for his record, how would Roberts be judged based on the promises he made in September 2005? Not that well.

Most troublingly, the Roberts Court has run roughshod over important legal precedents, not just in its ruling in January to free corporations in political campaigns but in many other ideologically divided decisions beginning as soon as Roberts' second term. And most of those rulings fit with a consistent agenda of favoring corporations over workers and consumers and of narrowing individual rights.

As a nominee, Roberts stressed the importance of following precedent —the legal principle known as *stare decisis* — in promoting both stability and evenhandedness. "I do think that it is a jolt to the legal system when you overrule a precedent," Roberts said. A judge should consider overruling a prior decision, he said, not because of personal disagreement, but only because of special factors such as the unworkability of the rule or the need to adapt to new circumstances.

Roberts has paid no more than lip services to those caveats as chief justice. By my count in *The Supreme Court Yearbook*, the Roberts Court has expressly overruled precedents eight times in Roberts' five terms: somewhat above the historical average of about one such decision per year. In at least half a dozen other decisions by my count, the court has bent precedent so badly as to approach an overruling.

Admittedly, two of these rulings were unanimous: an 8-0 ruling in 2006 favoring patentholders that tie an unpatented item to their patented product and a 9-0 decision in 2009 changing the procedure in constitutional rights suits against government officials. And in another 2009 decision, the court strengthened individual rights by limiting the authority of police to search a vehicle after arresting the driver. Significantly, Roberts was among four dissenters in that case.

The other overruling cases all came on 5-4 votes that pitted the conservative majority (Roberts, Scalia, Kennedy, Thomas, and Alito) against the liberal bloc (Stevens, Ginsburg, Breyer and either Souter or in the most recent term Sotomayor). In 2007, the court buried a nearly century-old antitrust precedent that made it illegal for a manufacturer to dictate to retailers a minimum price for its product. In an otherwise insignificant case, the court decided that a missed deadline for filing a notice of appeal — in this case, because of wrong information from the court — requires dismissal of the appeal, no exceptions permitted.

Among the more controversial rulings, the court in 2009 trashed a Burger Court precedent by allowing police to initiate an interrogation of a suspect without notifying his or her lawyer. As Justice Stevens noted in dissent, the new rule gives a criminal suspect less protection than a defendant in a civil suit, who cannot be questioned by the opposing lawyer without notice to counsel.

The *Citizens United* campaign finance decision in January drove a huge loophole through a century-long rule barring corporate spending in federal campaigns. In a concurring opinion, Roberts sought to justify the majority's decision to overrule two precedents, the most recent from 2003. Roberts posited a new and troubling justification for overruling prior decisions: "when a precedent's validity is so hotly contested that it cannot reliably function as a basis for decision in future cases." In effect, this criterion invites what Roberts said five years ago is impermissible: overruling a past decision because of personal disagreement.

The court finished its term in June with its decision to use the post-Civil War Fourteenth Amendment to extend the newly created Second Amendment individual gun right to state and local governments. That ruling explicitly overturned decisions from the late 19th century, written with the Fourteenth Amendment still in recent memory. And it built on the 2008 decision in the Washington, D.C., *Heller* case that itself rejected a 70-year-old precedent rejecting an individual right under the Second Amendment.

Among the bent precedents is the 2007 decision upholding a federal ban on so-called "partial birth abortions." The ruling rode past the *Roe v. Wade* requirement that abortion regulations include an exception if necessary to protect a woman's health. In the same, tumultuous term, Roberts led the court in rejecting many voluntary school integration plans and reducing to insignificance a central provision of the McCain-Feingold campaign finance law on election-time TV advertising. Other decisions significantly narrowed high school students' free speech rights and taxpayers' ability to challenge government actions on Establishment Clause grounds. All came on 5-4 votes in a term with the highest percentage of one-vote decisions *ever* in the court's history.

Dissenting in the school integration case, Justice Breyer added a tart comment from the bench that applies all the more three terms later. "It is not often in the law that so few have so quickly changed so much," Breyer said. With Roberts so young and the conservative majority so often so entrenched, the prospect is for more jolting changes ahead.

Roberts confounded many, perhaps most Supreme Court watchers at the end of the 2011-2012 term by casting the decisive vote to uphold most of President Obama's health care reform, the Affordable Care Act. Disappointed conservatives in particular viewed Roberts as having engaged in some specious legal reasoning primarily to avert political attacks on the court during a presidential election year.

Taking One for the Team
(*Jost on Justice*, June 29, 2012)

The Supreme Court will not be a major political issue in the presidential election between Barack Obama and Republican Mitt Romney. That is the important secondary implication of Chief Justice John G. Roberts' surprising decision to join with the court's liberal bloc in upholding Obama's signature domestic policy achievement, the Affordable Care Act, even as he rejected its premises on two counts as unconstitutional and un-American.

Whether or not that was Roberts' motivation, he has enough political savvy to recognize the effect and enough concern about the court's institutional standing to be glad of it. Roberts' vote to keep the health-care law essentially intact answers the politicians and pundits who, along with a growing number of Americans, saw the court as overtly partisan, toeing a Republican line.

Before saving Obamacare, however, Roberts sided with Republican politicians, libertarian legal scholars, and the conservative commentariat in criticizing it. The individual health insurance mandate, Roberts said, amounted to "cradle to grave regulation" by a government of supposedly limited powers. "This is not the country the Framers of our Constitution envisioned," he snapped.

Unconstitutional as well was the way that the Democratic-controlled Congress and the Democratic president decided to expand the federal-state Medicaid program to ensure health care for more of the nation's poor. The federal government would be paying for the expansion, but Roberts said the provision allowing the government to withhold Medicaid funds from any state that did not go along was unconstitutionally coercive. "A gun to the head," he termed it.

With those two passages, Roberts put himself on the side of that part of public opinion reflexively opposed to mandates and Washington. He also established, thanks to the votes of his four fellow conservatives in dissent, important legal markers for the future.

The federal government's powers to regulate interstate commerce, we now know, cannot extend to forcing people to buy health insurance – or cars or broccoli. It is hard to imagine the next case where this will be important, but putting the fanciful broccoli analogy into *U.S. Reports* amounts to a signal victory for the libertarians who dreamed it up.

More importantly, Roberts and six other justices, including liberals Stephen G. Breyer and Elena Kagan, established an outer limit to the federal government's Spending Clause power to use federal money to get states to go along with federal policies. The Court had never before found a federally imposed condition on federal money to be unconstitutional. That once-theoretical possibility is now real and — as lawyer Kevin Russell pointed out on *SCOTUSBlog* — could cast a shadow over federal anti-discrimination laws that threaten states with loss of federal money if they do not comply.

With these legal victories, it is no wonder that conservatives and libertarians view their glass as at least half full. "Lose the battle, win the war," wrote Jonathan Adler, law professor at Case Western Reserve University, also on *SCOTUSBlog*'s free-for-all after the decision was announced. In like vein, Ilya Shapiro, editor in chief of the *Cato Supreme Court Review*, proclaimed, "We won everything but the case."

Justice Ruth Bader Ginsburg spoke for all four liberals in complaining that Roberts' disquisition on the Commerce Clause was unnecessary if he was going to uphold the individual mandate as a constitutionally valid tax. Roberts' response is singularly unconvincing. He explained that he would not have been forced to construe the act's penalty as a tax but for finding its major rationale invalid.

Once construed as a tax, however, the "exaction" from the relatively small number of Americans who do not have insurance but can afford it is clearly within Congress's power. As Roberts noted, the Court's precedents make clear, for example, that the federal government can tax a lottery even if it has no power to run one.

The political consequences of declaring the insurance mandate to be a tax can only add to its unpopularity. "ObamaCare Taxes the American People and the House Will Repeal It," House Republican Leader Eric Cantor declared in the press release announcing the scheduled July 11 vote on scrapping the bill altogether. The release is good short-term politics even if the move is doomed to fail in the Democratic-controlled Senate – and in any event would be vetoed by Obama.

For many legal scholars, Roberts is also unconvincing in rejecting the individual mandate as an exercise of Congress's Commerce Clause power. Ginsburg recapitulated the argument that the "shared responsibility" provision forces health care customers to prepay for care through insurance rather than risk imposing the cost of unforeseen and uncompensated care on others. Roberts conceded that states could impose the requirement through their police power; Ginsburg countered that Congress has powers commensurate with the nationwide nature of the problem.

Roberts' tie-breaking vote to uphold the law takes the court out of the political cross-hairs of Democrats and progressives. The indignant denunciations from some conservatives will soon be forgotten, especially when Roberts returns next term as the conservative leader of a conservative Court. For the moment, however, Roberts took one for the team — the Court — even if none of his colleagues thanked him for it.

Conciliator in Chief?

(*Jost on Justice*, June 26, 2014)

Supreme Court justices appeared to be divided and in search of a compromise when they heard arguments two months ago on police authority to search a suspect's cell phone after an arrest. But there was no division and barely a hint of compromise when Chief Justice John G. Roberts Jr. announced the unanimous decision this week [June 25] instructing police to "get a warrant" before searching a cell phone except in very limited emergency circumstances.

Roberts is only first among equals, of course: he has facetiously rued the Framers' decision to give the chief justice only one vote. But surely he must have played an important role in conference in getting eight often fractious colleagues to join in a forceful affirmation of privacy rights for the digital era. As NBC's Pete Williams aptly remarked, the decision was "surprising" precisely because it was both "unanimous and so bold."

A chief justice also can be bold, however, by exercising restraint. And Roberts showed this kind of bold restraint in two other of the week's decisions as well as earlier in the term. Roberts shares the generally conservative views of the court's four other Republican-appointed justices, but twice this week he refused to join conservative colleagues who were voting to undermine or overrule Supreme Court precedents defended by liberals on and off the court.

In both of those cases, the court's decisions were unanimous and favored conservative constituencies: businesses in one, anti-abortion groups in the other. But Roberts formed majorities with the court's liberal justices to avoid the kind of "shock" to the legal system that he had warned against in his confirmation hearings back in 2005.

In *Halliburton Co. v. Erica P. John Fund, Inc.*, Roberts unapologetically reaffirmed the quarter-century-old "fraud on the market" doctrine that forms the basis for the modern securities fraud class action. Roberts acknowledged the continuing criticism of the doctrine and of its effects in facilitating costly litigation for businesses that they say brings few real benefits for investors. But he insisted that the court considered all those views in its seminal case *Basic, Inc. v. Levinson* (1988); any policy concerns, he said, were properly addressed to Congress, not the court.

The ruling does help securities fraud defendants by giving them an early opportunity to prevent suits from being certified as class actions.

But three conservatives — Scalia, Thomas, and Alito — wanted to go further and voted to overrule *Basic* outright.

In somewhat like vein, Roberts wrote for the court in its decision *McCullen v. Coakley* striking down a Massachusetts law establishing a 35-foot buffer zone around abortion clinics. Roberts said the law violated the First Amendment by burdening more speech than necessary, but only after accepting the state's interest in protecting access to clinics and reaffirming precedents subjecting similar laws only to "intermediate" instead of "strict" constitutional scrutiny.

Four justices — Scalia, Kennedy, and Thomas in one opinion and Alito separately — insisted the law improperly singled out opponents of abortion and called for applying the often fatal strict scrutiny. In his opinion, Roberts all but laid out road maps for legislators to follow in enacting abortion clinic protections that can pass constitutional muster.

Those three decisions contribute to the term's remarkable statistic. Out of 65 signed decisions so far, 41 have come on unanimous votes — more than 60 percent. With only two decisions remaining, the unanimity score is guaranteed to be significantly higher than the Roberts Court's previous high of 49 percent in Roberts's first term. True, the unanimous results have papered over doctrinal disagreements, as in this week's cases, but the record recalls to mind Roberts's confirmation hearing hope for more unified decisionmaking.

Roberts still knows how to be an activist. He led the term's early 5-4 decision in *McCutcheon v. Federal Election Commission* to strike down the federal law establishing "aggregate" contribution limits for individuals in federal campaigns. And this week, he voted with conservatives Scalia, Thomas, and Alito in the recess appointments case, *National Labor Relations Board v. Noel Canning*, to impose a more drastic limit on the practice than established by the five-vote majority formed by liberals plus Kennedy.

Setting those cases to the side, Roberts's stances during the term recall the aversion to 5-4 rulings that he voiced to CNN's Jeffrey Rosen, in an interview for *The New Yorker*. "I do think the rule of law is threatened by a steady term after term after term focus on 5-4 decisions," Roberts said. "I think the Court is ripe for a similar refocus on functioning as an institution, because if it doesn't, it's going to lose its credibility and legitimacy as an institution."

The term's two remaining cases, to be decided on Monday [June 30], might seem likely candidates for 5-4 decisions. In *Sebelius v. Hobby Lobby Stores, Inc.*, private companies are claiming a religious exemption from the Obamacare requirement to include coverage for contraceptives in employee health plans. In *Harris v. Quinn*, home health workers classified as state employees are challenging a requirement to pay dues to the union that represents them in collective bargaining.

Statistics are hardly the full measure of a court, and one term is only that. As the court wraps up this term, however, Roberts appears to be playing a more conciliatory role than in some in the past.

Roberts voted with the conservative majority in the term's final two decisions, but the term ended with the second lowest number of 5-4 decisions for any year since Roberts took office in September 2005.

#RetiredJustices

Three moderate Republicans appointed to the court in three different decades – John Paul Stevens, Sandra Day O'Connor, and David H. Souter – played pivotal roles on the Rehnquist and Roberts Courts. Here are columns on each, starting with O'Connor's post-retirement reflections on the court's momentous decision in Bush v. Gore *(2000).*

O'Connor's Belated Regrets
(Jost on Justice, May 5, 2013)

After nearly 35 years on the Supreme Court, Justice John Paul Stevens thought back to his first term to list the one vote he most wanted to have back. Stevens joined with moderates Potter Stewart and Lewis F. Powell Jr. in the pivotal opinion in *Griggs v. Georgia* (1976) that allowed states to resume the death penalty under procedures to narrow its use to defendants most deserving of execution.

"I thought at the time," Stevens told NPR's Nina Totenberg in September 2010, three months after his retirement, "that if the universe of defendants eligible for the death penalty is sufficiently narrow so that you can be confident that the defendant really merits that severe punishment, that the death penalty was appropriate." Over the years, however, Stevens said the court expanded the cases eligible for the death penalty, undermining his original premise. "I really think that the death penalty today is vastly different from the death penalty that we thought we were authorizing," he said.

Stevens is not the only justice to have a change of mind after leaving the bench. Powell famously expressed regrets about his decisive vote in *Bowers v. Hardwick*, the 1986 case that upheld state anti-sodomy laws. "I think I probably made a mistake in that one," he told a group of New York University law students in October 1990, three years after retiring. A full generation of gay men paid the price for Powell's mistake by living under a legal cloud until the court reversed the decision 17 years later in *Lawrence v. Texas* (2003).

Now comes retired justice Sandra Day O'Connor to express regrets about her vote in another, even higher-profile case: *Bush v. Gore*, the 5-4 decision in December 2000 that gave George W. Bush the presidency by blocking a popular vote recount in the election-deciding state of Florida. The court "took the case and decided it at a time when it was still a big election issue," O'Connor told the *Chicago Tribune* editorial board on April 26. "Maybe the court should have said, 'We're not going to take it, goodbye.'"

"It turned out that the election authorities in Florida hadn't done a real good job there and kind of messed up," O'Connor continued. "And probably the Supreme Court added to the problems at the end of the day."

Like Powell, and unlike Stevens, O'Connor cannot rationalize her vote after the fact on the basis of unforeseeable developments. The stakes in *Bush v. Gore* could not have been clearer: not only the White House but also public confidence in the court itself. And the path to a decision that could have safeguarded public confidence in the court was available: the proposal by Justices David H. Souter and Stephen

G. Breyer to send the case back to Florida with instructions to adopt uniform criteria for the further recount.

O'Connor chose instead to join with Justice Anthony M. Kennedy in the pivotal opinion that stopped the election recount on the basis of a previously undiscovered federal constitutional right to uniformity in state election tabulations. O'Connor's cryptic comments more than a decade later shed no light on why she did not join Souter and Breyer in letting the recount proceed. As one other alternative, O'Connor could have taken the route she now says might have been best: she could have voted to dismiss the case without a ruling — in effect, saying "Goodbye." That would have provided a decisive fifth vote for letting the recount go on.

The two senior veterans of the Supreme Court press corps are taking opposite views of O'Connor's after-the-fact regrets. In a column on the *New York Times* blog *Opinionator*, the newspaper's now semiretired Linda Greenhouse is lightly scornful of O'Connor's comments, noting that her change of heart comes too late to make a difference. Shortly after the original decision, Greenhouse wrote in the *Times'* house organ, *Times Talk*, that *Bush v. Gore* marked the first time in three decades of covering the court that she viewed it as having issued a truly partisan decision.

From the opposite perspective, Lyle Denniston, now with *SCOTUSblog* after more than 50 years of covering the court, stoutly defends the court's decision. In his view, the court had no alternative but to hear Bush's appeal of the Florida Supreme Court's decision. The public would not have been content to let lower courts decide what had evolved into a constitutional crisis, Denniston argues in a posting on *Constitution Check*, the blog of the National Constitution Center. And he has contended in other settings that the court's decision was right on the merits and that Bush's narrow victory in Florida has been confirmed by subsequent journalistic efforts at a complete recount.

On the court's decision to take the case, O'Connor's regrets are beside the point. With only four votes needed to grant certiorari, O'Connor's vote was surely unnecessary. But those, like Denniston, who argue that a complete recount would not have mattered overlook the effect on the court itself, as Stevens explained in his dissenting opinion. "Although we may never know with complete certainty the identity of the winner of this year's Presidential election," Stevens wrote, "the identity of the loser is perfectly clear. It is the Nation's confidence in the judge as an impartial guardian of the rule of law."

Some court-watchers speculated in the presidential election year of 2008 that David Souter might be interested in quitting the court for the solitude of his New Hampshire cabin. Still, Souter's decision to retire in spring 2009 came mostly as a surprise.

Souter: A Principled Justice

(*Jost on Justice*, May 5, 2009)

David Souter will not be remembered as a great or near great justice. He will leave the Supreme Court at the end of his nineteenth term with relatively few landmark majority opinions bearing his name. His dissenting opinions tend to be long in legal prose and footnotes and short in soaring rhetoric or memorable quotes. And many conservative Republicans will of course remember him as a traitor to their cause and to the president who appointed him, George H.W. Bush.

Souter deserves better. In an era of increasing ideological polarization on the court, he stands out as a judge's judge: judicious in temperament, rigorous in legal reasoning, faithful to constitutional tradition, and stalwart in defense of the court as a legal instead of a political institution.

Nothing exemplifies Souter's belief in the court's role better than the decision that many conservatives count as an historic betrayal: his critical vote along with Justices Sandra Day O'Connor and Anthony M. Kennedy in 1992 to reaffirm the landmark abortion rights ruling, *Roe v. Wade*. Souter's contribution to the jointly authored plurality opinion stressed the danger that a reversal in the face of intense political opposition would cause what he called "profound and unnecessary damage to the Court's legitimacy, and to the Nation's commitment to the rule of law."

From various accounts — including that of CNN senior editor Jeffrey Toobin in his book *The Nine* — Souter believed that the court inflicted that kind of damage on itself with its 2000 decision in *Bush v. Gore*. According to Toobin, Souter viewed the decision to cut off the Florida vote recount and hand the presidency to George W. Bush as a blatantly partisan act by the five conservative, Republican-appointed justices in the majority.

Toobin wrote that Souter considered resigning — a report disputed by Souter's original sponsor, New Hampshire's former Republican senator Warren Rudman. Souter himself has never publicly addressed the report. Indeed, Souter is famously media-averse. He dislikes having his picture taken and vowed that video cameras would be allowed in the Supreme Court's courtroom only over his dead body.

Indeed, Souter has been very much the anti-modern justice: using a fountain pen instead of word processor to write his opinions, carrying his apple and yogurt lunch to the office in a plastic bag, and preferring his remote New Hampshire cabin to the social and political life of the nation's capital.

Fittingly, Souter's most distinctive jurisprudential contribution is in fact rooted in history: his strict view of the separation of church and state, whether speaking for a majority or in dissent. In his first important vote on the issue, Souter cast a critical vote (along with Kennedy) to bar even "nondenominational" prayer at high school graduation ceremonies. In his concurrence, Souter carefully reviewed the history of the Establishment Clause to conclude that the Framers intended to bar government support not merely for one particular denomination over another but for religion in general. He then added that reviewing supposedly nondenominational prayers would thrust the courts into "comparative theology" — a task beyond the competence of the federal judiciary.

A decade later, Souter spoke for the majority in barring religiously-motivated displays of the Ten Commandments in government buildings. In many other cases, however, Souter found himself at odds with the Rehnquist Court's willingness to permit government aid to religion. And two years ago, he led four dissenters from the Roberts Court's decision to block taxpayer suits using the Establishment Clause to challenge federal expenditures as improper aid to religious programs or institutions.

Souter also relied on history to dissent from a second major departure by the Rehnquist Court: the use of state sovereignty principles to limit private suits against state governments for violating federal laws. Dissenting in the 1996 decision that launched the new jurisprudence, Souter argued that the Rehnquist-led majority was misreading the Framers and distorting the court's own precedents.

The 1992 abortion decision prompted speculation that O'Connor, Kennedy, and Souter would form a lasting triumvirate in the court's ideological center. That did not come to pass. Souter moved to the left, while O'Connor and Kennedy reverted to their accustomed positions at the centermost point of a predominantly conservative bench.

In the succeeding 17 terms, Souter has been a reliable member of a liberal bloc more often than not in dissent in the court's most important decisions. On the bench, he has used carefully structured questioning to challenge the conservative bloc's apparent inclinations — for example, in colloquies this week defending the continuing validity of the Voting Rights Act's key section against the open skepticism from Chief Justice John G. Roberts Jr. and Justice Antonin Scalia.

Souter has not voted in lockstep, however. He departed from the liberal bloc in writing the 5-4 decision permitting police to make a custodial arrest for a minor traffic arrest and the 5-3 decision striking down the punitive damage award in the *Exxon Valdez* oil spill.

The Supreme Court's legitimacy, Souter wrote in the abortion decision, "depends on making legally principled decisions under circumstances in which their principled character is sufficiently plausible to be accepted by the Nation." Likewise for a justice's legitimacy. On that standard, Souter has acquitted himself well: a justice as principled as he was unprepossessing, on the bench or off.

John Paul Stevens signaled his likely retirement in fall 2009 by selecting only a single law clerk – the number allowed for retired justices – instead of the usual complement of four. With the term's arguments concluded, Stevens made his decision official in April 2010.

"Learning on the Job"
(*Jost on Justice*, April 14, 2010)

As a federal appeals court judge in Chicago in the 1970s, John Paul Stevens sat on a case challenging political patronage — the long established practice of awarding government jobs on the basis of political affiliation. Stevens initially saw no grounds for a constitutional attack, but after research and argument wrote an opinion finding the practice a violation of First Amendment political rights.

None of Stevens' colleagues joined the opinion. But Stevens stayed on the bench long enough to see his view adopted, at least in part, in three Supreme Court decisions.

Stevens told that story in remarks at a forum in his honor sponsored by Fordham University Law School in 2005. Stevens related the episode to his view of the judicial role. "Learning on the job is essential to the process of judging," Stevens said.

Perhaps no justice in history better exemplifies than Stevens the importance, or the impact, of learning on the job. In a 34-year Supreme Court career that will end as the third longest of any justice, Stevens evolved from a centrist Republican and frequent maverick to a leader of the Court's liberal bloc and an effective coalition-builder in a number of critically important decisions.

In interviews while weighing his retirement, Stevens discounted the "evolution" theory. He insisted he was and remains a "conservative," his views largely unchanged as the Court changed around him. His protestations must be taken with several grains of salt.

Stevens' record is full of seemingly inconsistent decisions that can be reconciled only with difficulty. He voted in 1978 to strike down the race-based admissions program at the University of California-Davis Law School, but approved a more nuanced racial preference system at the University of Michigan Law School in 2003. In like vein, Stevens voted in 1980 to strike down a federal minority-preference government contracting program but shifted sides to support a more carefully structured program in 1995.

In one of his first abortion-related cases, Stevens in 1977 helped to uphold a state's refusal to pay for nontherapeutic abortions for indigent women. Barely three years later, he led four dissenters when the court approved the Hyde Amendment's broader federal ban on abortion funding. He went on to become a strong defender of abortion rights, playing a behind-the-scenes role in the final form of the 1992 decision that left *Roe v. Wade* on the books.

Stevens wrote the so-called *Pacifica* decision in 1978 that gave the Federal Communications Commission (FCC) the green light to ban "seven dirty words" on radio and television. Two decades later, he led a nearly unanimous court in 1997 in overturning Congress's attempt to ban indecency on the Internet. When the FCC came back before the court defending its ban on "fleeting expletives," Stevens voted in 2009 to reject the policy, saying *Pacifica* never envisioned such sweeping censorship.

On one issue, however, Stevens acknowledges a change of views: capital punishment. In his first term, Stevens was part of a triumvirate of "centrist" justices — along with Potter Stewart and Lewis F. Powell Jr. — that paved the way in 1976 for the return of capital punishment. The decision in *Gregg v. Georgia* permitted judges or juries to impose the death penalty under a system of "guided discretion."

With 32 years' experience under that system, Stevens concluded in 2008 that the effort to impose the death penalty with complete evenhandedness and assured reliability had failed. The risk of error and the risk of discriminatory application, Stevens wrote in *Baze v. Rees*, make the costs of capital punishment far greater than benefits he found to be "negligible." Justice Antonin Scalia wrote separately in the case to mock Stevens' use of his personal "experience" in reaching that position.

Without referring to Stevens by name, Justice Clarence Thomas has also mocked what conservatives regard as the tendency of justices to shift to the left over time. "I'm not evolving," Thomas is said to have promised after his contentious confirmation in 1991. And he has not. The same death penalty cases that caused Stevens to change his stance have left Thomas unmoved; he consistently votes to reject death penalty challenges no matter how strong the evidence of irregularities or injustice.

Over time, Stevens also learned from experience the ways of wielding influence within the court's cloistered walls. As the leader of the court's four liberals for the past 15 years, Stevens helped forge five- or six-vote majorities that guaranteed rights for Guantanamo detainees, preserved affirmative action in higher education, barred capital punishment for mentally retarded or juvenile offenders, and protected gay rights in the bedroom and in the political process. He also dissented eloquently when the fortified conservative majority under Chief Justice John G. Roberts Jr. slid around precedents to limit racial diversity in public schools and grant corporations unlimited spending rights in election campaigns.

In looking for the next justice, President Obama said he would be looking for attributes he identified in Stevens: independence, integrity, and "a fierce dedication to the rule of law." And the president added one more: "a keen understanding of how the law affects the daily lives of the American people." For that, the next justice must do what Stevens did himself: learn on the job.

#SittingJustices

With Souter's and Stevens's retirements, Supreme Court justices were for the first time in history divided along an ideological fault line that corresponded exactly to the party of the president who appointed them. Four Republican-appointed justices – Roberts, Antonin Scalia, Clarence Thomas, and Samuel A. Alito Jr. – form a conservative bloc on many of the most divisive issues, while the Democratic-appointed justices – Ruth Bader Ginsburg, Stephen G. Breyer, Sonia Sotomayor, and Elena Kagan – comprise a liberal wing. Justice Anthony M. Kennedy, the moderate conservative appointed by President Ronald Reagan in 1987, often casts a decisive vote: most often with the conservatives, but more than occasionally with the liberals.

Scalia's Injudicious Temperament

(*Jost on Justice*, Dec. 13, 2009)

Justice Antonin Scalia has a well developed capacity for indignation that he directs at any number of targets, including Congress, "living constitutionalists," and international law advocates. But even long-time Scalia watchers seemed surprised early in the current Supreme Court term when Scalia chose Jewish war veterans for one of his signature from-the-bench outbursts.

Scalia professed incomprehension during the Oct. 7 arguments in *Salazar v. Buono* that Jewish war veterans could feel slighted at the designation of a Christian cross — with no other religious symbol — as a national memorial to World War I veterans. The eight-foot high cross, originally erected by the Veterans of Foreign Wars but later given official recognition by Congress, sits atop a hill in a remote location in the Mojave Desert in California.

"The cross doesn't honor non-Christians who fought in the war?" Scalia asked of the lawyer representing a plaintiff who views it as an unconstitutional government endorsement of religion. The cross, Scalia continued, "is the most common symbol of the resting place of the dead."

In all seriousness, ACLU attorney Peter Eliasberg felt obliged to explain to Scalia, a devout Roman Catholic, that the cross may be a common symbol for Christians, but not for others. "I have been in Jewish cemeteries," Eliasberg said. "There is never a cross on a tombstone of a Jew."

Scalia remained unconvinced. His voice rising, Scalia insisted that the idea that the cross honors only Christian war veterans was "an outrageous conclusion."

The episode comes to mind these days as Scalia's legacy during 23 years on the Court is being examined thanks to the first full-length biography of the justice. In *American Original*, Joan Biskupic, the longtime Supreme Court reporter for *USA Today*, provides a scrupulously fair account of Scalia's life and views.

Biskupic, a friend and colleague for 20 years, has informed her narrative with several interviews with Scalia himself and with six of

Scalia's current or former colleagues. She accurately describes his reputation for brilliance, his strongly held legal views and his apparently increased influence in the four years since the appointments of Chief Justice John G. Roberts Jr. and Justice Samuel A. Alito Jr.

Along with those positives, however, Biskupic also presents the major elements of the less favorable view of Scalia the justice: his outsized ego, overbearing personality, and intellectual inconsistency. Tellingly, the most damning items come from Scalia himself or from other justices who simultaneously profess admiration for and exasperation with their irascible colleague.

"I love him," Justice Ruth Bader Ginsburg tells Biskupic, "but sometimes I'd like to strangle him." Ginsburg and her husband are close friends with Scalia and his wife: the justices share a passion for opera; the families share festive holiday dinners.

Justice John Paul Stevens, the longest serving of the Court's current members, says all the justices admire Scalia's "writing ability and his style and all the rest." But, Stevens adds, "Everybody on the Court from time to time has thought he was unwise to take such an extreme position, both in tone and in the position."

From Biskupic's telling, Scalia's dogmatism may be traced as far back as his years as a student at a Jesuit-run, all-male military academy, where the school newspaper once described him as "an exemplary Catholic." Scalia's pre-ecumenical faith helps explains his blind spot to the Jewish war veterans' argument. So too his experience at an all-male military academy helps explain Scalia's scornful dissent when the Court in 1996 ruled the all-male Virginia Military Institute guilty of unconstitutional sex discrimination.

From Scalia himself, readers learn that despite his illustrious career he nurses long lingering resentments. More than 50 years later, Scalia still broods that Princeton rejected him because of his Italian immigrant background. (He went on to graduate first in his class from Georgetown.) Nearly 30 years after the fact, he remains "bitterly disappointed" that President Ronald Reagan passed him over for solicitor general in 1981. (He was appointed the next year to the federal appeals court in Washington.) And after Chief Justice William H. Rehnquist's death in 2005, Scalia evidently hoped for elevation to the post even while acknowledging the reasons for picking someone else.

Biskupic recounts some of the many examples of Scalia's argumentative questioning from the bench — and his response that Ginsburg can be just as bad. She quotes some of Scalia's inflammatory dissents — and his comment in a slightly different context that he is "not that nasty a fellow." And she notes, in the face of Scalia's denial, that he applies his "originalism" to constitutional cases selectively, upholding laws that he approves (abortion regulations) while striking down laws that he disapproves (the District of Columbia gun ban).

Throughout, Biskupic draws a portrait of a justice who is the very antithesis of the model judge of open mind and judicious temperament. Scalia came to the court on Rehnquist's elevation to the chief justiceship in 1986 and succeeded then to Rehnquist's place as the most conservative of the nine. When Rehnquist's bust was unveiled at the Supreme Court last week [Dec. 10], Roberts remembered his fellow conservative as "modest and unassuming," while the liberal Stevens recalled Rehnquist as "absolutely impartial" in all procedural matters.

Some day, Scalia will be honored with his a portrait in the Supreme Court building. There will be fond tributes, no doubt, but modesty and impartiality will likely go unmentioned.

Thomas's Disregard for Precedent
(Jost on Justice, Oct. 31, 2011)

As a Supreme Court nominee, Clarence Thomas presented himself as a cautious jurist committed to judicial restraint. "I have no agenda to change existing case law," Thomas told a Republican senator during his confirmation hearing after being asked about his critical views about school desegregation. "That's not my predisposition. It's not the way that I approach my job."

In his 20 years on the bench, however, Thomas has been a judicial activist of the first rank, a veritable bull in a china shop of Supreme Court precedents. More than any justice in recent memory — perhaps more than any justice in history — Thomas has time and again called for overruling prior decisions, some of them of recent vintage and some dating back decades or even centuries.

Thomas was a brand-new Supreme Court justice in fall 1991 when he first met a precedent that he did not like. In *Hudson v. McMillian* (1992), a case argued in November 1991 in Thomas's second week of oral arguments, Thomas contended in dissent that the Eighth Amendment's Cruel and Unusual Punishment Clause should not apply to a prison guard's deliberate beating of an inmate. For the majority, Justice Sandra Day O'Connor said that Thomas's dissent ignored a "settled rule" dating to 1977 that "unnecessary and wanton infliction of pain" violates the Eighth Amendment.

Thomas originally cast a lone dissenting vote in the case in the justices' conference, though fellow conservative Antonin Scalia later joined his opinion. (In her book *Supreme Conflict*, the conservative-leaning reporter Jan Crawford Greenburg, then with ABC News and now with CBS, cites that sequence to refute the notion that Thomas in his early years simply followed Scalia's positions.) In at least three dozen cases since then, however, Thomas has been all by himself in calling to overturn precedents.

A compilation in 2004 by Jason Rylander, a lawyer then with the progressive group Community Rights Counsel, lists 35 cases in which Thomas argued alone either in concurring or dissenting opinions for reconsidering settled precedents. The list begins with Thomas's questioning in *Georgia v. McCollum* (1992) of the rule established a year earlier that private litigants cannot use peremptory challenges to exclude potential jurors on the basis of race.

Rylander, now with Defenders of Wildlife, ended his list in 2004, a year in which Thomas argued in half a dozen cases for rethinking past decisions. In one of those, *Elk Grove Unified School District v. Newdow*, Thomas took the startling position that the Establishment Clause, the central pillar of the separation of church and state, should apply only to the federal government, not to the states. In another, *Sabri v. United States*, Thomas argued for reconsidering decisions broadly interpreting Congress's powers under both the Commerce Clause and the Necessary and Proper Clause.

Had Rylander continued the compilation, he could have added at least two more from the past two terms. In *Citizens United v. FEC* (2010), Thomas argued in a lone dissent for scrapping campaign-finance precedents that uphold mandatory disclosure of campaign contributions. And just this year, in *Brown v. Entertainment Merchants Association* (2011), Thomas argued in dissent that minors have no independent First Amendment right of access to speech that the government wants to censor. That approach would be at odds with the court's landmark student-speech ruling in *Tinker v. Des Moines Unified School District*. Writing the majority opinion in the case, Scalia noted that Thomas cited no case in support of his view.

Thomas is not always alone in his penchant for breaking precedent. In his first term, he joined three others, including Chief Justice William H. Rehnquist, in a dissenting opinion that called for a "re-examination" of the landmark abortion rights ruling *Roe v. Wade*. Thomas had studiously avoided all questions on abortion during the confirmation hearing. More recently, in *Parents Involved in Community Schools v. Seattle School District No. 1* (2007), he joined a plurality opinion by Chief Justice John G. Roberts Jr. that undercut the line of school desegregation decisions that Thomas had earlier appeared to accept.

Precedents are not sacrosanct. The court itself has stated that the principle of *stare decisis* — respect for precedent — "is not an inviolable command." Some of the court's greatest moments have come in rejecting decisions that were wrong when decided or wrong when reconsidered. Think *Brown v. Board of Education*, *Gideon v. Wainwright*, and *Lawrence v. Texas*.

Thomas's approach, however, sets him apart even from his fellow conservatives. In his confirmation hearing, Roberts acknowledged that overruling a precedent can be "a jolt to the legal system." As chief justice, Roberts has stopped short at times of officially overruling prior decisions. Thomas is less hesitant. As Scalia remarked to Thomas's biographer Ken Foskett, Thomas "doesn't believe in *stare decisis*, period.

As he marks his twentieth anniversary on the court, controversy still rages whether Thomas or law professor Anita Hill was telling the truth about Hill's accusations of sexual harassment. That controversy will likely remain unsettled. But Thomas's record over two decades shows that he has not been the justice that he promised to be during confirmation hearings. His record may cheer conservatives, but others will see evidence that Thomas reached the court only after a calculated dissembling before the Senate about his approach to legal issues. That may be a reflection on the confirmation process, but it is also, and more to the point, a reflection on Thomas himself.

Alito's Power of Positive Thinking
(Jost on Justice, Jan. 31, 2011)

Donald Specter had reached a critical point in his argument before the Supreme Court defending a lower federal court's order to reduce prison overcrowding in California when Justice Samuel A. Alito Jr. interrupted. "This is going to have," the justice began, but caught himself, "it seems likely to have an effect on public safety. And the experts can testify to whatever they want, but you know what? If this order goes into effect, we will see."

Specter, who directed the months-long trial for the Berkeley-based Prison Rights Project, knew that the three-judge court had actually concluded otherwise. "Well, based on the experience in the other jurisdictions," Specter answered, "the court found we wouldn't."

As noted at the time by law professor and Atlantic.com blogger Garrett Epps, Alito's comment during the Nov. 30 argument in *Schwarzenegger v. Plata* went against the normal rule requiring appellate courts, even the Supreme Court, to defer to findings by lower courts. But certitude has been Alito's hallmark in what is now [Jan. 31] five years since he joined the high court.

As predicted by Democrats and liberal groups who unsuccessfully tried to block his confirmation, Alito has staked out a position at the far right of the court's ideological spectrum, in some respects even more ideologically pure than fellow conservatives Antonin Scalia and Clarence Thomas. In the process, Alito has become the court's most powerful justice, enabling the conservative majority to shift American law to the right on such hot-button issues as abortion rights, campaign finance regulation, school integration and gun control.

True, Justice Anthony M. Kennedy plays a pivotal role by siding at times with the conservative bloc led by Chief Justice John G. Roberts Jr. and at times with the four-justice liberal bloc. That is the same role played for more than two decades by Alito's predecessor, Sandra Day O'Connor, who was famously depicted on the cover of the *New York Times* magazine as the most powerful woman in American government.

Alito wields power not by swinging from side to side but by standing fast. He flexed power from his first months on the court, when he cast the deciding votes in three cases that had to be re-argued after O'Connor's departure. With the other justices divided 4-4, Alito in effect became the one-man court in rulings in 2006 that weakened the "knock and announce" requirement for police, limited free-speech protections for public employees, and upheld Kansas's death penalty statute.

As the junior justice until Sonia Sotomayor's appointment in 2010, Alito voted last in the justices' private conferences, where cases are actually decided and opinions assigned. In that role, Alito literally cast the deciding votes in 5-4 rulings in the momentous 2006-2007 term that upheld a federal ban on a specific abortion procedure, weakened the McCain-Feingold campaign finance law, limited school districts' ability to promote racial diversity, and restricted taxpayer suits against government subsidies to religious groups. He was also the tie-breaker in the well-known Lily Ledbetter case, which made it harder to bring pay discrimination suits in federal courts until Congress reversed the ruling by statute.

All of those rulings went against the grain of what had seemed to be established precedent or dominant positions in lower courts. As in the prison crowding case, however, Alito is willing to find his own facts or make his own law. Writing for a 5-4 majority in an Arizona case challenging bilingual education in 2009, Alito found "documented, academic support" for the view that structured English immersion is the better educational technique, but failed to mention the dominant view among experts favoring dual-language instruction. In another 5-4 decision a year earlier striking down a minor part of the McCain-Feingold law, Alito relied in part on a lower court decision striking down a public campaign financing scheme without acknowledging that most federal court decisions have upheld such laws.

Alito wears his conservatism on his sleeve both on and off the court. He has been speaker or guest at fundraisers for conservative organizations, such as the Manhattan Institute and *American Spectator*, the conservative weekly. When questioned at the *American Spectator* event in November 2010, Alito told a reporter for the left-wing blog ThinkProgress that his attendance was "not important."

On the bench, Alito poses hard-edged questions like those in the prison crowding case, almost always reflecting a conservative bent. Jan Crawford, CBS's conservative-leaning Supreme Court correspondent, praised him in October as the court's "most insightful and strategic questioner." Less star-struck, First One @ One First blogger Mike Sacks described Alito in December as the conservatives' "enforcer."

When Alito took the bench in January 2006, Martin Lederman, then a professor at Georgetown University Law Center, identified more than 30 Supreme Court rulings where his predecessor, O'Connor, had cast pivotal votes. In a beginning-of-term preview last fall, Lederman, back at Georgetown after serving in the Justice Department, listed some of the areas where Alito's vote has already made a difference in bending or breaking past Supreme Court rulings. In apparently good health at age 60, Alito presumably has at least another decade to work with the conservative bloc to change some of the others.

Ginsburg: Knowing When to Leave
(*Jost on Justice*, March 18, 2013)

Fresh from celebrating her 80th birthday, Ruth Bader Ginsburg will take her place on the Supreme Court bench this week as the twelfth justice in history to serve past that milestone. Completing her 19th term, Ginsburg walks slower these days, but her age has not visibly affected her work as a justice, either in her questions on the bench or in her written opinions.

Still, Ginsburg must by now be contemplating her legacy. Like her admirers, she probably views her years on the court with a mix of satisfaction and disappointment. Ginsburg has done her work well, but, contrary to the title of Jeffrey Toobin's insightful profile in *The New Yorker* (March 11), she has not been not a "heavyweight" on the court.

Because of what Toobin calls "less fortunate timing," Ginsburg has been in dissent on many of the issues that most concern her: civil liberties, racial equality, and women's rights.

To safeguard her legacy, Ginsburg must now make the right decision about when to retire from the court. She has spoken often — most recently to Toobin — about wanting to stay until she is 82, the age at which her judicial hero Louis Brandeis retired from the court. Conveniently, she will reach that age in 2015, with Barack Obama, a civil liberties-minded Democrat, still in the White House. Asked by Toobin whether the party of the president is relevant to a justice's decision whether to retire, Ginsburg replied: "I think it is for all of us."

Ginsburg's place in history is assured not by her service on the court but by her role as a litigator in the 1970s in establishing a new constitutional right: the right to be free from governmental discrimination based on sex. Ginsburg graduated in 1959 from a top Ivy League law school, Columbia, but, despite a recommendation from the dean of Harvard Law School, was turned down for a clerkship by Justice Felix Frankfurter.

Ginsburg went on to found the *Women's Rights Law Reporter* while teaching at Rutgers Law School. In 1972 she became the first woman to gain tenure at Columbia Law School and also established the American Civil Liberties Union's Women's Rights Project. Already by then, Ginsburg had won the first of four women's rights rulings at the Supreme Court: a unanimous decision in 1971 striking down an Idaho law automatically favoring men over women in the appointment of administrators of estates (*Reed v. Reed*).

Ginsburg's next victory, *Frontiero v. Richardson* (1973), relied in part on her counterintuitive insight that laws that discriminate against women can also disadvantage men. The law at issue made it harder for a woman in military service to claim her husband as a dependent for purposes of health benefits than it was for a man to claim his wife. The court ruled the distinction unconstitutional but without a majority holding on the standard to be used in sex discrimination cases.

Only in Ginsburg's third case, *Craig v. Boren* (1976), did the court agree on what is now known as the "intermediate scrutiny" test: laws that discriminate on the basis of sex are unconstitutional unless they further an important governmental interest in a way substantially related to that interest. The law struck down in the case allowed girls to drink 3.2 percent beer at age 18 but boys only at age 21.

Ginsburg had argued for the more demanding "strict scrutiny" test, but over time intermediate scrutiny has proved to have effective bite in limiting sex discrimination. In her first term, Justice Sandra Day O'Connor, the first female justice, led a 5-4 majority in striking down the single-sex admissions policy at a state nursing school in Mississippi (*Mississippi University of Women v. Hogan*, 1982). A decade-and-a-half later, Ginsburg, as the court's second female justice, led a stronger, 7-1 majority in striking down the all-male admissions policy at Virginia Military Institute (*United States v. Virginia*, 1996). "Women seeking and fit for a VMI-quality education cannot be offered anything less," Ginsburg declared.

Unfortunately for Ginsburg's legacy, the VMI case stands all but alone as a memorable majority opinion. Instead, her memorable opinions of recent years have been in dissent, most notably her anguished attack on the 5-4 decision upholding the federal ban on so-called partial birth abortions (*Gonzales v. Carhart*, 2007). She can rightfully take credit, however, for using her dissent in the same year in *Ledbetter v. Goodyear Tire & Rubber Co.* to prompt Congress to overturn a decision making it harder to bring pay discrimination cases under federal law.

Like Ginsburg, Thurgood Marshall established his place in history before becoming a Supreme Court justice through the school desegregation litigation he directed at the NAACP Legal Defense Fund. As a justice, Marshall resisted delicate suggestions in the 1970s to retire with a Democrat, Jimmy Carter, in the White House. Marshall stayed for another 12 years but accomplished little; his successor, Clarence Thomas, now votes against the positions that Marshall worked and fought for.

Ginsburg told Toobin that she would stay on the court "as long as I can do the job full steam." By her own words, however, her stamina is not the only relevant consideration. Ginsburg's legacy will depend in part on whether she makes the right decision about the best time to step aside.

Breyer: The "Cold-Fish" Justice
(*Jost on Justice*, Aug. 17, 2014)

As a young lawyer, Ian Gershengorn minced no words in sizing up Stephen Breyer as a candidate for a vacancy on the Supreme Court. After plowing through a decade's worth of Breyer's work as a federal appeals court judge, Gershengorn reported to the Clinton White House that he had found "very little heart and soul" in Breyer's opinions. "Quite clearly," Gershengorn wrote in a memo co-authored with Tom Perrelli, "he is a rather cold fish."

Two decades later, Breyer is on the Supreme Court, and Gershengorn regularly appears before him as a deputy U.S. solicitor general. So, Gershengorn naturally took the chance to recant after his earlier evaluation surfaced last month in the release of some of President Clinton's White House papers.

"Everyone has regrets from his 20s," Gershengorn told The *Wall Street Journal*'s Supreme Court correspondent Jess Bravin. "Suffice it to say I have the highest respect for Justice Breyer and believe he has proven to be a terrific justice."

Gershengorn is entitled to his disavowal, but his evaluation proved to be spot-on at the time and looks as much true as false based on Breyer's 20 terms on the high court. Among The Nine, Breyer is on the cool end of the emotional spectrum, logical to a fault with little if any of the passion that one sees in Ginsburg or Sotomayor on the left, Scalia or Alito on the right, or even Kennedy in the middle.

Breyer left Clinton cold when he was interviewed in May 1993 for the vacancy that Ginsburg won instead on the strength of her emotion-laden life story. A year later, Breyer became the default choice for a second vacancy only after Clinton struck out with his hope to put a politician like George Mitchell or Bruce Babbitt on the court.

Belying Gershengorn's review to some extent, Breyer showed emotion at least twice during his Senate confirmation hearing, according to my account in *Supreme Court Yearbook*. When asked about affirmative action, Breyer spoke strongly about the need to do more to meet the "basic promise of fairness" in the Fourteenth Amendment after "years of neglect." He also signaled a strong commitment to women's rights, referencing his daughters Chloe and Nell seated behind him. "Think of some kind of rule that makes their life worse because they're women," Breyer said. "Wouldn't you say, but what kind of justification for that could there be?"

Breyer has proved to be a reliable vote for women's rights and racial justice throughout his tenure. He veers away from a liberal line on some other issues, however, notably First Amendment free speech issues and Fourth Amendment search disputes. In those two and other areas, Breyer displays his signature doctrinal commitment: pragmatism. "He is unapologetically pragmatic," Kevin Russell, a former Breyer law clerk and now a frequent Supreme Court advocate, remarked in a 20th anniversary profile in *USA Today.*

In Fourth Amendment cases, Breyer is likely to side with law enforcement, as in this year's 5-4 decision upholding a traffic stop based on an anonymous 911 call (*Navarette v. California*). In First Amendment cases, Breyer looks for reasons to uphold government regulation, as when he voted in dissent in 2011 to uphold California's ban on violent video games for minors (*Brown v. Entertainment Merchants Ass'n*).

Pragmatism can turn into hash, however, in a Supreme Court decision. When he wrote the main opinion in a case striking down parts of a law aimed at restricting sexual material on cable television, Breyer turned the court's precedents into a morass of generalities: "The Government may directly regulate speech," he wrote, "to address extraordinary problems, where its regulations are appropriately tailored to resolve those problems without imposing an unnecessarily great restriction on speech" (*Denver Area Educational Television Consortium v. FCC*, 1996).

More recently, Breyer provided nothing better than an unweighted multifactor approach for testing the powers of Congress when he wrote the decision upholding a federal law allowing civil commitment of mentally ill offenders (*United States v. Comstock*, 2011). In a dissent, Thomas said Breyer's "novel five-factor test" included no guidance on how to apply the decision to the next case.

Breyer's convoluted thinking is often on display on the bench as well. The one-time Harvard law professor is the master of the long-winded question and the hopelessly complex hypothetical. Often, he prefaces questions by saying he needs the answer to decide how he will vote. Other justices— perhaps most notably Alito on the right and Kagan on the left—use their questions more strategically to try to influence their colleagues' votes.

Perhaps most significantly, Breyer is Congress's best friend on the court. He served two tours as a staff assistant on Capitol Hill, helping to author the trucking and airline deregulation bills and the new system of federal sentencing guidelines. Statistics compiled by Yale law professor Paul Gewirtz in 2005 showed Breyer the least likely of the Rehnquist Court justices to vote to find laws passed by Congress unconstitutional. My count suggests he holds the same position on the Roberts Court.

Breyer has tried, in his book *Active Liberty* and elsewhere, to lay out an overall philosophy of the court's need to assist the process of self-government and to look to history and practice more than literal text to guide decisions. But his ideas have had nothing like the impact of those from his hot-tempered colleague Scalia. After two decades on the bench, the influence of the cold-fish justice is sometimes hard to discern.

Sotomayor: Wise Latina Justice
(*Jost on Justice*, Feb. 7, 2013)

Sonia Sotomayor notched her first courtroom victory as a prosecutor in New York City when a jury convicted a defendant in an episode stemming from an assault on his wife while riding the subway. The wife refused to testify, but the defendant was also charged with assaulting a fellow subway rider who had intervened to try to stop the beating.

Although gratified by the jury's guilty verdict, Sotomayor's heart sank when the judge said he was inclined to sentence the defendant to one year in jail. The defense attorney protested that the defendant had never been in trouble before and his family depended on him for support.

The judge then turned to Sotomayor, who — as she recounts in her insightful memoir *My Beloved World* — said she agreed with the defense lawyer. Jail would be a hardship for the family, Sotomayor acknowledged. Probation along with a treatment program for domestic abuse would be satisfactory. The judge went along with the recommendation.

Three decades later, opponents of Sotomayor's nomination to the Supreme Court in 2009 might have made something out of the case had they only known of it. Some critics labeled Sotomayor the "empathy nominee," playing off President Obama's listing of one of the attributes he had been looking for in a prospective justice. Sotomayor resisted the imputation. As a judge, she told the Senate Judiciary Committee, she based her decisions solely on the law.

Sotomayor reveals in her memoir, however, that empathy is in fact a deeply ingrained trait of hers. Chronicling her life up to her appointment to the federal bench in 1992, Sotomayor makes clear that she believes her "innate skills of the heart" help explain her success in rising from a crime- and drug-ridden Puerto Rican neighborhood in the Bronx to become the first Hispanic to serve on the highest court in the land.

"Whenever I make a new friend, my mind naturally goes to the question, what can I learn from this person?" Sotomayor writes midway through the 300-page memoir published last month [Jan. 15]. "There are very few people in the world whom you can't learn something from . . . ." Later, she explains how she came to realize that "leveraging emotional intelligence" was important to communicating with jurors along with remembering that there is a difference between what makes sense to a lawyer and what makes sense "to a human being."

Sotomayor's life parallels in some respects that of her Supreme Court colleague Clarence Thomas, who recounts in his memoir *My Grandfather's Son* how he rose from poverty to become the second African American justice. But the memoirs are as different in tone as night and day. Thomas's memoir is suffused with anger, resentment, and self-pity, not just in his account of his bitter confirmation battle but in the narrative of his childhood, adolescence and college and law school education.

By contrast, Sotomayor is forgiving and understanding even when confronted with hardships and prejudice of the same type that Thomas encountered. Her father was an alcoholic, who drank himself to death when Sonia was only eight, but Sotomayor depicts him nevertheless as loving and attentive. Her mother was distant and often insensitive, but Sotomayor gives her credit for instilling discipline and a love of learning. And when Sotomayor is admitted to Princeton as an undergraduate, she says she felt no envy or resentment toward her wealthier and better-prepared schoolmates. Instead, Sotomayor writes, she felt "only astonishment at how much of a world there was out there and how much of it others already knew."

From his Yale Law School experience, Thomas has taken away a lasting resentment toward affirmative action. His degree, he wrote, bears "the taint of racial preference." Sotomayor, by contrast, has openly called herself an "affirmative action baby" and bears her status as a badge of honor. She relates in the memoir her dinner at Yale with a law firm recruiter who asked her whether being Puerto Rican helped her get admitted. "It probably didn't hurt," Sotomayor replied. "But I imagine that graduating summa cum laude and Phi Beta Kappa from Princeton had something to do with it too."

Throughout the memoir, Sotomayor stresses discipline and perseverance as keys to her success along with confidence that she could do whatever she set out to do — just as she learned to manage her diabetes from the age of seven. Yet, unlike Thomas's self-portrait, there is no swagger in Sotomayor's account. Thomas wrote that it never occurred to him that he could not do the work of a Supreme Court justice. By contrast, Sotomayor writes that her knees were knocking the first time she presided over a courtroom. She used the same metaphor in a television interview to describe her first session on the Supreme Court.

Sotomayor closes her memoir by recalling a friend's rebuke from law school days that she never took firm stands, that she was always open to persuasion. Sotomayor takes the point that having principles is important, but wisely adds that equally important is being open to new understandings. "My highest aspiration for my work on the Court," she writes, "is to grow in understanding beyond what I can foresee."

Kagan's Future Path Unclear

(Jost on Justice, May 10, 2010)

Elena Kagan appears on a path toward Senate confirmation as the next Supreme Court justice, but her ability to move the court in the direction that President Obama hopes for remains to be seen. Indeed, her first effort in that regard failed.

In announcing his selection today (May 10), Obama stressed along with Kagan's academic credentials (Princeton, Oxford, Harvard) her reputation as a consensus-builder in six years as dean of Harvard Law School. Obama specifically pointed to Kagan's role in hiring conservative scholars for the school's ideologically fractious faculty as evidence of a judicial temperament open to diverse points of view.

Liberal advocacy groups have been pinning their hopes on Kagan as the silver bullet for pulling Justice Anthony M. Kennedy more often toward the four-justice liberal bloc and away from the bloc of four conservatives headed by Chief Justice John G. Roberts Jr. But as U.S. solicitor general, she ended on the losing side of the Court's 5-4 decision in January striking down a major provision of the McCain-Feingold campaign finance law and freeing corporations and unions to spend unlimited sums on congressional or presidential elections.

Obama referred to the case, *Citizens United v. Federal Election Commission*, in his remarks, noting that Kagan took on the case as her debut before the Court last September despite the odds against the conservative majority's upholding the law. But, echoing his earlier comments on the retirement of Justice John Paul Stevens, Obama said that Kagan understood that "in a democracy, powerful interests must not be allowed to drown out the voices of ordinary citizens."

Kagan had been regarded as the presumptive front-runner for the vacancy ever since last fall, when Stevens signaled his likely retirement by hiring only one law clerk for the coming term instead of the normal complement of four for a sitting justice. In his remarks, Obama indicated he was drawn to Kagan's life story: immigrant grandparents; her father a housing lawyer, her mother a public school teacher. He noted as well her firsts as a "trailblazing leader" — first female dean at Harvard Law School and now the first woman to serve as solicitor general.

In her academic career, Kagan produced only a limited paper trail: several law review articles on First Amendment issues, a pair on presidential power, and a few book reviews and speeches. They give conservative critics little ammunition for opposing her, but likewise leave liberal advocacy groups with only limited clues about Kagan's stands on specific legal issues. In her longest academic writing, she dissected the Court's free speech cases at length but offered no overarching theory of her own.

If confirmed, Kagan will come to the Court after service in all three branches of the federal government. She was law clerk to federal appeals court judge Abner Mikva and later to Supreme Court Justice Thurgood Marshall, both liberal icons. She served as special counsel to the Senate Judiciary Committee during the 1993 confirmation hearings for Justice Ruth Bader Ginsburg — and later wrote critically about Ginsburg's evasion of senators' questions. She then went on to work for Mikva as associate White House counsel during the Clinton administration.

Kagan will lack, however, the experience that the other eight justices have: prior service on a federal appeals court. Some conservatives are pointing to the lack of experience as a detriment. On the other hand, some Court watchers have been yearning for a justice to be selected from outside the judicial monastery. William H. Rehnquist — who served for 19 years as chief justice — and Lewis F. Powell Jr. in 1971 were the last justices to be nominated without prior judicial experience.

If she joins justices Ginsburg and Sonia Sotomayor as the third woman, Kagan would add to gender diversity, but otherwise she will make the Court less representative of the country as a whole. If she is confirmed, all nine justices will have attended either Harvard or Yale law school. (Stevens graduated from Northwestern.) She will be the seventh justice who counts the Boston-Washington corridor as home (all but Kennedy and Clarence Thomas). And Kagan would be the third Jewish justice — and, with six Catholics, leave the Court for the first time ever with no Protestant member.

Kagan's background marks her as a liberal from her childhood on Manhattan's Upper West Side through a college thesis on socialism and her campaign work for such Democrats as Rep. Theodore Weiss and 1988 presidential nominee Michael Dukakis. Republican senators looking for vulnerabilities will undoubtedly criticize her decision as Harvard dean to enforce the law school's policy barring military recruiters on campus to protest the "don't ask, don't tell" policy on gays in the military. (She changed the policy after the Supreme Court ruled against law schools by an 8-0 vote.) With that exception, however, Kagan gives potential opponents few easy targets for attack.

Among the four front-runners for the nomination, Kagan was the youngest; she turned 50 last month. She would be the youngest justice to take the bench since Clarence Thomas was appointed at the age of 43 in 1991. (Justice Antonin Scalia took office in 1986, six months past his 50th birthday.) Her relative youth — and the prospect of a 20- to 30-year tenure — was undoubtedly a factor in Obama's selection. Stevens retires after a 35-year evolution from moderate conservative to liberal leader. With limited evidence, predictions about Kagan's role should be made and considered with utmost tentativeness.

Kennedy's Power of Being Earnest
(Jost on Justice, Sept. 15, 2013)

Supreme Court Justice Anthony M. Kennedy was at his most serious and most earnest as the keynote speaker at the annual meeting of the American Bar Association (ABA) in San Francisco last month [Aug. 10]. Greeting his audience as "fellow adherents to the rule of law," Kennedy devoted the first half of a 26-minute speech to the national crisis in prison crowding before turning in the second half to the importance of civic education for young people.

Kennedy had all the usual statistics about overincarceration in the United States: 2.1 million prisoners nationwide, including 160,000 in his home state of California — an imprisonment rate seven times greater than in England, France, or Germany. But he quoted as well from the Gospels — "I was in prison and ye came unto me" — to stress the bar's responsibility to address the crisis. Despite the prisoner's offense, Kennedy concluded, "he or she is part of the family of humankind."

Kennedy was, if anything, even more didactic as he talked about instilling in young people a proper appreciation for "the meaning of freedom and its history." "You cannot preserve what you have not studied," the one-time constitutional law professor said. "You cannot protect what you do not comprehend. You cannot defend what you do not know."

Some in the press corps have been known to roll their eyes as Kennedy waxes lyrical in his speeches. His conservative critics — including his fellow justice, Antonin Scalia — sneer more pointedly when Kennedy veers into grandiloquence in his opinion. As one example, they cite Kennedy's opening paean to the "transcendent dimensions" of individual liberty in his opinion for the court in *Lawrence v. Texas* (2003) striking down laws against gay sex.

But make no mistake: Kennedy's tendencies toward pomposity are nothing to be trifled with. Today, after a quarter-century on the court, Kennedy is clearly its most powerful individual member. Year after year, he is the justice with the fewest number of dissenting votes. "It's the Roberts Court," NBC's Supreme Court correspondent remarked in his end-of-term wrap-up in June. "But Anthony Kennedy is the president and chief executive officer."

Kennedy is in fact more powerful than his former swing-vote colleague, Sandra Day O'Connor, who was given the title of "most influential justice" in Joan Biskupic's biography a few years back. O'Connor's tendency was to cast her often decisive vote in favor of splitting the difference between opposing views. Kennedy, by contrast, comes down hard on one side or the other: no muddled compromises in his majority opinions in closely divided decisions. Instead, as in *Lawrence*, Kennedy sets out explicit holdings, black-letter law for judges to follow with little of the case-by-case weighing that O'Connor often favored.

As a result, Kennedy's judicial legacy is of real, unmistakable consequence. And he has made his mark in areas that one might not have expected.

Gay rights is the most recent and most obvious example. Kennedy authored the 5-4 decision in June, *United States v. Windsor*, that struck down the federal Defense of Marriage Act (DOMA), which barred marriage-based benefits to married gay and lesbian couples. He also wrote the court's two previous gay rights landmarks: *Lawrence* and the earlier decision, *Romer v. Evans* (1996), that struck down a Colorado initiative barring the enactment of anti-gay discrimination laws.

Gay rights advocates opposed Kennedy when he was nominated to the court in 1987, noting that he had ruled against gay rights plaintiffs in five cases while on the federal appeals court in California. With a keener eye, they might have recognized a gay rights supporter waiting to come out. In the first of the cases, *Beller v. Middendorf* (1981), Kennedy upheld the military's policy of discharging homosexuals but only after acknowledging that "the choice to engage in homosexual action" might be "a fundamental right" entitled to "full protection as an aspect of the individual's right to privacy."

Kennedy has also made his mark on sentencing issues. He has been the pivotal vote in a series of decisions beginning in 2002 that bar the death penalty for mentally retarded defendants, for juveniles, or in child rape cases. Kennedy also wrote the 2010 decision barring life without parole sentences for juveniles in non-homicide cases and led the follow-on decision to bar mandatory life without parole terms for juvenile murderers.

As the court's most consistent First Amendment supporter, Kennedy can also take credit for the string of rulings under Chief Justice John G. Roberts Jr. generally backing freedom of speech. Indeed, according to insider accounts, it was Kennedy who prevailed on Roberts in the campaign finance case, *Citizens United v. Federal Election Commission* (2010), to turn a narrow ruling into a broad guarantee of political speech rights for corporations.

On the bench as in his writing, Kennedy is always in earnest. Other justices engage in an occasional joke or witticism, but Kennedy hardly ever if at all. He came to the court as a safe choice after the Senate rejected the combative conservative, Robert Bork, as outside the mainstream. Instinctively mild of manner, Kennedy might have been expected to recede to the background. Instead, with the court about to begin a new term, he once again is the justice that lawyers focus on as they fashion their arguments and the justice that court watchers watch as they handicap the term's cases.

2

#Supreme

"We are not final because we are infallible, but we are infallible only because we are final."

Justice Robert H. Jackson
(Brown v. Allen *(1953), concurring opinion)*

#ConfirmationProcess

Politics first reared its head in the Supreme Court confirmation process in 1795 when the Senate rejected President George Washington's nomination of John Rutledge as chief justice because of Rutledge's criticism of the Jay Treaty with Great Britain. Pure partisan politics underlay many of the rejected Supreme Court nominations in the 19th century, but legal ideology began to play a more prominent role beginning in the early 20th century. The Senate can go only so far in learning a nominee's legal views, however, because the politically savvy nominee will steer clear of any comment about how he or she will rule in future cases.

Full Disclosure
(*CQ Weekly*, July 18, 2005)

Loose lips sink ships . . . and Supreme Court nominations. That appears to be the rule Republicans plan to follow in guiding President Bush's eventual choice for the high court through a potentially rancorous Senate confirmation process.

Politically, the tactic makes sense. Robert H. Bork failed to win confirmation in 1987 because of what he said about his legal views. Four years later, Clarence Thomas survived in part because of what he refused to say: his views on abortion.

Democratic senators, however, have good reasons to resist the tactic. Neither history nor constitutional principle limits the Senate's right to examine a judicial nominee's views on legal issues. And a decade ago both Ruth Bader Ginsburg and Stephen G. Breyer demonstrated in their confirmation hearings that a nominee can disclose much about his or her legal philosophy without crossing the ethical line against pre-judging a future case.

No one who listened closely to those two confirmation hearings — as I did — should be surprised by the moderately liberal course of Ginsburg's and Breyer's votes and opinions over the past decade. What the Senate heard was what the country got. Conversely, no one who read Thomas' pre-Supreme Court writings and speeches should be surprised by the doctrinaire brand of conservatism he has espoused as a justice. But Thomas evaded senators' questions in the pre-Anita Hill phase of his confirmation hearing — most famously, by maintaining that he had never "debated" the issue of abortion.

Less than nine months after his confirmation, Thomas voted (in dissent) to overrule *Roe v. Wade*. If Thomas had acknowledged to the senators his willingness to throw out legal precedent — since repeated on several other well-established constitutional rulings — it is doubtful he would have been confirmed. The country got what the Senate never had a chance to hear.

The White House is sending mixed signals about what role it thinks the Senate should play in finding successors to Justice Sandra Day O'Connor — and perhaps later to Chief Justice William H. Rehnquist.

Bush and White House aides have been talking with senators on both sides of the aisle in advance of any decisions. At the same time, Fred Thompson, the former Tennessee senator tapped to manage the confirmation process in the Senate, is saying that nominees should not be pressed to answer any question that would indicate how they would decide a particular case or kind of case.

Senate Democrats want broader questioning. "The No. 1 thing we look for are the person's views," Charles E. Schumer of New York told *The Washington Post*. The Democrats have no other choice, really. Short of an ethical snafu, they need to probe the nominee's views to determine whether there are grounds to oppose confirmation. But the Democrats are also making constitutional sense.

The Senate has a role to play in seating justices on the nation's highest court. "Advice and consent" is not exercised with a rubber stamp. And at a time when legal issues are both so important and so divisive — and the Supreme Court's delicate balance up in the air — the president's nominees are not entitled to a lifetime seat solely on the basis of a legal resume and a presidential say-so.

Historically, the Senate has not been a rubber stamp. In the 19th century — before the advent of formal confirmation hearings — nearly one-third of Supreme Court nominations failed, most of them because of what historian Peter Comiskey calls their "politicolegal views."

In modern times, Republican and Southern Democratic senators sharply questioned Thurgood Marshall and Abe Fortas in the 1960s about their views on liberal Warren Court decisions. Rehnquist faced contentious hearings when nominated as an associate justice in 1971 and when he was up for promotion to chief justice in 1986.

But the mother of all Supreme Court confirmation fights was the battle over President Ronald Reagan's nomination of the confirmed conservative Bork to succeed the centrist Lewis F. Powell Jr. in 1987. To this day, Bork and his defenders insist that he was — as they put it — "borked" by Democrats and liberal interest groups that distorted his views and savaged his character.

In fact, Bork's 30 hours at the witness table provided what *CQ Weekly* described then as "an unusually rich debate over legal philosophy." His rejection by a lopsided 42-58 vote showed that the Senate considered him outside the legal mainstream. What the Senate heard, it did not like.

The Senate needs to hear from Bush's nominees, within the limits of judicial ethics and impartiality, to judge their views about the law and the Supreme Court's role. With both sides saying there is so much at stake in choosing the next justices, it would be odd to limit the Senate's role by depriving senators of the information they need before giving their consent to the president's choice.

Confirmation Class
(CQ Weekly, Jan. 30, 2006)

Are Senate confirmation hearings for Supreme Court nominees an idea whose time has gone? From opposite perspectives, partisans say that such proceedings have become meaningless exercises because the nominees do not give straight answers or that they are harmful because opponents use the hearings to politicize the process and smear worthy nominees.

Both indictments are true, but the prescription is wrong. Improve the process if possible. But flawed as they are, the confirmation hearings serve a valuable purpose. Certainly, the Senate Judiciary Committee's five days of hearings for Judge Samuel A. Alito Jr. were a disappointment — both as television drama and as a foreshadowing of his constitutional decision-making.

Alito was boring and repetitive, his answers scripted and deliberately obscure. The senators were too often predictable and verbose. Alito may have given the senators more evasive responses than real answers, but the senators who managed to ask good questions usually failed with their follow-ups.

After Alito finished his third day on the witness stand, Democrat Joseph R. Biden Jr. of Delaware went so far as to suggest that confirmation hearings be scrapped. "We should just go to the floor of the United States Senate, debate the relative merits of the positions of the nominee, and vote," he said on NBC's "Today."

For their part, Republicans asserted that Democrats were poisoning the judicial confirmation process with their attacks on Alito. Speaking before the Judiciary panel's party-line vote last week to recommend Alito's confirmation, Tom Coburn of Oklahoma warned that, "We will not have good people come before this committee if we continue this process."

As a historical matter, however, the confirmation hearing cannot be blamed for the politicization of Supreme Court nominees. Nominees did not appear before the Senate until 1925; Senate debates on confirmation were closed until 1929. But there was plenty of hardball politics without a public process. Twenty-two nominations failed in the 1800s for a variety of philosophical or political reasons. And still in the pre-hearing era, Louis Brandeis won confirmation in 1916 only after a bruising battle — ostensibly over his pro-consumer views, but also tinged with anti-Semitism. [*Clarification:* The Senate held a committee hearing on Brandeis, but he did not testify.]

Nominees themselves benefited from some of the early confirmation hearings. Brandeis had no official forum to respond to attacks. But Harlan Fiske Stone used his appearance before the Senate in 1925 to answer criticism of his role as attorney general in prosecuting a sitting senator. Felix Frankfurter similarly succeeded in 1939 in rebutting criticism of his work for the American Civil Liberties Union.

In like fashion, Alito used his 18 hours on the witness stand to answer an array of criticisms that had accumulated in the two months after President Bush nominated him. Make of those answers what you will, but Alito gave the Senate — and the public — a full-throated reply to accusations about his character, his ethics and his judicial ideology and record.

"People would view it as unfair for senators to form a judgment if they hadn't heard from the nominee," says Michael Comiskey, a political scientist at Pennsylvania State University and author of a book on the Supreme Court confirmation process. "Now, we've heard his explanation, and people can form their own judgments after having heard both sides."

Biden and others, however, say Alito ducked substantive questions on such issues as abortion rights and executive power. On this score, Biden must take part of the blame himself. In the back-to-back hearings for Chief Justice John G. Roberts Jr. and Alito, he was one of several senators who appeared more interested in hearing themselves talk than in asking direct questions and careful follow-ups.

In any event, Alito revealed a lot by what he said — and what he didn't say. He respects precedent, but refused to call the *Roe v. Wade* abortion rights decision a "super-precedent" or "settled law." He said the president is not above the law, but left himself plenty of room for giving the current president a wide constitutional berth in the pending and coming cases on executive power.

Most broadly, Alito revealed himself — as several liberal commentators remarked — as a judge who focuses on legal issues to the near exclusion of their real-life stakes. In any number of disputed cases, he opted for technically defensible legal positions with little regard for the values that the applicable law was designed to protect. Republican senators were satisfied with what they heard; Democrats were not. That's politics. Those political judgments would be less well informed without the confirmation hearing.

Some day, senators may ask better questions, nominees may give better answers, and judicial politics may be less contentious. Until then, the confirmation process — like Winston Churchill's definition of democracy — is the worst possible system except for all the others.

Confirmation Show Must Go On

(Jost on Justice, July 19, 2009)

The Founding Fathers did not decide that the Supreme Court would have nine justices. That goes back to 1869. They did not decide that the court would begin each term on the first Monday in October. That goes back to 1917.

The Framers also did not decide that Supreme Court nominees would appear in front of a Senate committee before a vote on their confirmation. That practice goes back only to 1925. And only since the 1960s have senators made extensive use of the procedure to try to learn the nominee's legal views and to air their own views on the hot legal issues of the day.

So the constitutional design does not depend on the Supreme Court confirmation hearing. We would not break faith with the Framers to dispense with a practice with so much evasion and circumlocution by the nominee and so much political posturing by the senators.

Despite the bad reviews, however — and the reviews for Judge Sonia Sotomayor's four days on the witness stand were poor at best — the show must go on. President Obama and his advisers took all the time they needed to explore the nominee's record and views before making a selection. Both the Senate and the public were entitled to their chance to see and hear the nominee for themselves before entrusting her with lifetime appointment to the Supreme Court.

There's no denying that, despite her impressive academic and professional qualifications, Judge Sotomayor was less than stellar on the Broadway of the political stage. She may have been "disciplined and good humored" (Jeffrey Rosen of *The New Republic* in *The New York Times*), but to many she appeared to be "over rehearsed" (David Broder, *Washington Post*). Perhaps Sotomayor "accomplished *her* goals" (attorney Andrew Pincus in *The Wall Street Journal*, emphasis added). But "it is not at all clear what all this accomplished" (law dean Erwin Chemerinsky, also in the *Journal*). "A kabuki dance," (Mark Shields, *PBS NewsHour*).

Sotomayor and her White House handlers bear principal responsibility for this lifeless performance. It was a decision born of politics, not judicial ethics, to present herself as a legal automaton who simply follows precedent as long as *stare decisis* says to. No wonder that one senator asked her whether judging amounts to nothing more than following a recipe in a cookbook.

Sotomayor rightly began with and returned often to her life story: a good one, to be sure. But again it was nothing but politics that led her to emphasize her early years as a prosecutor and then to claim all but complete ignorance of the legal positions that the Puerto Rican Legal Defense and Education Fund took during her 12 years with the organization, including service as chair of the litigation committee.

Senators on both sides of the dais, however, must share in the responsibility for the unedifying spectacle. Veteran Democrats Herb Kohl of Wisconsin and California's Dianne Feinstein opened by complaining about the limited information from the most recent nominees: John Roberts and Samuel Alito. But among all the Democrats only Feinstein succeeded in eliciting a nugget of useful information: Sotomayor's agreement that the woman's health remains a "compelling consideration" in testing the validity of abortion regulations.

For their part, Republicans went on and on and on about the "wise Latina woman" speeches, well after the questions were yielding any useful information or perspective. One longed for Judiciary Committee Chairman Patrick Leahy to bang the gavel and say, "Asked and answered. Let's move on."

More substantively, no Republican senator recognized the patent inconsistency in stressing the power of elected legislators, not courts, to make laws but at the same time pressing Sotomayor to interpret the Second Amendment to limit gun control laws enacted by elected state and local governments. And no Republican senator gave Sotomayor credit for her decision in the New Haven firefighters case to follow the apparent precedent and to uphold the decision by local officials in the case.

Of course, the show lacked drama from the outset. Sotomayor's nomination by a still popular president was assured of confirmation in a Senate with a 60-vote Democratic majority. Republicans found no smoking guns in her record apart from the "wise Latina" speeches. By the end, even her critics were conceding her to be a mainstream judge with no evident problems of temperament in this setting at least.

What kind of justice will Sonia Sotomayor be? Democrats hope and Republicans expect that she will fit in comfortably with the court's liberal bloc — still only four strong in most instances. Perhaps. But University of Texas law professor Sanford Levinson may be quite right in his end-of-show prediction to the *New York Times* that Sotomayor will be the same "basically cautious person" on the bench that she was on the stand. The hearings may not have told us what we wanted to know, but they quite possibly told us all there is to know about Justice Sonia Sotomayor.

Don't Count on Candor

(Jost on Justice, Jan. 9, 2012)

When John Marshall Harlan appeared before the Senate Judiciary Committee in 1955 for confirmation to the Supreme Court, Sen. James Eastland, the race-baiting Mississippi Democrat, wanted to ask about the court's still new school desegregation decision. But no matter how Eastland phrased the question, Harlan was giving no hints about his views on the ruling. "I should not be asked to forecast how I will decide cases when they arise before me," Harlan said.

Two years later, William J. Brennan Jr. was pressed for his views on the legal status of the Communist Party from Sen. Joseph McCarthy, the red-baiting Wisconsin Republican. Brennan — like Harlan before him, already serving on the court under a recess appointment — similarly resisted being pinned down. "I simply cannot venture any comment whatever that touches upon any matter pending before the court," Brennan said.

The Harlan and Brennan hearings, recalled in a new law journal article by political scientists Dion Farganis and Justin Wedeking, mark the beginning of the modern Supreme Court confirmation process. Not until the 1950s did it become standard practice for Supreme Court nominees to appear in person before the Senate Judiciary Committee for a confirmation hearing. Indeed, the Senate held no committee hearings at all until the nomination of Louis Brandeis in 1916 — and Brandeis did not himself testify in a hearing that featured sharp criticism of his progressive views.

Today, the Supreme Court confirmation process is widely criticized — indeed, mocked — as a meaningless charade. Back when he chaired the Senate Judiciary Committee, Joe Biden famously described confirmation hearings as "a Kabuki dance." In the critics' view, every nominee since Robert Bork's ill-fated candor in 1987 has taken shelter in judicial ethics to turn aside any effort to learn his or her views on legal issues. "No hints, no forecasts, no previews," Ruth Bader Ginsburg said in her opening statement in 1993.

The critique seems to assume some golden age of Supreme Court confirmations when nominees answered senators' questions freely, giving them all the information they needed for knowledgeable votes. Farganis, a professor at Elon University in North Carolina, and Wedeking, a professor at the University of Kentucky, demonstrate in their article in *Law and Society Review* that the idea of the once fully forthcoming confirmation hearing is largely myth — some truth to it, but no more than some.

The researchers took on the monumental task of reading and encoding all of the confirmation hearings from Harlan through the most recent: Bush nominees John G. Roberts Jr. and Samuel A. Alito Jr. and Obama nominees Sonia Sotomayor and Elena Kagan. Nominees' answers were categorized and then counted as "fully forthcoming," "qualified," "not forthcoming," or non-responsive ("non-answer").

The numbers confirm some decline in candor since the Bork hearings, though the very next nominee — Anthony M. Kennedy — was among the most forthcoming. But Farganis and Wedeking attribute the relatively slight decline in candor to another, even stronger trend: the increasing number of questions from senators touching on the nominees' personal views.

Beyond the researchers' numbers, the senators' increased inquisitiveness can be seen quite dramatically in a law library with the printed volumes of confirmation hearings. The Harlan and Brennan hearings are printed along with four others in a single volume. The Bork hearings mark the beginning of multi-volume hearings. Bork's spans seven volumes; two decades later, Roberts's confirmation hearing fills eight volumes, Alito's 10.

Some of the hearing records' length stems from outside witnesses, but the nominee now routinely spends more time in the witness chair than in the past. The hearing for Charles Whittaker in 1957 was so perfunctory that a former Supreme Court law clerk, the future chief justice William H. Rehnquist, was prompted to write a law review article critical of the confirmation process. Byron R. White was asked six, non-challenging questions in 1962.

The court — and the confirmation process — became more politicized in the 1960s. Senators asked more and more questions, more and more confrontational — arguably fulfilling their constitutional duty to determine whether to render their "advice and consent" to the president's choice. Equally, however, the nominee has some obligation to the judicial oath he or she hopes to take not to prejudge the issues that are to come before the court. The Supreme Court nominee's pledge card is necessarily limited to a promise to endeavor to decide cases fairly and impartially on the basis of the evidence and the law.

This restriction does not mean that the confirmation hearings are useless. No one reviewing the confirmation testimony of Ginsburg or Stephen G. Breyer could be surprised by their moderately liberal records on the court. Both, for example, strongly endorsed the existing constitutional precedents on abortion rights. By contrast, the qualified responses that Roberts and Alito gave on *Roe v. Wade* foreshadowed the position they took only one term later to uphold a federal ban on so-called partial birth abortions in a decision that undercut one of *Roe*'s major premises.

As with democratic government itself, the process is not perfect. But the process gives senators enough information to make a meaningful choice whether to confirm a nominee or not. Senators can probe; nominees can duck. And the justice who seemingly departs from his or her confirmation statements can at least be held accountable in the court of public opinion. Critics who find this unsatisfactory yearn for some ideal that cannot exist — and never has.

#LifetimeTenure

The Constitution provides that the judges of the Supreme Court and "such inferior courts" as Congress may establish "shall hold their Offices during good Behaviour...." Thurgood Marshall famously remarked that he was "appointed for life" and intended to "serve my term." Ill health, however, forced Marshall to retire in 1991; he died two years later. Several other justices have chosen to retire when an ideologically compatible president could name their successors. The unsavory political gamesmanship is one reason why I favor a proposal to limit justices to 18-year terms of active service, with lifetime tenure as "senior justices" thereafter. Alas, the proposal is probably a political non-starter.

Judicial Retirement Strategy
(*CQ Weekly*, Feb. 19, 2007)

Chief Justice Earl Warren tried to time his retirement so President Lyndon B. Johnson could appoint his successor before the 1968 election. But Senate Republicans filibustered Johnson's effort to put Abe Fortas in the top job, allowing President Richard M. Nixon to make the pivotal appointment of Warren E. Burger the next year.

Other justices have had more success in timing their departures for political effect. Republican Potter Stewart's decision to retire in 1981 gave his vacancy to Ronald Reagan to fill (with Sandra Day O'Connor). Byron R. White, at the time the court's only Democratic appointee, decided to leave in 1993 so Bill Clinton could name his successor (Ruth Bader Ginsburg).

Such episodes illustrate that politics plays a big part not only when justices join the court, but also when they leave. But new details about Chief Justice William H. Rehnquist's conversations with O'Connor as they both weighed retirement add a new twist: One justice — Rehnquist, in this case — influencing the timing of another's departure.

The events, as reported by Jan Crawford Greenburg of ABC News [now CBS News] in her recent book *Supreme Conflict* suggest that the gravely ill Rehnquist might have intentionally misled O'Connor about his own likely tenure so as to ease her off the court earlier than she wanted. And even the hint of manipulation helps make the case for a proposal to limit active service on the Supreme Court to 18 years. By providing for a vacancy every two years, the proposal might reduce the Armageddon-like nature of some recent confirmation battles.

Rehnquist reportedly had his eye on confirmation politics in June 2005. As Greenburg tells the story, O'Connor approached the chief justice earlier in the year as she began thinking about retiring to care for her ailing husband, John. At the time, Rehnquist suggested that they talk again at the end of the term. Rehnquist, suffering from thyroid cancer, knew from his doctors that he probably had less than a year to live, but he had not told his colleagues. When O'Connor approached Rehnquist a second time, he surprised her by saying that he intended to stay for another term. And, according to Greenburg, Rehnquist pointedly added: "I don't think we need two vacancies."

In Greenburg's view, Rehnquist effectively forced O'Connor to retire then or wait two years, longer than she wanted. She took the first option. But then Rehnquist died two months later, creating the situation he had supposedly wanted to avoid.

Greenburg does not accuse Rehnquist of being deliberately misleading, but one conservative commentator saw the implication — and applauded. "If it is true that William Rehnquist effectively pushed Sandra Day O'Connor out the door," political science professor Matthew Franck wrote for *National Review Online*, "this fact would count as the last great service he did for his country."

Most court watchers, however, would probably disapprove of one justice manipulating another's retirement decision. And Rehnquist's shielding information about his health had that effect, intentional or not.

Whatever the reasons, the political calculations that retiring justices make would appear to serve no legitimate constitutional purpose. In the modern era, justices often stay or leave depending on who is in the White House. And the president and Senate view each nomination as a chance to shape the court for years to come.

Law professors Roger Cramton and Paul Carrington want to reduce the stakes by setting an 18-year limit on justices' active service. The still life-tenured justice would then assume "senior status," available for temporary assignments to lower federal courts or even to the Supreme Court itself if a sitting justice was recused from a case. Cramton and Carrington developed the proposal in part because some aging justices have not carried their fair share of the court's work. More important, however, they say current arrangements create "incentives for strategic behavior" that may not be in the court's best interests — or the public's.

Skeptics argue that this proposal would have cut short the careers of many distinguished justices. But several justices made their marks in fewer than 18 years, including Robert H. Jackson, John Marshall Harlan, and Lewis F. Powell Jr. And there seems to be little doubt but that any group of nine justices would have sufficient experience and knowledge to handle the court's work even if none had served for 20 or 30 years.

The Cramton-Carrington idea has support from law professors spanning the ideological spectrum. Their rationale is that, while no proposal can eliminate politics from Supreme Court successions, an orderly biennial vacancy could help make the court broadly responsive to changing political conditions and also lower the temperature on confirmation battles.

This is an interesting concept, probably worth an airing, but it has little prospect of serious consideration in Congress. Neither political party is likely to see much advantage in such a reform, and most scholars believe it would require a constitutional amendment. Thus, the process of replacing justices of the Supreme Court will probably remain unchanged, with all the resulting human drama that entails.

Too Much of a Good Thing?

(Jost on Justice, March 15, 2009)

The news that Justice Ruth Bader Ginsburg had been diagnosed with pancreatic cancer raced through legal and judicial circles in a cyber-instant on February 5. With Chief Justice William H. Rehnquist's death from thyroid cancer in September 2005 still fresh in mind, Ginsburg's medical bulletin prompted immediate research on survival rates for pancreatic cancer and ghoulish speculation about her likely successor.

The overall statistics are grim: the one-year survival rate is 20 percent; for five years, only 4 percent. But a month later, Ginsburg's prognosis appears more favorable than the norm. The 1-centimeter lesion originally detected in a CAT scan in late January turned out to be benign. A smaller tumor found during surgery was malignant, but it was removed. Surgeons found no evidence that cancer had spread to other parts of the body.

Ginsburg survived colon cancer 10 years ago without missing a single argument. She was back on the bench in late February, her performance seemingly unaffected. With the favorable news, however, comes the reminder that life tenure for Supreme Court justices means that turnover comes not at any regular or any logical intervals, but according to medical vicissitudes or personal predilections of the individual justices.

This is the law of succession in hereditary monarchies and personal dictatorships, but not in constitutional republics. Of course, the Constitution provides life tenure for federal judges — and for good reason. Life tenure is a good thing for ensuring the independence of the federal judiciary. But too much of a good thing may not be so good. And there are good arguments that given the unique role that Supreme Court justices have come to play in the American system of government, life tenure for The Nine is just that: too much of a good thing.

One statistic frames the issue: recent justices have been serving longer on average than justices did in most of U.S. history. As pointed out by eminent legal scholars Paul Carrington at Duke and Roger Cramton at Cornell, the average tenure of justices during the court's first 180 years — from 1789 through 1970 — was about 14 years; for justices who have retired since 1970, it is around 26 years.

Two factors contribute to the trend. Justices appear to be living longer. A fair number of early justices lived into their 70s, but recent justices are staying even longer: Lewis F. Powell Jr. retired three months before his 80th birthday; William J. Brennan Jr. and Thurgood Marshall retired at 83, Harry A. Blackmun at 85. And Rehnquist was one month shy of 81 when he died.

Presidents also seem to be appointing somewhat younger justices. Consider Byron R. White (44 when appointed), Rehnquist (47), and Clarence Thomas (43). Not to mention John G. Roberts Jr., appointed at age 50 as the youngest chief justice since John Marshall was appointed at age 45.

So justices start earlier and live longer. And with few exceptions they stay on the court as long as possible. This conclusion emerges from the recent paper, "Modern Departures From the Supreme Court," by Santa Clara University professors Terri Peretti and Alan Rozzi. They set out to examine whether justices time retirements to allow an ideologically compatible president to appoint an ideologically compatible successor. They conclude that so-called "strategic retirements" are the exception, that justices in fact continue to serve because they do not want to lose their position or influence.

There are exceptions: Potter Stewart in good health made way for President Reagan to appoint a Republican; White in good health gave

President Clinton the chance to name a Democrat. And occasionally justices' efforts to time their departures fail. Earl Warren tried to give President Johnson the chance to name his successor, but the Senate balked. William O. Douglas wanted to stay long enough for a Democrat to name his successor, but senility intervened.

Carrington and Cramton have helped assemble a diverse group of legal academics — liberals and conservatives alike — to argue that these statistics demonstrate a problem of institutional unaccountability. With long tenure and infrequent turnover, the court becomes out of touch — not as suggested by the crude attacks on "unelected judges," but isolated to some extent and deprived of the benefit of "new blood" at regular intervals.

Moreover, with no regular turnover, each nomination and each confirmation assumes an outsized political significance. Every president sees each nomination as the chance for a long-lasting legacy; likewise, interest groups and senators in both parties see each confirmation as a battle for lasting control of the court. And this is true whether or not justices deliberately play into the political gamesmanship.

The solution proposed by the Carrington-Crampton coalition is a hybrid form of term limits for the justices: 18 years of active service on the court, followed by life tenure as a senior justice; senior justices could serve on trial or appellate courts or even on the Supreme Court itself if a regular justice is recused. Judicial independence is preserved, but regular turnover — a new justice every two years — provided.

The obstacles to the proposal are foreboding: inertia, tradition, and the absence of any party or interest group with strong motivation to push it. Perhaps — as the old joke goes — you can't get there from here. But the logic is strong: strong enough for Congress to take a look.

Overstaying Their Welcome
(Jost on Justice, Oct. 2, 2010)

Brennan and Marshall. Their names were linked while on the Supreme Court and remain lastingly connected years after their deaths. William J. Brennan Jr., the affable Irishman and architect of the Warren Court's most important decisions. Thurgood Marshall, the gruff African

American crusader against racial segregation and first of his race on the Supreme Court.

Democratic presidential contenders — Al Gore in 2000, Barack Obama in 2008 — cited Brennan and Marshall as the models for their possible Supreme Court nominees. Liberal advocates regularly lament the lack of a comparable liberal on the court today.

Marshall's work in directing the litigation strategy leading up to *Brown v. Board of Education* has already been lionized in several creditable biographies. Brennan's life and work are now being told in a new, exhaustive biography: *Justice Brennan: Liberal Champion* by Seth Stern and Stephen Wermeil. (Disclosure: Stern, a *Congressional Quarterly* reporter [update: now with Bloomberg], and Wermeil, a professor at American University's Washington College of Law, are colleagues and friends.)

The Brennan biography, written by Stern and based on Wermeil's extensive interviews with the justice and access to his voluminous files, is touching off a new round of debate over the Warren Court's burst of liberal activism from the late 1950s until Warren's retirement in 1969. Today's conservatives answer criticism of the Roberts Court's reversals of precedent by likening them to the Warren Court's.

The comparisons are inapt, as this biography makes clear. With Brennan the mastermind behind the scenes, the Warren Court overturned old and poorly reasoned precedents that had allowed systematic injustices to go uncorrected. No one today would seriously argue against the decision in *Baker v. Carr* (1963) to use federal judicial power to establish the "one person, one vote" principle in legislative redistricting or the ruling in *Gideon v. Wainwright* (1962) to require appointment of counsel for indigent defendants in state criminal cases.

History has already judged those rulings and many other activist decisions of the Warren era as both necessary and beneficial. Eight months after the Roberts Court's ruling in *Citizens United*, it is reasonable to predict that history's judgment on freeing corporations to spend unlimited sums in political campaigns will be, at best, ambiguous.

The Brennan biography, however, supports a different line of criticism of both him and his fellow liberal Marshall. Both justices arguably stayed on the court too long.

By the mid-1970s, Brennan the private conciliator was becoming the public scold. His dissents were becoming, as he acknowledged later, "much too sharp and acid." For years, Brennan had made a point of taking new justices under his wing — helping orient them and laying the groundwork for gentle persuasion in future cases. But not long after Sandra Day O'Connor joined the court in 1981, Brennan made the unseemly and unwise decision to mock one of her early opinions in his dissent.

As for Marshall, Brennan privately considered his performance a disappointment. "What the hell happened when he came on the court, I'm not sure," Brennan is quoted as saying, "but he doesn't seem to have had the same interest." As with Brennan's dissents, Marshall was an occasional scold in the justices' internal deliberations — sometimes addressing his colleagues as "massa" in a deep slave dialect, according to the book.

Both men had health problems in the late 1970s, but both chose to stay on the bench. Brennan was persuaded in part by his family, who wondered what he would do with himself in retirement. Although unmentioned in the book, Marshall is famously reported to have bluntly rebuffed an inquiry from the Carter White House about his possible departure.

With a Democrat in the White House and a Democratic majority in the Senate, either or both of the justices might have retired with an expectation of a compatible successor. Both stayed on for a combination of personal and institutional reasons; their contributions over the next decade are in some sense negligible. Brennan lived long enough to see his successor, David H. Souter, emerge as an often likeminded justice; Marshall regretted his successor, Clarence Thomas.

The episodes buttress the arguments made for the proposal to modify justices' tenure by limiting their active service on the court to 18 years. As previously suggested here ("Supreme Court Tenure: Too Much of a Good Thing?," March 2, 2009), the proposal would promote healthy turnover at the court and defuse confirmation battles somewhat by reducing the stakes (the risks) of each new appointment. Despite support from a range of legal experts, however, the proposal is a dead letter politically. Neither party wants to give up the chance for a president to appoint a justice — a Roberts or a Kagan — who can serve for decades.

In his farewell letter this year, John Paul Stevens offered a mild apology to his fellow justices for his 34-year tenure. "If I have overstayed my welcome," he wrote, "it is because this is such a wonderful and unique job." Stevens was both sharp and collegial to the end, but his example is the proverbial exception that proves the rule. Age and wisdom may sometimes go hand in hand, but sometimes the better part of wisdom may be recognizing when they do not.

#ExtrajudicialActivities

Supreme Court justices have taken on political roles off the bench since the very first chief justice, John Jay, was asked by President George Washington to negotiate a post-revolutionary treaty with Great Britain. The Jay Treaty, narrowly ratified by a politically divided Senate, may have averted war with Britain, but no justice would likely accept such an assignment these days. Questions about the justices' extrajudicial activities arose recently, however, when the public interest group Common Cause complained about speeches that Antonin Scalia and Clarence Thomas had given to political groups. I was moved to dissent when a prominent law professor and ex-Supreme Court law clerk called for easing the strictures against the justices' engagement with the political world.

Justices' Off-Bench Roles
(*Jost on Justice*, Feb. 21, 2011)

Within a week of President John F. Kennedy's assassination on Nov. 22, 1963, President Lyndon B. Johnson created a commission to investigate the slaying and leaned hard on Chief Justice Earl Warren to agree to serve as chairman. Warren reluctantly took on the assignment and over the next seven months led a highly limited review of evidence gathered by others that concluded — just as Johnson wanted — that Lee Harvey Oswald had acted alone: no conspiracy.

Warren apparently managed to juggle the commission's work with his Supreme Court duties, but the commission's report is now recognized as woefully inadequate. The fault was not Warren's: the CIA withheld important evidence of Oswald's activities and connections. But wherever the blame may lie, Warren's extrajudicial assignment did no good for him or for the court.

No sitting Supreme Court justice has taken on an analogous off-the-bench assignment since then, apart from the chief justice's statutorily designated position as chancellor of the Smithsonian Institution. In that role too, chief justices have not shined. Chief Justice William H. Rehnquist in 2001 helped authorize a whopping salary increase for the Smithsonian's general secretary, who resigned in 2007 after disclosures of absenteeism and authoritarianism. Despite the governance crisis, Rehnquist's successor, John G. Roberts Jr., that year helped water down recommended reforms, including a reduction of the chief justice's role to non-voting board member.

The lesson of these episodes seems clear: justices should stick to their knitting. But Noah Feldman, a Harvard Law School professor and former Supreme Court law clerk, argues that the justices should spend more time off the bench, even to the point of taking on political responsibilities and engaging in political activities.

The justices' "disengagement from public life," Feldman writes in an op-ed in *The New York Times*, stems from "the imagined ideal of the cloistered justice." This monastic imperative, he says, has real costs. "Isolated justices make isolated decisions," Feldman writes. The evidence: *Clinton v. Jones* (1997), with its naïve assumption that allowing a civil suit (see: Paula Jones) against a sitting president (see: Bill Clinton) would not interfere with his duties as chief executive (see: impeachment).

Feldman writes against a specific context: the current controversy over off-bench activities of conservative justices Antonin Scalia and Clarence Thomas. Common Cause is calling for an ethics investigation of Scalia's and Thomas's participation in events sponsored in 2007 and 2008, respectively, by the billionaire Charles Koch, bankroller of conservative and libertarian causes. And Scalia came in for widespread criticism — from the *New York Times* editorial board, among others — for his Jan. 24 appearance before a closed-door meeting of the House Tea Party Caucus.

With reason, Feldman describes the controversy as "suspiciously partisan." Common Cause, the campaign-finance reform group, is straining to argue that Scalia and Thomas were so beholden to Koch to require recusal from the case, *Citizens United v. Federal Election Commission* (2010), that freed Koch's company and others to spend freely on political activities. Scalia's reported lecture on constitutional interpretation is more problematic, but mainly because it was behind closed doors to an overtly partisan group.

Feldman is not content, however, to knock down the attacks on Scalia and Thomas. With a selective retelling of history, Feldman argues that Supreme Court justices have committed politics ever since Chief Justice John Marshall, who served as secretary of state for the last month of John Adams' presidency after having assumed his position on the court. Charles Evans Hughes accepted the Republican nomination for president in 1916 while still serving as an associate justice. And Robert Jackson took a year's leave in 1945-46 to serve as chief prosecutor at the Nuremberg war crimes trials.

The brief overlap of Marshall's dual roles is *de minimis* and, in any event, unthinkable in present day. So too, given the realities of contemporary campaign finance, a justice's active quest for political office without leaving the bench. As for Jackson, he was praised for his opening and closing statements at the Nuremberg trials, but faulted for intemperance and weak cross-examination. And the court was left to decide cases for a full term with eight members and, after Chief Justice Harlan Fiske Stone's death in late April 1946, only seven — surely at some loss.

As a clerk to the reclusive justice David H. Souter, Feldman saw the monastic ideal at its extreme. He is right to think — without saying so — that the court could benefit from justices who come not from lower courts but from the political world. But he is wrong to excuse Chief Justice Fred Vinson for giving President Harry Truman a green light to seize the steel mills and wrong to lightly pass over Abe Fortas's poor judgment in advising LBJ while on the bench.

Feldman is especially wrong to argue for politically engaged justices with the court split as never before between Republican- and Democratic-appointed blocs. The current division pitting five conservative Republicans against four liberal Democrats feeds the cynical view that Supreme Court cases are in the end just politics. The justices can see and interact with the world in many venues: judicial conferences, college campuses, civic clubs, and so forth. But with every partisan appearance, a justice puts at risk his or her reputation as well as the court's commitment to equal justice for all.

#CamerasintheCourtroom

Television's early years in courtrooms were inauspicious. The Supreme Court in the 1960s reversed the high-profile convictions of Cleveland physician Samuel Sheppard and Texas financier Billie Sol Estes because of what the justices found to be inflammatory broadcast coverage of the trials. In 1981, however, the court acquiesced in Florida's statewide experiment of allowing TV and radio coverage of trials (Chandler v. Florida). *Cameras are now a regular part of news coverage in state courts, but the federal courts —and the Supreme Court in particular—resist.*

Not Ready for Prime Time
(*Jost on Justice*, Oct. 31, 2010)

Anyone following the contentious arguments over immigration policy is in for a real treat on Monday: a carefully organized debate, broadcast nationwide on C-SPAN (9 AM PDT), over Arizona's controversial new law aimed at cracking down on illegal aliens.

The participants will be two experienced lawyers: John Bouma, chairman of a big Phoenix-based law firm, representing Arizona, and Edwin Kneedler, a deputy U.S. solicitor general for the federal government. The forum will be a federal courtroom in San Francisco before a three-judge panel of the Ninth U.S. Circuit Court of Appeals.

One month later, the U.S. Supreme Court on Dec. 8 will be the forum for a similar debate over an earlier Arizona law that seeks to raise the penalties, for workers and employers alike, of hiring undocumented aliens. On that day, however, the only members of the general public who will be able to hear the arguments in real time will have to line up hours beforehand to claim one of the coveted 300 seats inside the courtroom.

Thirty years after the Supreme Court gave a green light to television coverage of state court trials, the court continues to close its doors to cameras. Whatever other courts may think about this no-longer-newfangled medium, the justices will have none of it, at least not yet.

The resistance continues despite the justices' awareness of the interest in the issue across in the street in the U.S. Capitol. The Senate Judiciary Committee in June approved a bill (S. 446) that would require the court to allow television coverage of oral arguments. A companion resolution (S. Res. 339), approved by the same, bipartisan 13-6 vote, would skirt separation-of-power issues by expressing "the sense of the Senate" that the court should allow TV coverage.

Both measures were sponsored by Sen. Arlen Specter, the Pennsylvania Republican-turned-Democrat now in the final months of his 30 years in the Senate. Specter has been dogged on the issue for years and has raised it at confirmation hearings for Supreme Court nominees.

With their confirmations at stake, Supreme Court nominees profess open-mindedness on the subject. "I don't have a set view on that," the future chief justice, John G. Roberts Jr., told Specter during his confirmation hearing in September 2005. "It's something that I would want to the listen to the views of — if I were confirmed — to my colleagues."

Less than a year later, however, Roberts had listened to his camera-shy colleagues and come around. "There's a concern about the impact of television on the institution," Roberts said in July 2006 to a conference of federal judges. "We're going to be very careful before we do anything that might have an adverse impact." In fact, the justices are not unanimous on the subject. Stephen G. Breyer says cameras will "inevitably" come to the court. Like Breyer, two other justices — Samuel A. Alito Jr. and Sonia Sotomayor — supported television coverage when they were serving on federal appeals courts.

The newest justice, Elena Kagan, voiced enthusiastic support for the idea in her confirmation hearing in June. "I think it would be a terrific thing to have cameras in the courtroom," Kagan said. "When you see what happens there, it's an inspiring sight."

With David H. Souter gone — he promised that television cameras would come in over his dead body — the avowed opponents on the court number three: Antonin Scalia, Anthony M. Kennedy, and Clarence Thomas. Kennedy fears some unstated negative effect on the court's "dynamic." Thomas too says it would be bad for the court without saying how. For his part, Scalia simply mocks the idea of open government by saying that the court's arguments should not become fodder for "entertainment."

Despite those views, the court opened the term with what seemed to be a major step into media sunshine. The court announced that audio recordings of oral arguments would now be available on the court's Web site by the end of the argument week. Previously, recordings were available only through the National Archives after the end of the term.

The move turned out, however, to be a head-fake. Without saying so, the justices at the same time discarded the practice of making arguments in major cases available on the same day. That practice, which originated with *Bush v. Gore* in 2000, had allowed radio and TV news outlets to air expanded, same-day coverage of big cases just when the public was paying close attention.

Ostensibly, the justices wanted to skirt the problem of deciding which cases warranted same-day release. The effect, however, has been to eliminate any news media interest in excerpting arguments a few days after. One suspects that at least some of the justices are pleased with that result.

With a lame-duck congressional session approaching, a coalition of open-access groups led by the American Civil Liberties Union is urging Congress to move on the issue after the election. "Allowing cameras to broadcast Supreme Court arguments will bring a crucial part of our government's proceedings to the vast majority of the American public for the first time," says Michael Macleod-Ball, the ACLU's legislative chief of staff and First Amendment counsel. With many other issues demanding lawmakers' attention, however, the prospects for action this year seem very slim.

Court's Obsession With Secrecy
(*Jost on Justice*, March 23, 2014)

Supreme Court Justice Antonin Scalia was apparently in full Scaliaesque mode when he spoke to the Georgia State Bar this month [March 14] on constitutional originalism. Scalia "ranted and ranted" that the Constitution grants no right to abortion or same-sex marriage, according to one of those in the audience. News accounts quoted Scalia as describing the idea of a "living Constitution" as "idiocy."

These days, many people interested in the issue might reflexively log on to You Tube to look for a video of Scalia's remarks. But don't bother. In accepting the speaking invitation, Scalia imposed his customary ground rule: no cameras, no tape recording. So you'll just have to rely on the brief news coverage of the speech or on second-hand accounts like the sharp critique delivered by Eric Segall, a law professor at Georgia State University in Atlanta who helped organize the event.

Scalia's ground rule is one of a dozen or so Supreme Court practices that severely limit information for the public about the nation's highest court and the nine life-tenured justices who serve on it. As Dahlia Lithwick, Supreme Court correspondent for *Slate* puts it, the court is "completely unknown and unknowable to 99 percent of the public."

Lithwick and Segall were among the participants in an hour-long indictment of the court's obsession with secrecy held last week [March 21] at New York University's Washington Center. The event was cosponsored by the Reporters Committee for Freedom of the Press and the newly organized Coalition for Court Transparency, an amalgam of press organizations and legal advocacy groups.

The program came against the backdrop of a renewed push to get the justices to let cameras into the courtroom for Supreme Court arguments. That issue has been percolating for at least 30 years, with no sign the court is likely to change its mind. To the contrary, the only minds being changed are those of new justices, including Sonia Sotomayor and Elena

Kagan. Both were open to the idea during their confirmation hearings but have been voicing doubts since joining the court.

The court's obsession with secrecy, however, goes much further. As one inexplicable example, most of the justices do not announce their speaking schedules or release the text of public speeches. Justice Anthony M. Kennedy was the keynote speaker at the American Bar Association's annual convention in August, but you won't find the text on the Supreme Court web site under "Speeches."

Segall finds it similarly inexplicable that the court does not announce the votes of the justices when it decides whether to review a case from a lower court. It takes four votes to grant certiorari, but the votes in individual cases are disclosed only in the handful of cases each year when one or more of the justices issue a public dissent from the court's refusal to take up a case.

The justices are just as opaque in regard to recusals. None of the justices issues an explanation when he or she steps aside in a case. The public is left to guess whether the reason is some financial interest, a familial conflict, or something else. And any efforts to look for financial conflicts in the justices' financial disclosure forms collides with the limited accessibility of the forms, which are available only in person in Washington, not on line.

The court is somewhat proud of its web site, relaunched with various improvements a couple of years ago. But there's not that much to brag about. Decisions are now available on line almost as soon as they are announced, and argument transcripts are posted within hours. But, despite the recent requirement for petitions and briefs to be filed electronically, these are not automatically posted on the court's web site itself. The best sources for briefs at the Supreme Court are private entities: the ABA and the utterly invaluable *SCOTUSblog*.

William Jay, a lawyer and an ex-Scalia clerk, noted one practice that only Supreme Court advocates would notice: the justices' occasional research outside the record in the case. Jay noted that when the court outlawed the death penalty for juvenile offenders, Kennedy cited in his majority opinion data gathered after briefing and arguments were completed. The parties had no notice of the extra-record research and, obviously, no opportunity to comment.

Of all the various issues, the question of cameras in the courtroom is easiest to raise in public. High courts in other nations allow video coverage — for example, Brazil, Canada, and the United Kingdom — with no apparent adverse effect. Justices have long warned of the risk of "showboating" by lawyers, but Sonja West, a law professor at the University of Georgia, notes that they are now raising a paternalistic fear that the public simply would not understand what was going on.

A court answerable to the public could not get away with so many violations of transparency or such attitudes. Segall proposes a radical step to get the court's attention. He wants Congress to refuse to fund the court until the justices improve their information practices. Congress is unlikely to go that far, so any major changes are likely to have to wait until a generation of post-Internet justices accustomed to instant transparency move into the Marble Palace at One First Street.

3

#Politics

The Supreme Court routinely refers to Congress and the president as the "political branches" of the national government. But, of course, the court's role is also political, at least in the larger sense of the word, however much the justices may try to rule solely on the basis of law. And the Roberts Court has had a direct effect on politics with controversial decisions in two areas: campaign finance and voting rights. I found the court's rulings examples of unwise and unwarranted judicial activism.

#CampaignFinance

Mark Hanna, the U.S. senator from Ohio who raised the cash that put William McKinley into the White House, famously summed up the relationship between money and politics. "There are two things that are important in politics," Hanna is reputed to have said. "The first is money and I can't remember what the second one is."

Hanna raised money primarily from corporations, which appreciated the pro-business policies that McKinley pursued as president. But when Theodore Roosevelt was accused of hitting up corporations for his 1904 campaign, he responded by supporting and eventually signing a bill to prohibit corporations from donating to presidential or congressional campaigns.

The ban on direct corporate contributions still stands, but the Supreme Court opened the door to corporate spending on federal elections with its 1976 decision, Buckley v. Valeo, that found a First Amendment right to engage in independent spending in federal elections. Congress in 2003 sought to rein in some corporate spending on federal elections with a provision that prohibited corporations from paying for election-time advertising on TV or radio except through separately established political action committees, not directly with corporate funds.

A constitutional challenge to that provision reached the Roberts Court in 2009 in a case called Citizens United v. Federal Election Commission. By then, the court's conservative majority had already signaled their belief that the First Amendment seriously limits the restrictions Congress or state legislatures can impose on campaign spending. The court's decision was stunningly bold and sparked vigorous debate.

Activist Blow for Corporate Speech
(Jost on Justice, Jan. 25, 2010)

The Roberts Court's decision to free corporations to spend unlimited amounts of their money in congressional and presidential campaigns is an undisputed instance of judicial activism and one of the least defensible in terms of judicial procedure, historical experience, or public policy.

The Jan. 21 decision in *Citizens United v. Federal Election Commission* belatedly vindicates the conservative advocacy group's right to produce and distribute through video-on-demand the documentary hit piece *Hillary: The Movie* during the 2008 primary season. The FEC had barred the plan because some of the group's financing had come from for-profit corporations. The corporate financing ran afoul of the so-called electioneering communications provision in the 2003 McCain-Feingold campaign reform law, which prohibited corporate or union financing of election-time campaign advertising on radio or TV.

In their ruling, the five-justice majority went beyond striking down that recently enacted federal law to throw out a 20-year-old precedent and the century-old premise of campaign finance permitting greater restrictions on corporations than on individuals. The conservative bloc fully understood the appearance of judicial overreaching in their decision. Between them, Justice Anthony M. Kennedy in the majority opinion and Chief Justice John G. Roberts Jr. in a concurrence devoted more than 30 pages to deny the suggestion.

The court's protestations that it had no choice may satisfy supporters of the decision, but less ideological observers are unconvinced. "There is such a long laundry list of other things they could have done," says Barry Friedman, a law professor at New York University and author of the new book, *The Will of the People*, on the Supreme Court and public opinion. "They so clearly didn't have to do what they did."

Justice John Paul Stevens listed some of those narrower ways to have decided the case. Citizens United originally had not asked to strike down the electioneering communications provision, but only to get out from under it. The court could have found, for example, that the provision did not apply to video on demand or that it did not apply to a not-for-profit corporation such as Citizens United as long as it received no or only minimal corporate funding.

As Stevens noted, that approach would have been consistent with Roberts' own definition of judicial restraint. "If it is not necessary to decide more, it is necessary not to decide more," Roberts has said and written both before and after his appointment as chief justice.

In his opinion, Roberts acknowledges the quote, but insists that in this case it *was* necessary to decide more. He and the other conservatives reach that conclusion only by exaggerating the impact of the provision. Repeatedly, they refer to the McCain-Feingold provision as a "ban" on political speech by corporations.

As Stevens notes, the provision only bars corporations (or unions) from using their own funds for campaign spending and only on radio or TV advertising close to an election. Even under the law, corporations or unions could form political action committees (PACs) to pay for election-time broadcast advertising. Kennedy is less than convincing in responding that forming a PAC is simply too much of a burden on political speech.

With an exaggerated view of the breadth of the law, Roberts responds tartly to Stevens that judicial restraint is not the same as "judicial abdication." The point is well taken. On numerous occasions, the court has gone beyond a narrow decision in a case to issue broad rulings to enforce constitutional rights. One example, directly pertinent here, is *New York Times v. Sullivan*, the landmark 1964 libel decision safeguarding a First Amendment right to criticize public officials (and, later, public figures).

In *Sullivan*, the court could have held that the segregationist Alabama official who sued the *Times* over a political advertisement in the newspaper had no case because he was never named in the ad. The court chose to go further and set a high, almost insurmountable barrier to libel suits by public officials. Undoubtedly, the justices were influenced by the larger stakes in the case. Sullivan's suit — filed at the height of the civil rights revolution — showed how local juries in the South could chill national publications such as the *Times* in their coverage of the most important domestic issue of the day. The *Times*, in fact, was facing so many libel suits in Alabama that it withdrew its correspondents from the state for a while to avoid service of process.

Citizens United reached the Supreme Court with no comparable threat to political speech at hand. Whatever the five justices may think, most Americans do not believe that corporations need more outlets for their political views. Neither history nor current events suggest that corporations lack effective avenues to make their views known and heard despite the century-old ban on direct campaign contributions to federal candidates, the bans on campaign spending in about half of the states, or McCain-Feingold's targeted restriction on direct corporate financing of radio and TV ads.

The effect of the court's decision remains to be seen. For now, the ruling is evidence that the conservative majority knows how to flex its muscles — and is willing to do so. Conservatives hope, and liberals rightly fear, that this will not be the last such occasion.

Four years later, the court struck down another campaign finance law. At issue this time was the federal provision dating from the 1970s that set overall or "aggregate" limits on an individual's contributions to candidates or political committees. The court had upheld the provision in 1976 with little discussion, but not this time.

More Money in Politics
(*Jost on Justice*, April 6, 2014)

Through more than 200 years, the Supreme Court invariably included a mix of justices who rose through legal and judicial careers and one or more justices with experience in elective politics. But when former Arizona legislator Sandra Day O'Connor retired in 2005, the court was left for the first time with no one who had ever sought elective office after their days in high school or college.

It is no mere coincidence that O'Connor's departure marks the court's turning point on issues of campaign finance regulation. O'Connor co-authored along with Justice John Paul Stevens what may prove to be the court's last decision supporting efforts by Congress and state legislators to limit the corrupting influence of uncontrolled money in politics. Her successor, Samuel A. Alito Jr., quickly joined the court's four other Reagan-era conservatives in what is now the Roberts Court's string of six decisions striking down federal or state laws aimed at limiting the corrupting influence of unlimited money in political campaigns.

The Roberts Court claimed its latest victim in a decision last week striking down so-called "aggregate" contribution limits to federal candidates or national parties and political committees. The 5-4 decision in *McCutcheon v. Federal Election Commission* [April 2] gives any well-heeled campaign donor the right to spread millions of dollars around to congressional candidates and national, state, and local parties in any given election cycle.

The ruling leaves in place the existing "base" limit on contributions to a single federal candidate: $5,200 per election cycle for a candidate who runs in a party primary and general election and $32,400 to a national party committee. But it wipes out the provision dating from the post-Watergate campaign finance law that established an overall limit on the donor's contributions.

For the current election cycle, the limit was $48,600 to candidates and $74,600 to political parties or committees — $123,200 in all. Under the new ruling, a donor theoretically could spread nearly $2.5 million around to 435 House candidates and 33 Senate candidates and perhaps another $1 million or so to party committees and political action committees (PACs).

The decision, written by Chief Justice John G. Roberts Jr., has an appealing logic, but only if one accepts an initial premise that distorts four decades of campaign finance precedents. In Roberts' reading, those precedents allow campaign contributions to be limited only as necessary to prevent quid pro quo corruption — which he helpfully defined in court as "this for that" — or the appearance of such blatant bribery-like vote buying.

Roberts acknowledged, at least for now, that federal law could limit the amount a donor could give to an individual candidate for Congress to prevent the corruption of that candidate. But if a donor could give that amount to nine candidates, Roberts asked, where is the harm in giving the same amount to a tenth? Or, under that logic, to a 435th?

Way back in 1976, the Supreme Court in *Buckley v. Valeo* (1976) upheld the principle of aggregate contribution limits as a way to prevent circumvention of the base limits. In a passage joined by six of the eight justices to hear the case, the court said the overall ceiling on contributions was needed "to prevent evasion" of the base limit. A donor could contribute additional sums to party committees, the court reasoned then, knowing that they would funnel the money to the specific candidate.

Roberts dismisses the passage as a single paragraph on an issue not fully briefed and then goes on to pooh-pooh the possibility of circumventing the base contribution limits so readily. The intricate arrangements needed, Roberts says, are speculative and unlikely. In addition, Roberts stresses that the Federal Election Commission (FEC) now has regulations that make it illegal for a donor to "earmark" a contribution to a party committee to benefit a specific candidate.

Roberts blithely disregards the FEC's permanent status of partisan gridlock — the inevitable product of the legal requirement for an equal number of Republican and Democratic appointees. Roberts cited one case in which the agency had found impermissible earmarking. In his dissent, Justice Stephen G. Breyer pointed more persuasively to eight cases in which the FEC had failed to enforce earmarking restrictions.

More broadly, Roberts simply ignores the political reality of campaign finance: influence-buying money, like water, will find its own level. As Breyer noted, the court in *Buckley* upheld contribution limits on the ground that they would help prevent "improper influence" on candidates, not merely quid pro quo corruption. And influence is what campaign donors seek to buy — and now will be able to buy in larger and larger amounts.

The new ruling marks the second time that Roberts, an adherent to judicial restraint in his confirmation hearing in September 2005, has presided over the overruling of a campaign finance precedent to strike down a law passed and reaffirmed by Congress. Four years ago, in *Citizens United v. Federal Election Commission* (2010), the court's precedent-breaking decision freed corporations or labor unions to spend unlimited amounts on their own in political campaigns.

In his dissent at the time, Stevens wryly observed that few Americans other than the court's majority would have worried about "a dearth of corporate money in politics." It is all the more true that few Americans want more money from well-heeled donors to flow to congressional campaigns. But that is what the Roberts Court, by a single vote, has now allowed — and most assuredly will occur.

#VotingRights

The Voting Rights Act of 1965 revolutionized U.S. politics by giving African Americans an effective remedy for the first time against the widespread racial discrimination in voting, especially in the South. Within a year after its enactment, the Supreme Court upheld the law in a nearly unanimous decision, including the provision requiring some southern states and other jurisdictions with a history of discrimination in voting to obtain "preclearance" for any changes in election laws or voting procedures.

Congress re-enacted the preclearance provision several times, and the Supreme Court upheld each re-enactment. But that was not good enough for the Roberts Court. The court in 2009 signaled that it had doubts about the preclearance provision and all but invited a new challenge if Congress failed to revise the law to reflect changed conditions in the South. Congress left the law unchanged, the court's suggestion notwithstanding. I wrote on the issue twice, first as the new case headed toward the Supreme Court and then after its decision.

Congress vs. Roberts Court

(Jost on Justice, May 29, 2012)

The Reconstruction Congress that proposed the Fifteenth Amendment to prohibit racial discrimination in voting recognized that recalcitrant states and localities might employ some ingenious devices, like poll taxes or literacy tests, to deny suffrage to newly freed slaves. The drafters feared, however, that putting specifics into the amendment could jeopardize ratification. So they made do with a prophylactic safeguard that gave future Congresses the power to "enforce" the amendment "through appropriate legislation."

Over the next century, states in the Deep South and elsewhere resorted to any number of ostensibly neutral but patently discriminatory devices to keep African Americans from voting. Only after decades of disenfranchisement of African Americans, often accomplished through brutal force, did Congress finally pass "appropriate" legislation: the Voting Rights Act of 1965.

Today, the Voting Rights Act is recognized as the essential instrument in gaining a nearly equal franchise for African Americans to that of white Americans. Paradoxically, it has been so successful that one of its two central provisions is now under constitutional challenge as no longer necessary. And that issue is only one step away from the Supreme Court, after a ruling this month (May 18) to uphold the act's so-called preclearance provision despite doubts raised by the high court itself.

The preclearance provision, section 5 in the act, requires covered states and localities to submit any change in election law or procedure to the U.S. Justice Department or a three-judge federal court in Washington before adoption. Five Deep South states are covered (Alabama, Georgia, Louisiana, Mississippi, and South Carolina), based on criteria included in the original act and tweaked several times since. Virginia was also originally covered in toto, but some local jurisdictions have used the act's so-called bailout provision, section 4(a), to get out of the requirement. Alaska and portions of other states have come under the requirement in the years since because of low registration of minority voters.

Evidently, the South of the early 21st century is much different from the South of the 1960s. Among those noting the difference is Chief Justice John G. Roberts Jr., writing in the decision three years ago that left the preclearance provision in place, at least for now. "Things have changed in the South," Roberts wrote for an all but unanimous court in *Northwest Austin Municipal Utility District No. 1 v. Holder* (2009). "Voter turnout and registration rates now approach parity. Blatantly discriminatory evasions of federal decrees are rare. And minority candidates hold office at unprecedented levels."

Congress, however, was not so sanguine in 2006 when it renewed the Voting Rights Act, including the preclearance provision, for another 25 years and by substantial bipartisan majorities. The ruling by the U.S. Court of Appeals for the District of Columbia Circuit in the new challenge, *Shelby County v. Holder*, cites some of the evidence that Congress heard before deciding to leave section 5 intact.

Writing for the majority, Judge David Tatel noted several modern instances of blatant racial discrimination in the covered Deep South states. As one example, Walker County, Texas, sought to lower black voting in 2004 by reducing early voting at polling places near a historically black university and threatening to prosecute students for illegal voting. In another, Kilmichael, Miss., abruptly canceled an election in 2001 when "an unprecedented number" of African Americans ran for office. Another: Webster County, Ga., redrew school board districts in 1998 after a majority black school board was elected for the first time.

Just as important in the appeals court's view are the instances of potential discrimination that have not been instituted thanks to the preclearance requirement. The Justice Department continues to use section 5 to block questionable election law changes by interposing objections – about 28 times per year. That rate has remained somewhat constant since 1965. In addition, jurisdictions sometimes withdraw proposed changes after the Justice Department requests more information. Congress counted about 800 such instances from 1990 to 2005.

The Justice Department also combats racial discrimination with the act's other central provision: section 2, which prohibits nationwide any election law change that has the effect of denying or abridge minorities' voting rights. Between 1982 and 2005, the government won 653 section 2 suits in covered jurisdictions – more than 25 per year. As Tatel noted, however, section 2 litigation is less effective than the preclearance provision at preventing racial discrimination because the remedy kicks in only after the questioned changes have been put into effect.

In dissent, Judge Stephen Williams saw no logic to continuing to single out some states and localities for disfavored treatment. He noted the paradox that the Supreme Court allowed Indiana to implement a photo-ID voting requirement, but the Justice Department has blocked similar laws in South Carolina and Texas. The majority's answer lies with statistics that show voting rights issues continue to crop up disproportionately in the Deep South states. And they note that the law has been revised to make it easier for jurisdictions to prove a clean voting rights record and get out from under the preclearance requirement.

Those considerations were good enough for Congress to pass and President George W. Bush to sign a long renewal of the Voting Rights Act. It remains to be seen whether they will be good enough for a Supreme Court that professes judicial restraint but often practices something else.

Fixing the Voting Rights Act?
(Jost on Justice, July 8, 2013)

The Voting Rights Act was not broken, but now, thanks to the Supreme Court, Congress and the Justice Department have to try to fix it. It is a daunting challenge, but perhaps not impossible.

The court's 5-4 decision in *Shelby County v. Holder* [June 25] to strike down a key provision of the 1965 law is long in praising the act's historic accomplishments and short in documenting its supposed present-day harms. Chief Justice John G. Roberts cites with statistics the dramatic improvements in voter registration and turnout among African

Americans in the Deep South. "There is no doubt," Roberts writes for the majority, "that these improvements are in large part *because of* the Voting Rights Act."

One might take that as an endorsement of the law and justification for Congress's decision in 2006 to extend the law for another 25 years, including the proven-to-be-effective enforcement mechanism: the preclearance provision in section 5 that applies to nine states and parts of six others. Instead, Roberts and his four conservative colleagues threw out the formula used to determine the states that have to preclear voting changes with the Justice Department or a federal court.

The harm from this provision, according to the majority, is its "drastic departure from federalism" and "from the principle that all States enjoy equal sovereignty." The Constitution supposedly forbids Congress from treating one state or group of states differently from others without very good reasons.

This may sound right in theory, but, as Justice Ruth Bader Ginsburg shows in a well documented dissent, it is not correct in practice. Congress routinely treats states differently, for reasons far less compelling than protecting the right to vote. Sports-related gambling is prohibited nationwide except for any state that allowed it in 1976 (read: Nevada). Appropriation measures often include obscurely phrased funding formulas designed to favor individual states or groups of states.

No less a figure than Michael McConnell, a conservative law professor and former federal judge, says the court's supposed principle is just "made up." "There's no requirement in the Constitution to treat all the states the same," McConnell remarked in an interview with NPR's Nina Totenberg. "It might be an attractive principle, but it doesn't seem to be in the Constitution."

Roberts says the other harm from the Voting Rights Act is that states and localities covered by the preclearance requirement are delayed or preventing from adopting "validly enacted laws." But the voting changes may or may not be validly enacted. The unchallenged Voting Rights Act section 2 makes it illegal for any jurisdiction, nationwide, to enact a voting change that has the intent *or the effect* of discriminating against a racial or language minority.

The Justice Department or federal court applied essentially the same standard in reviewing proposed changes. So, any changes that were disallowed — a vanishingly small fraction — had been found by an official body to be, in fact, illegal under federal law. A proper view of the preclearance requirement is that it prevented the enactment of invalid laws — a benefit in protecting voting rights, not a harm, as the Supreme Court conservatives believed.

The court made its decision, however, and Congress and the Justice Department now have to live with it. Roberts stressed that the preclearance requirement remains on the books and Congress is free to craft a new coverage formula.

Without a coverage formula, the preclearance requirement is — as Ginsburg wrote in her dissent — "immobilized." Political realities make it unlikely that Congress can enact a formula that recognizably identifies the worst of the bad actors in voting rights for preclearance coverage. But the possibility of salvaging something of the preclearance requirement is less remote than pessimistic lawmakers and realistic Capitol Hill observers depicted immediately after the ruling.

A *New York Times* editorial a few days later [June 29] pointed to some of the ways that Congress or the Justice Department can respond to blunt the impact of the court's decision. For starters, the *Times* noted that the act's "bail-in" procedure in section 3, untouched by the decision, allows the Justice Department to ask a court to extend the preclearance requirement to a designated jurisdiction upon proof of intentional racial discrimination in voting.

The *Times* notes that intentional discrimination is hard to prove, but it is not impossible. The state of Texas, as one example, was found to have intentionally discriminated against Latino voters in redrawing congressional lines in 2003. And minority group plaintiffs filed a federal court action after the latest ruling seeking to invoke section 3 to block Texas from implementing its voter ID law.

The *Times* suggests that Congress could make section 5 usable again by requiring preclearance for any state to have violated a federal election law in the last few years. Such an objective requirement would meet the Supreme Court's criterion that preclearance be based on "current conditions." It would impose preclearance again on most of the southern states and on others, but recidivist voting rights violators would have a hard time complaining about being unfairly singled out.

The Supreme Court won little praise for its decision to gut the Voting Rights Act. The only poll conducted so far found a majority of Americans opposed to the ruling, The court has given a lemon to Congress and the Justice Department; their job now is to make lemonade out of it.

Unsurprisingly, legislation to re-enact a pre-clearance provision failed to advance in Congress.

The Roberts Court proved to be more deferential to legislative bodies in other voting rights disputes: specifically, the historic but shameful practice of gerrymandering legislative districts and the new and equally shameful flurry of laws requiring photo IDs for would-be voters.

Surrender to Gerrymandering

(*Jost on Justice*, March 14, 2011)

It's that time of the decade again: time for legislative and congressional redistricting by state lawmakers or, in a few states, specially created commissions. The Supreme Court struck a major blow for political democracy a half century ago by establishing the "one person, one vote" rule for electoral districts. In the past decade, however, the court has failed to finish the job by leaving the time-dishonored practice of partisan gerrymandering effectively immune to judicial oversight.

The Warren Court started the reapportionment revolution with its 1962 decision, *Baker v. Carr*, despite the warning from dissenting justice Felix Frankfurter against venturing into a "political thicket." After retirement, Chief Justice Earl Warren said he considered the reapportionment decisions the most important of his 15-year tenure — outranking even *Brown v. Board of Education*, the landmark school desegregation case.

The Supreme Court entered the political thicket in the 1960s because the political process was broken. Rural-dominated state legislatures had failed to redraw districts for decades as population shifted to cities and suburbs. My home state of Tennessee had not reapportioned since 1901, despite a mandate in the state constitution to do so. As a result, a minority of voters — about 40 percent — were able to elect super-majorities in both the state Senate and state House of Representatives.

Urban officials and residents sued, claiming a violation of the Equal Protection Clause. The lower court dismissed the suit, citing the Supreme Court's earlier decision in a similar Illinois malapportionment case, *Colegrove v. Green* (1946), that federal courts had no jurisdiction over such claims.

In *Baker v. Carr*, the court said that federal courts could exercise jurisdiction over malapportionment cases even if they presented a "political question." The ruling sent the case back to a lower court, which forced the Tennessee legislature to redraw districts to give urban voters their constitutionally entitled due. By the end of the decade, state legislatures throughout the country had similarly been forced to redraw legislative and congressional districts to comply with the "one person, one vote" requirement that the court established in its later cases.

Two decades later, the court similarly opened the federal courthouse door to constitutional challenges to partisan gerrymandering, the practice of drawing district lines to help one's party or hurt the other. Indiana Democrats went to federal court alleging that the Republican-controlled legislature had drawn districts in 1981 in a deliberate effort to disenfranchise Democratic voters. The proof: under the GOP-drawn plan, Democratic candidates won 51.9 percent of the vote in the 1982 election, but only 43 out of 100 seats in the Indiana House.

In *Davis v. Bandemer*, the Court in 1986 said that federal courts could hear such claims despite the warning from Justice Sandra Day O'Connor that the ruling would invite federal litigation by the losing party in every reapportionment fight. On the merits, the Indiana Democrats lost their fight. But Justice Byron White's opinion for seven justices established a standard for future cases. "Unconstitutional discrimination occurs," White wrote, "only when the electoral system is arranged in a manner that will consistently degrade a voter's or a group of voters' influence on the political process as a whole."

Twice within the past decade, the court has been asked to strike down partisan congressional gerrymanders fashioned by Republican-controlled legislatures, first in Pennsylvania and then in Texas. In both cases, GOP lawmakers had used recognized tricks to minimize Democrats' chances at the polls: pairing incumbent Democrats in the same district; "packing" Democratic voters into some districts so their votes would be wasted; or "cracking" Democratic districts so that Democrats would be spread out and outvoted.

In both cases, Republicans won lopsided majorities in the House delegation in the next election: a 12-7 GOP edge in Pennsylvania in 2002; a 21-11 Republican advantage in Texas in 2004. But both times the Court found nothing unconstitutional in the overall line-drawing. In the Pennsylvania case, *Vieth v. Jubilerer* (2003), four conservative justices wanted to overrule *Davis v. Bandemer* altogether and bar gerrymandering challenges. Justice Anthony M. Kennedy refused to go that far, but could not come up with a standard for such suits. Nor could the four dissenting liberals agree on a single test. Three years later, Kennedy led a pivotal group of three justices in rejecting Texas Democrats' efforts to fashion a standard for gerrymandering cases (*League of United Latin American Citizens v. Perry*, 2006).

With no Supreme Court standard, partisan gerrymandering is all but certain to proceed apace in the current redistricting cycle. And Kennedy's hesitancy appears likely to steer the Court's course in any subsequent challenges. Tellingly, Kennedy had no such difficulty in fashioning a rule against racial gerrymanders. Kennedy spoke for the Court in *Miller v. Johnson* (1995) in holding that a district map was unconstitutional if race was "the predominant factor" in the design. Evidence of lawmakers' intent could be inferred, Kennedy said, from a district's departure from "traditional" principles, including "compactness" and "contiguity."

A workable standard to judge gerrymandering cases is not beyond the Supreme Court's ability if the justices only had the will. With the court on the sidelines, however, redistricting fights will again be waged according to the law of the political jungle and the constitutional goal of fair representation shortchanged for another decade.

The Roberts Court also deferred to lawmakers on the spate of laws requiring potential voters to show a photo ID before casting their ballots. State legislators approved the laws along party lines, with Republicans in support and Democrats opposed. Republicans said the laws were needed to prevent voter fraud. Democrats countered that the evidence of in-person voter impersonation was all but non-existent and that the laws were really aimed at reducing turnout among Democratic constituencies.

Making Every Vote Count
(*Jost on Justice*, Oct. 20, 2013)

"[E]lections for political office at the state or federal level are never decided by just one vote." Crawford v. Marion County Board of Elections (*Posner, J.*)

One vote actually can make a difference — even in elections, however rarely — but certainly in judicial decisions. So legal commentators naturally are making much of Judge Richard Posner's belated apology for his pivotal vote in the seminal federal court decision seven years ago to uphold state voter photo ID laws.

"I plead guilty to having written the majority opinion (affirmed by the Supreme Court) upholding Indiana's requirement that prospective voters prove their identity with a photo ID — a type of law now widely regarded as a means of voter suppression rather than of fraud prevention," Posner writes in his new book, *Reflections on Judging*.

Posner's confession of error, in the midst of the continuing debate over voter photo ID laws, would have earned him a gold star for candor but for his subsequent decision to deflect the blame to the lawyers in the case. The real blame, however, lies not with the lawyers and not even with Posner alone, but with the deferential stance that the Supreme Court itself has taken in reviewing laws that make it hard to vote.

Posner shifted the blame for his vote in an interview on HuffPost Live [Oct. 11] when he said the lawyers challenging the Indiana law failed to show that the photo ID requirement would actually disenfranchise people entitled to vote. "If the lawyers had provided us more information about the abuses," Posner told interviewer Mike Sacks, "the case would have been decided differently."

Understandably, the Washington lawyer who argued the case before the Supreme Court is taking exception to Posner's blame-shifting. Paul Smith, a veteran of voting rights litigation and an experienced Supreme Court advocate, notes on the American Constitution Society's blog that Indiana's Republican secretary of state, the law's chief sponsor, had acknowledged that the photo ID requirement would be "difficult" for many voters, including "elderly voters, indigent voters, voters with disabilities, first-time voters, [and] re-enfranchised ex-felons."

The lawyers challenging the law also emphasized the political facts of life behind it. The law was enacted in 2005 just after Republicans had gained control of both chambers of the state legislature and the governorship. Every Republican legislator voted for it, and every Democratic lawmaker voted against it. Posner himself acknowledged in his opinion that the potential voters most likely to be burdened by the law were people "low on the economic ladder" — and most likely to be Democratic voters.

Partisanship was also in evidence in the courts' handling of the case. The district court judge who upheld the law was a Republican appointee, as are Posner and his Seventh Circuit colleague who joined in the decision. The Democratic appointee on the panel, the late Judge Terence Evans, dissented. "Let's not beat around the bush," Evans wrote. "The Indiana voter photo ID law is a not-too-thinly-veiled attempt to discourage election-day turnout by folks believed to skew Democratic."

The partisan divide was muddied somewhat at the Supreme Court, as Justice John Paul Stevens joined with the Republican-appointed conservative bloc in 2008 in upholding the law. Writing for a plurality that also included Chief Justice John G. Roberts and Justice Anthony M. Kennedy, Stevens accepted the state's purported justifications for the law, including preventing voter fraud, and found the law's burdens not substantial enough to justify striking it down.

Stevens conceded that Indiana itself had shown no instances of in-person voter impersonation — the only kind of voter fraud that a photo ID can prevent — but claimed that history offered real-life examples. In the most recent instance cited by Stevens, however, an investigation in Washington State of 19 supposed "ghost" voters identified only one instance of in-person impersonation. For three liberal dissenters, Justice

David H. Souter argued that the state's "abstract interests" did not justify the "nontrivial burdens" imposed on would-be voters.

Voter ID laws are now on the books in 34 states and are surviving legal challenges, most recently in a unanimous decision by the Tennessee Supreme Court [Oct. 17]. The Roberts Court's decision in June that freed southern states from the Voting Rights Act's preclearance requirement has defanged the Obama administration's challenges to such laws in South Carolina and Texas. The plurality in the Indiana case left the door open to future legal challenges, but none is likely to succeed unless judges gets serious about requiring states to justify laws that inevitably impede the ostensibly sacred right to vote.

The court's precedents require states to show the precise interest to be served by any voting eligibility requirements and to weigh that interest against the resulting limitations on the right to vote. In his decision in the Indiana case, however, Posner was notably blasé about the limitations. Even "slight costs in time or bother or out-of-pocket expenses" may deter "many people" from voting, he wrote, but with no great concern. The benefits of voting to the individual voter," Posner opined, "are elusive."

The right to vote deserves better than that — from Posner and, all the more, from the Supreme Court. "Every vote counts," voters are regularly told on the eve of elections — and so too every vote that is not counted because never cast. In future voting rights cases, the Supreme Court needs to try to make that slogan actual reality and not just a platitude.

#MainJustice

The seal of the U.S. Department of Justice bears the Latin inscription, "Qui Pro Domina Justitia Sequitur" —translated as, "Who strives for Lady Justice?" The department strove for justice quite differently under two different presidents in the 2000s. The Bush Justice Department backed the president's controversial "war on terrorism" policies and retreated from the department's post-World War II support for racial justice. President Obama's appointment of Eric Holder as the first

African American attorney general signaled a return to traditional civil rights policies and a new approach on counterterrorism.

Politicizing Main Justice

(*CQ Weekly*, May 14, 2007)

Barely nine months after after he became attorney general, John Ashcroft issued a regulation designed to stop doctors in Oregon from prescribing lethal medications to people hoping to take advantage of that state's assisted-suicide law, which social conservatives find abhorrent.

That initiative — later struck down by the Supreme Court as beyond Ashcroft's expertise or statutory authority — got limited attention in the fall of 2001, when the nation was preoccupied by the al Qaeda attacks. But Ashcroft's effort then was one of the earliest, and clearest, signals that the Bush administration's Justice Department would gladly bend or stretch the law to advance the president's ideological, political and policy goals.

And so this spring's wellspring of outrage at the dismissals of eight United States attorneys is, in one sense, too little and too late. Evidence of the Justice Department's penchant for politicization has been steadily building for six years. The client-in-chief has had every opportunity to notice; since the pattern continues, the president himself must not be displeased.

In Bush's first term alone, Justice issued a memorandum, which it later disavowed, claiming a presidential power to torture enemy combatants. The department also devised a policy, repudiated by the Supreme Court, of holding enemy combatants at Guantánamo Bay to try to prevent judicial oversight of the detentions. And it approved the Republican-drawn redistricting of Texas, which the Supreme Court ruled violated federal voting rights by effectively disenfranchising some Hispanics.

Ashcroft, of course, came to the department after 20 years in statewide elected office in Missouri, where he became a favorite of the Christian right nationwide. When he bowed out after the president's re-election, some expected his softer-spoken successor, the career insider Alberto R. Gonzales, to smooth some of the department's rougher political edges. But the law continued to take a frequent backseat to ideology or partisanship in many instances. Gonzales vigorously defended the president's secret wiretapping of U.S. citizens in the face of widespread doubts about its legality. Justice lawyers handling a giant racketeering suit against tobacco companies were ordered to scale back the government's proposed penalty in the case. Lawyers in the civil rights division were blocked from bringing a challenge to Georgia's voter ID law.

However controversial, the department's stances on those issues at least had plausible and ascertainable defenses. But six months after the event, the public record has yet to disclose a coherent explanation, much less a convincing defense, of the reasons for the firings last year of eight federal prosecutors Bush had once picked, an unprecedented move in the middle of a presidential term.

Congressional Democrats have established that the administration began hatching its plan while Gonzales was still awaiting Senate confirmation — and preparing to invite a cadre of his White House counsel aides to join him at Justice. At the time, his chief of staff, Kyle Sampson, who was to become a central figure in the prosecutor purge, dismissed the notion that Gonzales would arrange for a White House mafia to run Justice. "I like to think he just did a dang good job of hiring us all in the first place," Sampson told *The Washington Post* in July 2005. Hardly anyone holds that thought today.

In his appearances on Capitol Hill, before the House Judiciary Committee last week and the Senate Judiciary panel last month, Gonzales has insisted that he understands the line between law and politics. But he's gained almost no congressional support. And the evidence grows that some of the prosecutors made it to the hit list either by pushing corruption cases against Republicans too hard or failing to do the White House's bidding on dubious voter fraud cases.

Other indications of the department's deep politicization have also surfaced. Sen. Sheldon Whitehouse, who was the U.S. attorney for Rhode Island in the Clinton administration, has produced figures to show that, in contrast to the tight restrictions under previous administrations, more than 400 people in the Bush White House were authorized to contact Justice officials about pending criminal investigations or cases.

The attorney general delegated hiring power for dozens of political appointees to two aides, Sampson and Monica Goodling, with no significant legal experience, according to a memorandum first reported by *National Journal*. And Justice has disclosed that Goodling, its former White House liaison, is under investigation for possibly taking partisan affiliation into account in hiring career federal prosecutors, which is explicitly barred by law.

The pervasive politicization at Justice is bringing forth some drastic proposals. Arnold Burns, a deputy attorney general in the Reagan administration, wrote a *New York Times* op-ed proposing that the attorney general be taken out of the Cabinet and hold the job for a fixed 15-year tenure. On the same page, Frank Bowman, a law professor and former federal prosecutor with no political ax to grind, urged Congress to consider impeaching Gonzales.

That is unlikely to happen; the Democrats have made clear they have no stomach to impeach anybody. So Gonzales is likely to stay on serving at the president's apparent pleasure — if hardly anyone else's.

Justice 2.0: Change to Believe In
(Jost on Justice, Feb. 13, 2009)

The Bush administration left a legacy of having distorted or deformed the mission of many executive branch agencies. The State Department was frozen out of Iraq diplomacy and reconstruction. The Environmental Protection Agency was forced to ignore global warming. The Interior Department was transformed from a steward to a despoiler of public lands.

No department suffered more, however, than the Justice Department. The Immigration and Naturalization Service, then part of Justice, grossly abused many of the aliens rounded up after 9/11. The Office of Legal Counsel produced legal opinions to give the president extraconstitutional powers as commander in chief and to define torture all but out of existence.

The FBI was silenced in its objections to the "enhanced interrogation" techniques being used on suspected terrorists. The civil rights division was turned into an employment center for right-wing ideologues. And, most embarrassingly, Attorney General Alberto Gonzales allowed the unprecedented, politically motivated midterm dismissals of at least half a dozen U.S. attorneys and then dissembled about the episode under oath before congressional committees.

Against that background, the Justice Department has nowhere to go but up under President Obama and the new attorney general, Eric H. Holder Jr. As a candidate, Obama sharply criticized the politicization of the Justice Department. As president-elect, he chose as one of his first Cabinet appointees the experienced and well-regarded Holder to head the department. In confirmation hearings, Holder and other senior Justice appointees assured the Senate Judiciary Committee that partisan politics will play no part in line-level hiring at Justice.

Significantly, Obama made Holder — a former federal prosecutor, local superior court judge and deputy U.S. attorney general— the point man on his first major policy initiative. Holder's Justice Department, not the Pentagon, was put in charge of reviewing the case files of the remaining 242 prisoners being held at the detention camp at Guantanamo Bay and fulfilling the pledge to close the facility within one year.

Another, less dramatic harbinger of change came two weeks later at the Supreme Court. The solicitor general's office moved on Feb. 6 to dismiss the Bush administration's appeal of a lower court order requiring stricter regulation of mercury emissions from power plants. The federal appeals court in Washington had rejected the Environmental Protection Agency's planned "cap and trade" system of regulating mercury as contrary to the Clean Air Act. The solicitor general's office now says the EPA will adopt a plan consistent with the act.

The solicitor general's office had escaped most of the controversy over the politicization of the Justice Department. Paul Clement, solicitor general during Bush's second term, won high praise from all sides not only as an accomplished advocate but also a straight shooter. Still, the solicitor general's office was enlisted to help advance Bush's political agenda at the Supreme Court.

Under Clement, the solicitor general's office sided during the 2006-2007 term with parents challenging racial diversity plans adopted by the Seattle and Louisville, Ky., school systems. It urged the court to overturn a century-old antitrust precedent against retail price fixing.

At the White House's direction, the solicitor general's office during the next term refused to back up the Securities and Exchange Commission in an important securities fraud case. And in another case last term and one pending now, it backed businesses over consumers and state governments in endorsing federal preemption of product liability suits in state courts.

The government's position prevailed in all the decided cases. Most were decided by five-justice majorities over dissenters' objections that the rulings either contradicted or disregarded established precedent. All were private suits that the Bush administration could have joined on either side or stayed out of altogether.

As the new solicitor general-designate, Elena Kagan comes to the post with credentials and reputation nearly as sterling as Holder's. As dean of Harvard Law School, she was widely admired by students and by professors from opposing ideological camps. Conservative blogs tried to rough her up in advance of her Feb. 10 confirmation hearings. The main exhibit was a brief she joined with other law schools challenging (unsuccessfully) the law that threatened a cutoff of federal funds to universities that barred military recruiters to protest the military's "don't ask, don't tell" policy.

Once confirmed, Kagan — like Clement before her — will be an advocate for policies often formed elsewhere. But one can confidently predict new stands on civil rights, consumer protection and government regulation. Still, in a worrisome sign for some civil liberties groups, Justice Department lawyers on Feb. 9 followed the Bush administration in endorsing the controversial "state secrets" privilege to block a suit by plaintiffs claiming they were tortured after being flown to other countries as part of the CIA's "extraordinary rendition" program.

Civil rights and civil liberties advocates may recall that a previous Democratic president, Bill Clinton, disappointed them on legal issues — for example, by signing a restrictive federal habeas corpus law and the Defense of Marriage Act. Those groups are giving Obama plaudits for his action on Guantanamo, but hawkish skeptics are noting that no one has been released yet. Obama's other legal policies are even less well formed.

Holder Wants to Accomplish More
(*Jost on Justice*, Aug. 12, 2013)

Attorney General Eric Holder appears to have served notice to his critics that he is not going anywhere soon by announcing a laundry list of criminal justice reforms in a speech to the American Bar Association (ABA) on Monday [Aug. 12]. At the top of the list is a sensible but likely controversial move to combat prison overcrowding by limiting the impact of harsh mandatory sentence provisions in run-of-the-mill federal drug cases.

In an address to the ABA's House of Delegates, Holder correctly noted the expensive and counterproductive practice of overincarceration in the United States — at the federal level and in many states. As Holder put it, the United States is "coldly efficient" at putting criminals behind bars *and* keeping them there. "Too many Americans go to too many prisons for far too long, and for no truly good law enforcement reason," Holder said.

With the highest incarceration rate of any country, the United States houses almost one-fourth of the world's prisoners but has only one-twentieth of the world's population, Holder noted. The federal prison population has increased 800 percent since 1980 while the country's population has increased only about one-third. The 219,000 federal inmates fill federal prisons 40 percent beyond their intended capacity.

Speaking in San Francisco, Holder passed over — at least in his prepared text — specific mention of California's own severe prison crisis. Two years ago, the Supreme Court upheld a well-documented order by a three-judge federal court that the state reduce prison population to 110,000 — or merely 30 percent above capacity. California Gov. Jerry Brown, once a liberal Democrat, insists the state has done enough by bringing the population down to 120,000. But the federal court refused to change its order and the Supreme Court earlier this month [Aug. 2] turned down the state's appeal.

As Holder aptly noted, federal prison overcrowding has been driven by an increase in federal drug prosecutions and in particular by the long mandatory minimum sentences enacted by Congress in the 1980s and '90s. Drug offenders comprise about half the federal prison population:

some are in for serious drug trafficking, but many — probably most — are not. But the mandatory sentencing laws give judges little leeway for tempering the excesses that Congress has enacted.

Congress cannot repeal prosecutorial discretion, however. So Holder is moving to ease the sentencing law by directing U.S. attorneys in most cases to omit from formal charges the specific quantity of drug seized or sold and thus to avoid triggering the mandatory minimum prescribed for specified quantities. That policy, he said, will apply to low-level, nonviolent drug offenders who have no ties to large-scale organizations, gangs, or cartels.

Holder said the Justice Department is also revising its policies for considering compassionate release for inmates who pose no threat to the public. The Bureau of Prisons already in April expanded compassionate release for medical reasons. Holder announced a further expansion for elderly inmates who did not commit violent crimes and who have served "significant portions" of their sentences. In addition, the Justice Department is looking into expanding diversion programs such as drug treatment or community service programs that serve as effective alternatives to incarceration.

Fittingly, Holder, the first African American to serve as attorney general, also addressed the continuing racial disparity in sentencing between white and black inmates. He cited one report, released in February, that indicates black male offenders in recent years have received sentences nearly 20 percent longer than those imposed on white males convicted of similar crimes. "This isn't just unacceptable," Holder said. "It is shameful." For now, the only reform is to direct a group of U.S. attorneys to examine the disparities and develop recommendations on how to address them.

Holder has been a political lightning rod, as almost any attorney general is bound to be. He reportedly considered leaving at the end of Obama's first term, but agreed to the president's request to stay. White House aides have grumbled, anonymously, that Holder has a political tin ear. As one example, Holder retreated in the face of overwhelming political opposition from his decision in November 2010 to try the accused 9/11 mastermind Khalid Sheikh Mohammed in a federal court in New York City. More recently, Holder antagonized the news media by allowing the Justice Department to issue an intrusive subpoena against the Associated Press in a leak investigation.

In announcing the criminal justice initiatives, however, Holder signaled that he and Obama are tied at the hip on the issues. Holder recalled Obama's work on such issues as a community organizer and in the Illinois legislature. He also noted the administration's successful efforts in Obama's first term to reduce the racial disparity in sentencing for crack versus powdered cocaine. And he made clear that "the president and I" had discussed and decided on the actions being taken and the proposals being studied.

The inside-the-beltway speculation about Obama's tenure resurfaced in the spring in, among other places, a long article in *The New York Times* [June 4]. Unnamed West Wing aides were described in the story as wishing that Holder would go. But his former spokeswoman Tracy Schmaler told the *Times* that Holder is determined to stay long enough to "accomplish what he would like to do so that he could leave on his own terms."

Update: Holder announced his intention to resign on September 25, 2014, after nearly six years in office, pending the confirmation of his successor. Liberal groups generally praised his service, while conservatives and Republicans on Capitol Hill were sharply critical. Holder had previously indicated his intention to leave office by the end of 2014 to return to private life.

4

#WarOnTerror

President Bush responded to the September 11 attacks on the United States by declaring a "war on terror." The rhetoric served as cover for unfortunate policies that called into question the United States' respect for the rule of law.

The World Is Watching
(*CQ Weekly*, Feb. 25, 2008)

War is hell, and President Bush's "war on terror" has been no exception.

His administration has worked around the U.S. courts and brushed off global criticism since Bush's decision in 2001 to hold suspected "enemy combatants" at the naval base at Guantánamo Bay, Cuba — supposedly outside the reach of the courts or the Constitution. And it has rebuffed Congress by refusing to say that waterboarding is torture, although the practice is barred under both U.S. law and international treaties.

With that record as background, the administration may seem to deserve commendation for finally announcing formal charges this month against six people being held at Guantánamo. The 21-page "charge sheet" details how Khalid Sheik Mohammed and five others allegedly helped plot and carry out the Sept. 11 attacks.

In announcing the charges, Air Force Brig. Gen. Thomas Hartmann, the legal adviser to the U.S. military tribunal system created for the Guantánamo detainees, gave repeated assurances that the proceedings would "follow the rule of law." The defendants, Hartmann says, will be accorded rights including the presumption of innocence, the "beyond a reasonable doubt" standard for conviction and an automatic appeal.

But hardly anyone outside the administration is applauding. A wide range of critics, among them Democratic presidential candidate Barack Obama, say the Guantánamo Six will not receive the same procedural rights accorded those in regular courts martial or in civilian courts. And Mohammed's interrogation by the CIA, using what it called "enhanced" techniques (including waterboarding), gives the tribunal the unpleasant task of deciding whether to admit evidence obtained as a result of such techniques — or rule against the U.S. government with the whole world watching.

A "clean team" of military and FBI interrogators tried to moot the issue by re-interviewing Mohammed and other high-value detainees after they were transferred to Guantánamo recently from secret CIA prisons, according to the *Los Angeles Times* and *The Washington Post*. But the "lingering taint" will be a problem for the tribunals, says Robert Chesney, a national security expert at Wake Forest University Law School [now, at the University of Texas Law School]. "It obviously would have been easier if they had done it this way from the beginning," he told the *Post*.

Indeed, much would have been easier had the Bush administration chosen a different route from the beginning, according to Scott Silliman, a Duke University Law School professor who spent 25 years as a military lawyer. Responsibility for implementing Bush's executive order dispatching enemy combatants to Guantánamo for adjudication fell to Paul Wolfowitz, a deputy Defense secretary at the time. As Silliman notes, Wolfowitz is not a lawyer, and the issue was not "a high priority" for him. Nothing got done for more than two years.

Putting the detainees at Guantánamo — an idea pushed by John Yoo, the executive power super-hawk who was then deputy director of the Justice Department's Office of Legal Counsel — backfired in 2004 when the Supreme Court ruled that the base was not beyond federal courts' jurisdiction. And the decision to bypass regular military courts for second-class military commissions backfired when the court ruled that the commissions' composition and procedures did not comply with the Uniform Code of Military Justice or the Geneva Conventions.

The administration then pushed Congress to write a 2006 law loosening the standards for admitting evidence obtained after "cruel, inhuman or degrading" treatment and limiting federal appeals court review of trials held by the commissions. The Supreme Court heard arguments challenging that law in December. A decision is due by June. Meanwhile, the administration wants the justices to stop the federal appeals court in Washington from carrying out its ruling that it must see all, not just some, of the military's evidence whenever it reviews a conviction from a Guantánamo commission.

The administration is asking the public to believe the Guantánamo Six case will proceed, as Hartmann puts it, "very much like a normal trial." Not so, say critics such as Eugene Fidell, president of the non-governmental National Institute of Military Justice, because hearsay evidence will be allowed, defense lawyers' access to classified information will be limited, and the proceedings will be run by a military judge rather than a more independent civilian jurist.

Hartmann says the accused terrorists' defense will be "very well" resourced. The defense lawyers disagree. The military apparently will provide only one lawyer for each of the six, though each can retain additional civilian counsel. Whatever the size of the defense teams, their logistical hurdles are daunting, according to Army Col. Stephen David, the chief defense lawyer for the military commissions. "You're not growing the garden in northern Indiana," he told *The Washington Post*. "You're growing the garden on the moon."

Silliman downplays the defense lawyers' concerns and some of the due-process shortcuts and says he's confident in the professionalism of all the trial's participants. Still, he declines to forecast a satisfactory outcome. "History will be the judge of whether we've done this right," he says, "and that chapter has yet to be written."

Gather Evidence for History to Judge

(*Jost on Justice*, Jan. 30, 2009)

When President Franklin D. Roosevelt ordered the internment of Japanese Americans living on the West Coast, Americans accepted his explanation that the move was necessary for national security. But Americans did not know – and did not learn for nearly 40 years – just how flimsy was the military's claimed justification for trampling on civil liberties.

In fact, reports prepared for Roosevelt by naval intelligence and by the State Department concluded that the vast majority of Japanese and Japanese American were – as one of the reports put it – "pathetically loyal" to the United States. And no less a domestic security hawk than FBI Director J. Edgar Hoover opposed the internment, writing to the attorney general that no evidence of disloyalty had been found among Japanese Americans.

The evidence from those buried government documents emerged in the 1980s. It served as the basis for reopening the trials and overturning the convictions of, among others, Fred Korematsu and Gordon Hirabayashi. And it also provides the basis for what is now history's judgment about the internments. They were doubly wrong: as unnecessary for national defense as they were unacceptable as legal policy.

History will be the judge of the detention and interrogation policies that the Bush administration initiated after the Sept. 11, 2001, terrorist attacks on the United States. President Bush and Vice President Cheney repeated their views as they left office. The prolonged detention of hundreds of foreigners at the Guantánamo Bay Naval Base and the "enhanced interrogation" techniques used on some number of them were necessary for national defense and legal under the law.

President Obama has also made his views clear. "We reject as false the choice between our safety and our ideals," he said in his inaugural address. Those ideals – "the rule of law and the rights of man" – "still light the world," Obama said, "and we will not give them up for expedience's sake."

Obama gave substance to his view the very next day by signing executive orders to limit the "enhanced interrogation" techniques such as waterboarding that were used against some detainees. The president also ordered the closing of the Guantánamo prison camp within one year and forbade the secret prisons that the CIA had operated for some "high-value" detainees.

Despite those actions, Obama is showing no appetite for investigating what the Bush administration did to those ideals in the name of national security in the seven-plus years after 9/11. "My orientation is going to be to move forward," he said on ABC's "This Week" before inauguration. For a new president with a plateful of problems –recession at home, two wars abroad – Obama's stance makes political sense. Obama has already run against Bush – and beat him soundly.

History has bigger interests, however. History needs to know all the details of how these policies were formed and how they were carried out. And the best time to begin gathering this evidence and compiling that record is now, while memories are still fresh and interest still high.

For that reason, some Democrats on Capitol Hill and some advocates and observers are calling for a joint congressional-presidential commission to examine the policies that the Bush administration pursued in its so-called war on terror. The purpose, according to House Judiciary Committee Chairman John Conyers, D-Mich., sponsor of one such proposal, "is not payback, but to uphold the rule of law, allow us to learn from our national mistakes, and prevent them from recurring."

Administration supporters naturally see the proposed commission as nothing but payback – a history written by victors, with predictable findings and self-serving conclusions. Their view gains credence from the calls by some critics on the left for war-crime prosecutions of those responsible for the detention and interrogation policies, up to and including Bush and Cheney.

Those trials are not going to happen. The new attorney general, Eric Holder, has made clear his opposition to criminalizing policy differences. For that very reason, trials will not tell the full story of the Bush administration's policies.

Administration supporters also say that the record is already complete, that nothing remains but the debate. In fact, many questions remain – including a full accounting of the interrogation techniques, the secret prisons and the government's "rendition" of detainees to other countries. In addition, a commission – its members chosen for their knowledge, judgment and independence – can draw conclusions that will carry greater weight than the partisan debates of today.

Similar inquiries have served valuable purposes. The Kerner Commission's chilling warning about racial injustice in the late 1960 gave impetus to efforts to deal with those issues. The Church Committee's documentation of CIA abuses in the 1970s helped close the door to some of the worst practices. A commission on the anti-terrorism policies pursued by the Bush administration – and its predecessors – could help the nation come to terms with the past and form a consensus on how best to preserve America's cherished ideals in the future.

The full history of the "war on terror" remains to be written. And as of early fall 2014 the military commission trial of Khalid Sheikh Mohammed and his co-defendants remained mired in pretrial proceedings with no date set for the beginning of the actual trial.

#Torture

The Bush administration subjected some number of "high-value" prisoners to what it euphemistically called "enhanced interrogation techniques," ranging from stress positions and sensory deprivation up to and including mock executions and waterboarding. The Justice Department's Office of Legal Counsel issued a controversial memo – later rescinded – that found the practices to be legal. After taking office, President Obama repudiated the policies but rejected calls for a full accounting. That allowed Bush alumni and supporters to continue defending what was done. My views came through clearly in several columns.

Coming Back to Haunt
(Jost on Justice, March 27, 2009)

When Binyam Mohamed was returned to Britain in February after nearly five years in the Guantánamo detention camp, his allegations that a British intelligence agent had colluded in his torture overseas rocked the British government. Now, a month later, Attorney General Patricia Schotland has formally directed Scotland Yard to investigate the allegations. Not satisfied, a spokesman for the opposition Liberal Democrats is demanding an independent judicial inquiry — in his words — "to ensure that trust in government and international respect for Britain is restored."

Contrast the events in Britain with the muted reaction in the United States in the past two weeks to the most compelling evidence to date that the Central Intelligence Agency systematically tortured high-level al Qaeda captives while held in secret prisons overseas. The evidence comes from a two-year old report by the International Committee for the Red Cross (ICRC), which interviewed the 14 prisoners after they were transferred to Guantánamo in September 2006. The report, leaked to University of California journalism professor Mark Danner, explicitly concluded that the interrogation techniques "constituted torture" and "cruel, inhuman or degrading treatment" — both violations of the Geneva Conventions governing treatment of wartime captives.

Granted, the allegations of torture are hardly new. Human rights groups, lawyers for prisoners, and journalists have been documenting the abusive techniques used against suspected terrorists by military and CIA interrogators almost since the opening of the Guantanamo prison camp in January 2002. *The Washington Post*'s Dana Priest was awarded the Pulitzer Prize for her stories in 2005 confirming the existence of the CIA's secret prisons and casting doubt on the U.S. government's official denials of torture.

Still, the ICRC report comes, in Danner's words, with exceptional "authenticity and credibility." As to its credibility, the ICRC is officially charged under international law with monitoring compliance with the Geneva Conventions. It safeguards its neutrality by keeping its reports confidential, sharing them only with the governments involved. Indeed, the ICRC responded to Danner's accounts by expressing regret about the disclosures.

As to the authenticity of the report, Danner notes that ICRC representatives obtained detailed and parallel accounts of the interrogations when they interviewed the 14 prisoners separately in

December 2006. According to Danner, the ICRC report specifically writes off the possibility that the prisoners fabricated the accounts since they had been isolated from each other.

Given that background, news of the ICRC report might have been expected to produce a surge of outrage, protest, and controversy. Instead, Danner's articles — a full account in the April 9 issue of *The New York Review of Books* and a condensed op-ed on March 15 in *The New York Times* — seem to have turned into hardly more than a two-day story. A handful of newspapers published editorials calling for an independent investigation. The American Civil Liberties Union and other human rights groups did the same. But one looks in vain for any palpable reaction from the White House, the Justice Department, or Congress.

In the first press briefing after the story broke, White House press secretary Robert Gibbs skirted the only question about the report by noting that President Obama had already changed the rules regarding detainees. Two days later, Attorney General Eric Holder told reporters he was "mindful" of the stories, but evinced little interest, according to the account by Congressional Quarterly's Keith Perine. Specifically asked whether an investigation was under way, Holder replied, "I wouldn't say that."

For his part, CIA Director Leon Panetta is on record opposing any criminal prosecutions of the CIA agents responsible for treatment that — according to the ICRC report — entailed beatings, denial of solid food, sleep deprivation, exposure to extreme temperatures, and forced nudity. "I would not support, obviously, an investigation or prosecution of those individuals," Panetta told the Senate Intelligence Committee on February 26. While pledging to cooperate with the committee's investigation, Panetta said he believed the agents "did their job . . . pursuant to the guidance that was provided them, whether you agreed or disagreed with it."

In Britain, Binyam Mohamed is taking a similar view of the MI5 agent who, according to his account, fed questions and information to Pakistani officials during his captivity in 2002 and who, he surmises, must have known he was being tortured. "I'm very pleased that an inquiry is taking place," Mohamed said in a statement issued by his lawyers on March 26. But, Mohamed added, "I feel very strongly that we shouldn't scapegoat the little people or blame Witness B [the unnamed agent] – he was only following orders."

Danner's op-ed in the Sunday *Times* hit breakfast tables just as former Vice President Dick Cheney was telling CNN's John King on "State of the Union" that the Obama administration was making the United States less safe by abandoning the Bush administration's anti-terror policies. As Danner points out, however, the evidence of torture creates an apparent dilemma for keeping the al Qaeda 14 in captivity. The torture will taint and possibly jeopardize any prosecutions, but — as Danner concedes — many of them likely have "blood on their hands." The Obama administration, Danner writes, is "haunted" by what its predecessor did. So, he might have added, are we all.

The Obama administration released the previous Justice Department opinions upholding the "enhanced interrogation techniques." Legal experts found them unpersuasive; so did I.

Torture Memos, Tortured Logic
(*Jost on Justice*, April 24, 2009)

The lawyer as litigator owes a client zealous advocacy in the courtroom. But the lawyer as counselor owes the client more: sound, independent judgment about proposed conduct, with frank and fully informed warnings about any doubts, legal or otherwise.

These elementary teachings in any legal ethics course can readily be applied to the controversy over the "enhanced interrogation techniques" used by CIA agents in questioning the so-called high-value al Qaeda detainees captured after 9/11. A lawyer defending any of the agents in court would have to pull out all the stops to get the agents off. But the lawyers in the Justice Department's Office of Legal Counsel (OLC) called on to advise the CIA about the legality of the proposed techniques needed to be more skeptical — all the more because they were representing not the agents, but the United States government itself.

The OLC's "torture memos" written in 2002 and 2005 and now released by President Obama show that the Bush administration lawyers failed in this basic, ethical obligation. On a quick read, the memos are chilling in the carefully calibrated approval of the techniques: confinement in cramped box, OK, if limited to two hours; sleep deprivation, OK, up to 72 hours or maybe longer; "walling," OK, up to 30 times; waterboarding, OK, for 20 minutes at a time.

The memos are even more disturbing in the patent legal errors that emerge from a closer reading. In one mistake already known, the lawyers erred in advising that the Geneva Conventions do not apply to the al Qaeda captives. As the Supreme Court ruled in 2006, the treaties' so-called Common Article 3 applies to all wartime captives, even those like the al Qaeda operatives who do not abide by the internationally recognized laws of war.

The lawyers were also on shaky grounds in advising that CIA interrogators would be protected from laws against torture as long as they did not specifically intend to inflict severe bodily harm. That argument would be no better than a dubious defense in the courtroom — and, for that reason, bad advice beforehand.

Since the release of the memos on April 17, legal commentators have pointed out many other mistakes. As widely observed, the memos approved waterboarding without noting that the United States has itself prosecuted persons who inflicted that technique on U.S. service personnel. That omission exemplifies the broader failure of relying solely on the CIA for information. As noted by Brian Tamahana, a professor at St. John's University School of Law in New York City [now Washington University Law School in St. Louis], on the *Balkinization* blog, the interrogation techniques are deemed not to inflict severe injury on the circular ground that the CIA says they won't.

Even if those assurances were taken at face value, the OLC lawyers sanction each of the proposed techniques with no consideration of their cumulative effect. And they approve the techniques in part because U.S. service personnel undergo them in training without recognizing that the training is designed to prepare U.S. service personnel to resist torture.

The lawyers also engaged in specious reasoning to conclude that the proposed techniques satisfy a "shock the conscience" test. That test, the lawyers reasoned, prohibits only "arbitrary" conduct that has no "reasonable justification" in furtherance of a "legitimate" government objective. The interrogation of the al Qaeda captives meets that test, the lawyers continued, because it was aimed at preventing a "grave threat" of supposedly imminent attack.

On that line of reasoning, virtually any interrogation technique — genital electric shocks, for example — would seemingly pass muster too. And in approving the imminent threat rationale, the lawyers raise no concern that the justification must be continually re-examined — or else it amounts to a blank check with no expiration date.

In one final omission, the memos never ask about the consequences of possible disclosure — as a good lawyer would have warned was all but inevitable. Indeed, over the past few years, the techniques have leaked out, at great cost to the government's standing at home and abroad.

Obama repudiated the memos on his second day in office. The lawyers who wrote or signed them — Steven Bradbury, Jay Bybee, and John Yoo — have moved on: Bybee to a federal judgeship, Yoo back to academia, and Bradbury to the private sector job market. Despite calls for accountability from the political left, they are unlikely to face criminal prosecutions. Nor does impeachment for Bybee seem likely. But the investigation still under way by the Justice Department's Office of Professional Responsibility could recommend some ethical sanction.

Of the three, only Yoo continues to publicly defend the memos. Bradbury and Bybee are largely out of sight. But Bybee is reported to have evinced some doubts in a gathering of his former law clerks to mark his fifth year on the Ninth U.S. Circuit Court of Appeals. As reported in *The Recorder*, a San Francisco-based legal newspaper, a former clerk quoted Bybee as saying he was proud of the memos his clerks had been writing for him — and then added: "I wish I could say that of the prior job I had."

A review by the Justice Department's Office of Professional Responsibility concluded that Yoo and Bybee were guilty of "professional misconduct" in preparing the memos. Yoo and Bybee both adamantly insisted their actions were proper. In a 69-page report issued on Feb. 18, 2010. David Margolis, a career Justice Department lawyer serving as associate deputy attorney general, rejected the ethics office's finding of misconduct despite what he called the "flawed" reasoning in the memos. "While I have declined to adopt O.P.R.'s findings of misconduct," Margolis wrote, "I fear that John Yoo's loyalty to his own ideology and convictions clouded his view of his obligation to his client and led him to author opinions that reflected his own extreme, albeit sincerely held, view of executive power while speaking for an institutional client." The decision came out even as Yoo was out promoting those views in a book tour.

Strong Presidents Don't Need Torture
(*Jost on Justice*, Feb. 16, 2010)

Constitutional law professor John Yoo is out promoting his new book and its stout defense of the need for a strong president in times of national emergencies. But the demonstrators in orange jump suits outside his recent appearance in Washington, D.C., were a reminder that Yoo's thesis has an inevitable subtext: his authorship of the later-repudiated Justice Department memo claiming a presidential power to commit torture.

Yoo makes no mention in *Crisis and Command* of either of the two infamous torture memos that he drafted in 2002 and 2003 as deputy director of the Justice Department's Office of Legal Counsel under President George W. Bush. Having returned to the University of California-Berkeley law school, Yoo makes his case for a strong presidency by citing assertive chief executives viewed favorably by history: chiefly, Washington, Jackson, Lincoln, and FDR. And he contrasts them with failed presidents, such as James Madison and James Buchanan, who took a less expansive view of their powers.

Despite all the indicia of respectable scholarship, the book is to some extent an academic sleight of hand. For one thing, Yoo neglects to tell readers of his belief that the president enjoys unbounded power as commander in chief over the detention and interrogation of enemy combatants — even to the point of violating domestic law and international treaties against torture.

Even in the covered material, however, Yoo glosses over the critical distinction between the use of presidential power in institutional conflicts — with Congress or the states — and the misuse of presidential power against individuals. It is one thing to commend Franklin Roosevelt for skirting neutrality statutes to lead the nation into a just and necessary war. It is another to defend Roosevelt for the internment of Japanese Americans or the summary convictions and executions of German saboteurs.

Yoo begins with the first president, George Washington, and his assertion of a critical foreign affairs power vis-à-vis Congress in 1793 in issuing a proclamation of neutrality in the war between Britain and France. Two of the framers, Alexander Hamilton and Madison, debated whether Washington had overstepped his powers. As Yoo says, Hamilton's view defending Washington's action has prevailed.

History similarly judges Andrew Jackson to have been right in two important tests of presidential power when he was in the White House. Jackson stared down a Senate censure over his decision to withdraw government funds from the corruption-plagued National Bank. And he stood up against John Calhoun and others who claimed for the states a power of "nullification" over federal laws that they disapproved.

Turning to the Civil War, Yoo says that both Buchanan and Abraham Lincoln believed that Southern states had no power to secede from the Union. Lincoln succeeded where Buchanan failed, Yoo says, because he thought — unlike Buchanan — that the president could use force against the secessionists. Then, during the war, Lincoln stretched his powers as commander in chief to issue the Emancipation Proclamation, even though Congress had a different approach on freeing the slaves.

History judges Lincoln right on both counts, but it gives no agreed verdict on Lincoln's suspension of the writ of habeas corpus — ratified by Congress only after the fact — and his detention of thousands of suspected saboteurs, spies and Confederate sympathizers. Whether justified or not, it should be noted that Lincoln countermanded some of the harsher decisions by military tribunals. And the war was won not by jailing secessionists in the North but by besting the Confederate Army on the battlefields in the South.

Franklin Roosevelt's actions in the run-up to World War II demonstrated a resolve similar to Lincoln's to use presidential power to confront a threat to national security. As commander in chief, FDR helped forge the alliance that defeated Germany and Japan. But history gives him no credit for the decision to send 120,000 Japanese Americans to concentration camps. And it is jarring to hear Yoo cite with approval the Supreme Court's discredited decision, *Korematsu v. United States*, upholding Roosevelt's action.

The Supreme Court brought no credit to itself either in upholding FDR's use of truncated procedures against the German saboteurs captured in June 1942 in New York and Florida, who were convicted within two months and put to death even before the justices had time to issue a formal opinion on their appeals.

Yoo says the Bush presidency must await history's verdict, but for his part reaffirms his support for all of the post-9/11 policies as consistent with the historical precedents of Washington, Lincoln and FDR. Again, though, Yoo makes no distinction between the use of force to confront and defeat the nation's enemies on the battlefield and the use of ad hoc procedures against captured "enemy combatants" that skirt constitutional rights and international law.

Yoo himself is awaiting the verdict from an internal Justice Department investigation on whether he violated legal ethics in providing the advice that permitted the use of waterboarding and other "enhanced interrogation techniques" and that depicted the president in any event as above the law in ordering those policies. He defends those memos, rescinded by the Bush Justice Department itself, as his best judgment as a lawyer. Perhaps they were. But history provides no basis, even in Yoo's telling, for believing that a strong president needs arbitrary powers, much less the right to use torture, to keep the country safe and secure.

Throughout the debate, President Bush insisted he never authorized torture. In his memoir, he was no more forthcoming.

Bush's Incomplete Memoir
(*Jost on Justice*, Nov. 22, 2010)

In his final weeks in office, President George W. Bush was beset with what he describes in his memoir *Decision Points* as a "flood" of pardon requests submitted by people who "pulled me aside" to special plead for some friend, family member or former colleague. At first "frustrated" and then "disgusted," Bush resolved "that I would not pardon anyone who went outside the formal [Justice Department] channels."

It is a good story, but — as the *New York Times* reporter Charlie Savage notes — "incomplete." In fact, as Savage wrote on the Times' blog *The Caucus*, Bush granted a batch of 20 pardons on Dec. 23, 2008, including at least four who went outside the Justice Department channels.

As with the self-enhancing version of his pardons policy, so too with Bush's description of one of the most momentous of his decision points: his personal authorization for CIA and military interrogators to use "waterboarding" on suspected terrorists. The four-page account (pp. 168-171) so oversimplifies the events before and after Bush's directive as to be at the very least "incomplete" — and, for any lesson-drawing purposes, simply wrong.

Bush traces the origins of the CIA's "enhanced interrogation techniques" to the capture in March 2002 of Abu Zubaydah, purportedly a close associate of al Qaeda leader Osama bin Laden, and his initial questioning by FBI agents. As Bush tells it, the FBI interrogation ran dry and the CIA proposed to take over in a secret location with additional techniques. "At my direction," Bush writes, "Department of Justice and CIA lawyers conducted a careful legal review." That review found all the techniques constitutional and lawful. Even so, Bush ruled out two that "went too far," but approved the others, including waterboarding.

To Michael Scharf, a law professor at Case Western Reserve University in Cleveland who has studied and written extensively on the issue, the account hardly begins to tell the story. In Scharf's account in a law review article and his forthcoming book, *Shaping Foreign Policy in Times of Crisis*, it was not Bush, but Vice President Dick Cheney and his lawyer, David Addington, who drove the legal review — determined to find the interrogation techniques lawful.

Cheney succeeded by the bureaucratic ploy of cutting out potential opponents. As Scharf explains, the interrogation program was classified "need to know" instead of merely "top secret." The effect was to keep the plan from the top lawyers of each of the military services and, most significantly, the State Department's legal adviser, the office most expert in interpreting the U.S.-signed treaties banning torture. The "careful" legal review that Bush describes was, in Scharf's words, "completely one-sided."

Unmentioned by Bush, the memos upholding the techniques — and twisting the previous view of waterboarding as torture — have been rescinded. Whatever its legal basis, Bush credits the waterboarding and other of the torture-like techniques used on Zubaydah with breaking his resistance. CIA interrogators supposedly gained pivotal information that led, eventually, to the capture of 9/11 mastermind Khalid Sheikh Mohammed in March 2003. And KSM provided information "vital to saving American lives" that "almost certainly would not have come to light without the CIA's enhanced interrogation program."

Nowhere does Bush mention the later downgrading of Zubaydah's importance. In court filings, the government now disclaims any allegation that Zubaydah is a member of al Qaeda or played a role in the September 11 or other attacks on the United States. Nor does Bush acknowledge the sharp dispute about the supposedly invaluable intelligence gained from the enhanced interrogation techniques.

The most telling refutation comes from former FBI agent Ali Soufan, who helped interrogate KSM for three months (March-June 2002) before the CIA took over. In successive op-ed articles in the *New York Times* in April and September 2009 and comments elsewhere, Soufan labels the puffed-up accounts of the intelligence gained from the enhanced interrogation techniques as "false claims." He says that KSM was providing "actionable intelligence" under traditional techniques and notes that KSM has boasted of providing false information to later interrogators. As for Zubaydah, Soufan similarly says no intelligence was gained that was not or could not have been gained from regular interrogations.

As with waterboarding, Bush is incomplete in describing some of the administration's other post-9/11 legal policies. He describes his early decision to treat the Guantánamo detainees as outside the protections of the Geneva conventions (pp. 166-167) with no mention of the State Department's position that in fact they were covered by the U.S.-signed international accords. He describes the creation of the "military commissions" to try Guantánamo detainees (p. 167) with no mention of the departures from the procedures for regular military tribunals. And after acknowledging the Supreme Court's decision in *Hamdan v. Rumsfeld* (2006) striking down the military commissions, Bush claims that Congress solved the problem with legislation passed later that year (pp. 177-179). But he does not mention the court's later ruling, *Boumediene v. Bush* (2008), which found unconstitutional the critical provision in the law to limit judicial review of the reconstituted military commissions' decisions.

Bush's acknowledgment of having authorized waterboarding has prompted calls from human rights groups, including Amnesty International and the American Civil Liberties Union, to prosecute him for violating U.S. law against torture. An administration that has already given a pass to the lawyers who wrote the torture memos is hardly likely to take on a former chief executive. But the American people still deserve the complete torture story — and they have gotten nothing close to that from Bush's first-person account.

The killing of the al Qaeda leader Osama bin Laden on May 1, 2011, renewed the debate on the use of torture. Some Bush alumni, including Yoo, contended that the controversial interrogation techniques helped get the information needed to track him down. Their account was factually suspect, but, more important in my analysis, logically flawed.

No Stopping Point on Torture
(*Jost on Justice*, May 9, 2011)

Nearly a century and a half after the fact, Robert Redford has renewed the debate, in his movie *The Conspirator*, over whether the government was right to prosecute and execute Mary Surratt for conspiracy in the assassination of President Abraham Lincoln.

Historical debates over wartime policies like this one are peculiarly durable because the legal and ethical issues are so stark and the stakes so high in getting the answer right or wrong. So decades from now, Americans will still be debating whether the U.S. government under

President George W. Bush was right to use torture against some number of "high-value" detainees in the so-called global war on terror.

The debate, which has gone on inconclusively since the first disclosure of the Bush administration's "enhanced interrogation techniques," resumed last week after the killing of al Qaeda's founder and leader Osama bin Laden [May 1]. Former vice president Dick Cheney and former Justice Department official John Yoo, among others, re-emerged into public view to credit the success in the decade-long hunt to the former administration's policies, including what Yoo called "tough" interrogation techniques.

The Bush alumni's argument rests on one dot out of the many that were connected only after years of painstaking intelligence gathering and surveillance. Writing in the *Wall Street Journal* (May 4), Yoo contends that the key to the success was learning the identity of Bin Laden's trusted courier, known as Abu Ahmed al-Kuwaiti, from two al Qaeda detainees subjected to the tough interrogation: Khalid Sheikh Mohammed, the architect of the 9/11 attacks, and his successor, Abu Faraj al-Libi.

The argument has several weak spots. First, al-Kuwaiti's identity apparently was first gleaned not from KSM or al-Libi, but from Hassan Ghul, a detainee captured in Iraq, held at a secret CIA prison, and, yes, subjected to some coercive interrogation. Ghul's information was "the linchipin," one U.S. official told the Associated Press, but he did not put the courier in direct contact with Bin Laden. Second, by this account KSM and al-Libi helped identify al-Kuwaiti and his significance not by answering questions but by refusing. Their determined silence about al-Kuwaiti convinced CIA agents they were on to something.

Whatever KSM and al-Libi said or did not say about al-Kuwaiti, critics of the Bush administration policies emphasize that the clues came not during or immediately after their rough treatment, but some time later. The time interval, they contend, shows that conventional interrogation yielded the crucial information, succeeding eventually where waterboarding did not.

The reply to that argument: waterboarding is not designed to elicit information in the moment, but to secure cooperation later. That reply has a flaw as well: it would prove that torture — once applied — always "works" whenever useful information is obtained later regardless of the methods used.

For now, the arguments are raging without a full disclosure of the facts and circumstances surrounding the KSM and al-Libi interrogations or the intelligence and surveillance that ensued. Writing in *The New Republic* (May 5), lawyer and law professor Joseph Marguiles, a leading critic of and litigator against the Bush administration detention policies, called last week for President Obama himself to confirm whether torture was used to find bin Laden or not.

Marguiles reviews the authoritative but contradictory statements issued after Bin Laden's death by presumptively knowledgeable current or former officials. Jose Rodriguez, head of the CIA's counterterrorism center from 2002 to 2005, tells *Time* that the "lead" information definitely came from KSM and al-Libbi. Sen. Diane Feinstein, the California Democrat who heads the Senate Intelligence Committee, says "none" of the intelligence came from what she called "harsh interrogation practices."

History suggests that this argument will continue even after (if?) the facts are fully laid out. But facts are unnecessary to expose the overarching flaw in defending torture based on bin Laden's death. The argument simply has no stopping point.

Pressed with the legal and ethical arguments against torture, defenders of the practice resort to the "ticking time bomb" hypothesis. A prisoner with information about some large and imminent threat to life and limb, the argument goes, should be questioned without restraint until the information is divulged. The hypothesis is more the stuff of fiction than of real life, but in any event does not fit the hunt for Osama bin Laden.

In hiding somewhere, Bin Laden was a threat, but not a ticking time bomb. Nor was the torture of second- or third-level operatives close enough in time or place to match the hypothesis. And to defend the use of torture to track down bin Laden is to suggest that the same techniques could be applied to track down al Qaeda's next leader — and the next and the next until the war ends.

As history, *The Conspirator* plays loose with some of the facts, but the liberties do not detract from the film's lesson that Surratt should have been tried in a civilian instead of a military court. Whatever the facts in the hunt for bin Laden, the lesson to draw is that the best stopping point for the use of torture, in line with American law and values alike, is before it ever begins.

Judging CIA on Torture
(*Jost on Justice*, March 16, 2014)

Confession may be good for the soul, but apparently not for the Central Intelligence Agency. Nearly eight years after the supposed end of the CIA's "enhanced interrogation techniques" era, the agency is resisting coming clean about what it did. And it is blocking the Senate Intelligence Committee from releasing its own report on the now repudiated torture-like practices.

This is the real import of the she said/he said dispute that erupted last week [March 11] between the CIA and Sen. Diane Feinstein, the California Democrat who has long been a friend of the CIA as chairman of the Senate Intelligence Committee. In an astonishing 15-minute floor speech, Feinstein charged that the CIA had illegally — indeed, unconstitutionally — spied on the Intelligence Committee as it prepared what has been described as a harshly critical report.

Brennan fired back in a matter of hours with a denial of sorts. "When the facts come out on this, I think a lot of people who are claiming that there has been this tremendous sort of spying and monitoring and hacking will be proved wrong," he said in a passage added to a previously scheduled speech.

Setting aside the details of this dispute for a moment, here is the most important passage from Feinstein's speech. The Intelligence Committee's preliminary report on the CIA's interrogation practices, conducted by two staffers and completed shortly after Feinstein became chairman of the committee in 2009, was, in her word, "chilling."

"The interrogations and the conditions of confinement at the CIA detention sites were far different and far more harsh than the way the CIA had described them to us," Feinstein declared. Put differently: the CIA lied to us, and we are the Congress of the United States.

That preliminary report persuaded the committee to approve, on a bipartisan 14-1 vote, a full investigation of the CIA's role in interrogation techniques that include practices long considered to be torture, such as waterboarding, sleep deprivation and prolonged stress positions. Nearly five years later, the report — described as 6,300 pages long — is still awaiting release.

The hold-up is at the CIA, which is reviewing the report ostensibly to guard against disclosure of any legitimately classified information (think: intelligence sources and methods). But one need not be a reflexive cynic to suspect that the agency is sitting on the report for more substantive reasons.

The further news from Feinstein's speech is that the CIA itself came to very critical conclusions about its conduct in an internal review commissioned by Leon Panetta in 2009 when he was CIA director. As Feinstein put it, "the Internal Panetta Review had documented at least some of the very same troubling matters already uncovered by the committee staff."

The committee's access to the Panetta review is at the heart of the dispute that Feinstein aired —she says reluctantly— on the Senate floor. Committee staffers found the review among the mass of documents the CIA provided using search tools also provided by the agency, according to Feinstein's account. She acknowledges that she does not know whether the review was provided intentionally by the CIA, unintentionally by the CIA, or intentionally by a whistle-blower.

Regardless, Feinstein insists the committee staffers did nothing wrong in uncovering the Panetta review. But Robert Eatinger, then the agency's acting general counsel, thought otherwise. He went so far as to refer the matter to the Justice Department for a possible criminal prosecution. And, it would seem, he must have authorized the search of the committee's computers in January that drove Feinstein first to complain and then, with no apology forthcoming, to take to the Senate floor.

Eatinger, unnamed in Feinstein's speech but readily identified from public records, has no clean hands in this dispute. The career CIA lawyer is named more than 1,600 times, often unfavorably, in the Intelligence Committee's still unreleased study.

As Feinstein explained, this was not the first access dispute between the committee and the CIA. Back in 2010, the committee staff discovered that the CIA had removed various documents from those it had previously made available. When Feinstein complained, the agency said it was done at the White House's orders. But the White House denied issuing any such direction, Feinstein said.

In a credibility contest, anyone who knows the CIA's history will readily decide whether Feinstein or the agency is most likely to be lying. "The CIA doesn't do that sort of thing," former CIA lawyer John Rizzo declared last week on WAMU's Diane Rehm Show [March 13]. It fell to David Corn, Washington bureau chief of *The Nation*, to recall for listeners that the CIA indeed lied in the 1970s about Chile and in the 1980s about Iran-contra.

For observant Catholics, confession — "Forgive me, Father, for I have sinned" — is the key to absolution: "Te absolvo." Rather than confessing, the CIA is now disputing some of the conclusions in the Senate committee's unreleased study even though, according to Feinstein, some of them "are clearly acknowledged in the CIA's own Internal Panetta Review."

The time has come for this controversy to be put to rest and, as Feinstein stressed, "to ensure that an un-American, brutal program of detention and interrogation will never again be considered or permitted." If it cannot confess, the least the CIA can do is get out of the way for the Senate to render its judgment.

When finally released in December 2014, the Senate Intelligence Committee's report renewed without settling the debate over the CIA's interrogation tactics. The majority report by the panel's Democrats said that the tactics were "brutal and far worse" and more detainees subjected to the tactics than previously described. Feinstein said the tactics amounted to torture "under any common meaning of the term." The report also found no evidence that the tactics had produced useful intelligence. In their report, Republicans defended the agency and insisted the tactics had been essential in countering or thwarting terrorist threats. CIA Director John Brennan split the difference by saying that the interrogations conducted with what he called "EITs" did produce usable intelligence but that it was "unknowable" whether the information could have been obtained without the techniques.

#Guantánamo

The United States acquired lease rights to establish a naval base at Guantánamo Bay, on the southeastern end of the island of Cuba, at the end of the Spanish-American War. No one then could have imagined that a century later it would be used as a controversial prison camp for suspected terrorists captured by U.S. forces halfway around the world. And a century from now perhaps no one will understand why the Bush administration worked so hard – and, ultimately, unsuccessfully – to deny legal rights to the prisoners held there. Or why the Obama administration failed to fulfill the president's promise – on his first full day in office – to close the prison camp within one year.

The Curious Kurnaz Case
(*CQ Weekly*, Dec. 17, 2007)

Murat Kurnaz is a free man today in his adopted home, Germany, after having spent nearly five years in the Guantánamo Bay prison camp as a wrongly suspected terrorist. He is free despite the procedures that the Bush administration has established for trying "enemy combatants" held at that naval base in Cuba. And his hard-earned freedom represents what even the administration's supporters concede is a strong argument against the legal policies now being challenged for the third time before the Supreme Court.

Kurnaz appears to have been a victim of guilt by misassociation — including his friendship with a supposed suicide bomber who's actually alive and not even under suspicion in Germany. Misinformation is a common risk in any criminal justice system, but it has been magnified by the administration's short-circuiting of legal process for enemy combatants.

The German-born son of a Turkish guest worker, Kurnaz says he rediscovered the Muslim religion in the fall of 2000. A year later, and three weeks after the Sept. 11 attacks, he traveled to Pakistan on a religious excursion with a friend, Selcuk Bilgin. Kurnaz connected with a Muslim missionary group, visited various holy sites and studied the Koran. In November he was arrested by Pakistani police and then turned over to the United States. He was brought to Guantánamo in January 2002.

The U.S. government's supposed evidence for believing Kurnaz to be an enemy combatant remains partly classified, but both the German government and U.S. District Court Judge Joyce Hens Green have concluded Kurnaz is innocent. That's why German Chancellor Angela Merkel pressed President Bush hard enough to win Kurnaz's release in August 2006.

Diplomacy was necessary because legal process had failed — even after Judge Green concluded in January 2005 that the government had failed to show that Kurnaz had taken up arms against the United States or otherwise intended to attack American interests. "No one gets out of Guantánamo by any legal process," one of his lawyers, Seton Hall law professor Baher Azmy, remarked in a story in the Washington Spectator this summer. "Because there is none."

Kurnaz was judged to be an enemy combatant by a Combatant Status Review Tribunal, the special military panels the administration has created to hear the Guantánamo detainee cases. But the CSRTs are not models of due process. The detainee is not afforded a lawyer, but a "personal representative" designated by the military. As Solicitor General Paul D. Clement conceded before the Supreme Court this month, the representative is not bound by lawyer confidentiality but would be obliged to report any intelligence information obtained from the detainee. And neither the detainee nor the representative is entitled to see all the government's evidence. As Judge Green explained, the classified document that the CSRT apparently relied on "was never provided to the detainee, and had he received it, he would have had the opportunity to challenge its credibility and significance."

Fortunately for Kurnaz, the Supreme Court ruled in 2004 that Guantánamo detainees may challenge the legality of their detentions in federal court. Azmy entered the case in August and was provided a transcript of his client's CSRT hearing. The strongest evidence in the transcript: Kurnaz's association with a supposed suicide bomber, his friend Bilgin. "I don't need a friend like that," Kurnaz said at the hearing. But, while locked up in Cuba, Kurnaz had no way to prove his innocence. Within days, however, his lawyers secured affidavits from Bilgin's German lawyer confirming that Bilgin was alive and from a German prosecutor stating that investigators had no evidence against him of terrorist activity.

The new evidence was not enough to win Kurnaz's release. The administration kept fighting the detainees' cases in court and in Congress. At Bush's request, last year Congress wrote a law barring federal courts from considering detainees' habeas corpus petitions. Instead, there is only limited appeals court review of the decisions rendered by CSRTs. And under the terms of a 2005 law known as the Detainee Treatment Act (DTA), new evidence — as in Kurnaz's case — may not be used to challenge a tribunal verdict.

Representing the detainees before the Supreme Court this month, former Clinton administration Solicitor General Seth Waxman cited the Kurnaz case to illustrate his argument that the review process is a constitutionally inadequate substitute for habeas corpus. Afterward, Robert Chesney, a pro-administration national security expert at Wake Forest Law School [now, University of Texas], called Kurnaz's case "perhaps the strongest argument" that DTA review is not an adequate substitute for habeas review. "A bang-up anecdote," remarked Jan Crawford Greenburg, ABC's Supreme Court correspondent, even while tentatively predicting a Bush administration victory.

Her forecast emphasized the mixed signals sent at the argument by the court's pivotal justice, Anthony M. Kennedy. Most observers, however, predict another administration defeat. The decision in *Boumediene v. Bush* is due by June. By then, Kurnaz's memoir, *Five Years of My Life: An Account From Guantánamo*, should be on bookstore shelves.

In fact, Kennedy wrote the majority opinion that dealt the Bush administration another defeat by ruling the limitations on habeas corpus rights unconstitutional. "We hold that petitioners may invoke the fundamental procedural protections of habeas corpus," Kennedy wrote. Roberts led three other conservatives in dissent. The ruling proved, however, to have more symbolic than practical value. Despite some favorable trial-level rulings, the federal appeals court for the District of Columbia rejected most of the pleas by Guantánamo detainees to be released. By summer 2014, some 149 prisoners were still being held at Guantánamo, some of them for more than a decade.

#ProsecutingTerrorists

The Bush administration's plan for getting tough with suspected terrorists was to try some of them in hastily established military commissions (read: pseudo-courts) instead of in the well established federal civilian courts. The result: delays, delays, and more delays in the military system even while the government was successfully prosecuting dozens of terrorism cases in federal courts. Despite that record, Republicans in Congress and national security hawks criticized the Obama administration for favoring civilian over military trials.

Taking Flak on National Security
(Jost on Justice, Jan. 11, 2010)

The good will from President Obama's inauguration lasted only as long as it took him to reaffirm his campaign pledge to close the Guantánamo Bay prison camp on his second full day in the White House. One year out, national security law remains a political battlefield, with Republicans and conservatives mounting partisan attacks grounded more in ideology than in evidence or reason.

The GOP critique depicts Obama as a feckless chief executive more interested in legal niceties than counterterrorism. Exhibit No. 1 is the decision to prosecute Umar Farouk Abdulmutallab, the foiled Christmas Day bomber on Northwest flight 253, in federal court instead of before a military commission.

The criticism comes from such Bush administration alumni as former vice president Dick Cheney and White House political guru Karl Rove as well as sitting GOP officeholders. "We must treat these terrorists as what they are — not common criminals, but enemy combatants in a war," said Sen. Christopher (Kit) Bond, the Missouri Republican and ranking member on the Senate Intelligence Committee.

One former Bush administration official, however, is OK with the decision: Robert Gates, secretary of defense in Bush's last two years in office and held over in the post by Obama. Gates was reportedly consulted in advance of the Justice Department's decision to prosecute Abdulmutallab and raised no objection.

The Republican critics appear blind to the poor record of the military commission system created up by the Bush administration either in intelligence-gathering or terrorist-prosecuting — as well as its use of civilian courts to prosecute many suspected terrorists. Most specifically, in a case virtually identical to Abdulmutallab's, the Bush administration prosecuted shoe bomber Richard Reid in federal court after his failed attack on a Boston-bound flight in December 2001.

Reid was indicted on eight terrorism-related counts in January 2002, pleaded guilty in October, and was sentenced to a life prison term that he is now serving in a maximum security prison within the United States. When reminded of this recent history, Republican critics can say only that the Bush administration made a mistake.

Attorney General Eric Holder says that Abdulmutallab similarly faces a possible life sentence if convicted under the six-count indictment that the government obtained on Jan. 6. Apart from any possible sentence, however, the Republican critics say that the administration has given up valuable leverage in obtaining useful intelligence from Abdulmutallab by vesting him with the legal rights of the criminal justice system, including the right to a lawyer instead of the diminished procedural protections of the military commission system.

As the *New York Times* reporter Charlie Savage has pointed out, however, Abdulmutallab has the right to counsel in the military commission system under Supreme Court rulings that rejected the Bush administration's efforts to bar federal court scrutiny of the system. In addition, the GOP critics disregard the likelihood that a defense lawyer will encourage, not discourage, Abdulmutallab to provide information to the government in the hope of getting some favorable consideration as the prosecution proceeds.

In any event, White House press secretary Robert Gibbs says the government did obtain "useable, actionable intelligence" before Abdulmutallab decided to stop talking once he was provided counsel. There is no public record from Reid's case eight years ago that the Bush administration turned him before putting him into the criminal justice system.

Abdulmutallab's training in an al Qaeda camp in Yemen opens a second target for Republican critics: Obama's now deferred promise to close Guantánamo within a year. Yemenis comprise nearly half of the 200 or so detainees still held at Guantánamo. Some of the Yemenis already released have been returned to their home countries, including one who is now said to be the head of al Qaeda in the Arabian Peninsula. Inconveniently for the GOP critics, he was released on Bush's watch, not Obama's.

Obama, who had already been working to strengthen Yemen's scrutiny of ex- Guantánamo detainees, promptly put a hold on any more releases to Yemen. Obama also quickly demanded and then released a review of how Abdulmutallab came to board a U.S.-bound flight, with explosives, despite the warning that U.S. diplomatic and intelligence personnel received from Abdulmutallab's father, a respected Nigerian banker.

The report disclosed "human" and "systemic" failures ranging from a misspelling of Abdulmutallab's name to a delay in sending a cable about the interviews with his father. The mistakes occurred down in the federal bureaucracy, but Obama personally assumed responsibility for them. By contrast, Bush was slow to acknowledge any Oval Office oversight in failing to pick up on pre-9/11 warnings from the intelligence community of a possible attack from al Qaeda.

Politics, it is often said, stops at the water's edge. The adage is perhaps honored more in the breach than in the observance, and thus it has been for Obama's first year in office. Still, even seasoned political observers may cringe at the degree of partisanship from Republicans toward a Democratic administration that has Abdulmutallab locked up and a crash program under way to plug the holes in the airline security system that allowed him to board flight 253 in the first place.

Congress put its unhelpful second-guessing on terrorism cases into law at the end of its 2011 session. Obama signed the measure into law at the end of December despite, as he wrote in a signing statement, "serious reservations" about the provisions regulating the detention, interrogation, and prosecution of suspected terrorists.

The Meddlesome Congress
(*Jost on Justice*, Dec. 5, 2011)

The Senate made a gallant effort last week to justify its former reputation as the world's greatest deliberative body as it tried to define the government's authority to detain suspected terrorists. The week began with a bipartisan compromise fashioned by two senators with experience generally taking the high road on the issues and ended on Dec. 1 with a thorough, and well-reasoned, floor debate.

Despite those indicia of legislative statesmanship, the detention provisions included in the National Defense Authorization Act represent a step backward in the United States' war against al Qaeda. Once again, Congress wants to micromanage the Obama administration's enforcement tactics against al Qaeda members by limiting prosecutions in federal courts in favor of trials in the still unproven system of military commissions. In addition, the Senate majority apparently hopes courts will allow use of military-style detention and interrogation against suspected terrorists even if they are U.S. citizens arrested within the United States.

True, the two sections at issue could have been worse. In section 1032, the bill supposedly mandates military detention for persons "determined to be part of al Qaeda or associated forces" who "have participated in a planned or actual attack or attempted attack on the United States or its coalition partners." But it allows the administration to waive that requirement if it shows that a waiver would best serve the interest of national security.

The mandatory military detention provision would not apply to U.S. citizens or lawful permanent residents. But in section 1031, the bill leaves unclear whether the general authority to detain suspected members of al Qaeda, the Taliban, or associated forces applies to U.S.

citizens. An earlier version had been written to apply to U.S. citizens unless prohibited by the Constitution.

In fashioning the compromise, Sens. Carl Levin, D-Mich., and John McCain, R-Ariz., chairman and ranking member respectively of the Armed Services Committee, said it was designed to leave the law on the issue unchanged. In effect, that would leave as the last word on the subject the Supreme Court's somewhat cryptic decision in *Hamdi v. Rumsfeld* (2004). That ruling allowed military detention of a U.S. citizen captured abroad but left unanswered the question of military detention for a citizen arrested within the United States.

In Senate debate last week, California Democrat Dianne Feinstein, who chairs the Senate Intelligence Committee, passionately argued against allowing indefinite military detention of U.S. citizens. "This country is special because we have certain values, and due process of law is one of those values," Feinstein said. "So I object. I object to holding American citizens without trial."

From the opposite side, South Carolina Republican Lindsey Graham, a former military lawyer, argued with equal force in favor of allowing military detention for U.S. citizens: "I am just saying, to any American citizen: If you want to help al Qaeda, you do so at your own peril," Graham said. "You can get killed in the process. You can get detained indefinitely."

Feinstein's amendment failed on a mostly party-line 45-55 vote. Three Republicans voted in favor: Illinois moderate Mark Kirk and the libertarian-minded Mike Lee of Utah and Rand Paul of Kentucky. But the amendment fell short because 10 Democrats joined 45 Republicans in opposing it.

Feinstein succeeded, however, with a second amendment that makes explicit that the provision has no effect on existing authority to detain U.S. citizens. Adopted with only one dissenting vote, the amendment effectively leaves it to the courts to answer the question left unresolved in *Hamdi*. In debate, Feinstein said both Levin and McCain had promised to defend that version of the legislation in conference with the House.

The House version of the defense authorization bill is more stringent in several respects, including in its provision to require military commission trials for all suspected terrorists. The House version also would bar transferring suspected terrorists captured abroad into the United States and make it harder for the administration to transfer any of the current Guantánamo detainees to other countries. The Senate's bill generally leaves those issues untouched.

The preference in both chambers for military over civilian trials for suspected terrorists elevates ideological posturing over fact-based decision-making. As Feinstein and others pointed out, the government has successfully prosecuted hundreds of suspected terrorists since 9/11, under presidents of both parties: Republican George W. Bush and Democrat Barack Obama. That list extends from "shoe bomber" Richard Reid, serving a life sentence for his foiled aircraft bomb attempt in December 2001, to Faisal Shahzad, also serving a life sentence for his attempted Times Square bombing in May 2010.

Major administration officials, including Defense Secretary Leon Panetta, CIA Director David Petraeus, and FBI Director Robert Mueller, argued against those provisions as the bills moved through the House and Senate. After the Senate action, White House officials raised the possibility of a veto.

The administration gave way earlier this year, however, when Congress prohibited bringing any Guantánamo detainees to the United States for trial in civilian courts. The result has been to slow the trial of Khalid Sheikh Mohammed and the other alleged 9/11 co-conspirators. Facts and logic notwithstanding, Obama may well find he has little choice again if Congress insists on dictating where best to prosecute suspected al Qaeda members.

#DeathbyDrones

President Obama went beyond the Bush administration in deploying one counterterrorism tactic: the use of unpiloted aircraft (a/k/a drones) to target suspected terrorists overseas. Viewed from 30,000 feet in the air, the tactic seems to offer the prospect of taking out bad guys with clean kills and without putting U.S. service members in harm's way. Viewed from the ground, the "death by drone" program looks more dubious. And the administration was slow to lay out the facts for Americans – and the world at large – to judge.

Laying Out the Facts
(Jost on Justice, Oct. 3, 2011)

When Thomas Jefferson and his fellow revolutionaries declared the American colonies' independence from England, they began by explaining the need to lay out their reasons, in factual detail, for such a momentous decision. "A decent respect to the opinions of mankind," Jefferson wrote, "requires that they should declare the causes which impel them to the separation."

What was true then is true today. The United States' national identity demands that its actions, at home and abroad, satisfy in some sense "the opinions of mankind," both at home and abroad. So the Obama administration owes it to Americans and the rest of the world to lay out in detail its case for the targeted killing of Anwar al-Awlaki, a U.S. citizen and al Qaeda leader, in a missile strike by a CIA-controlled drone aircraft in the Yemeni desert last week [Sept. 30].

Much is known about Awlaki (sometimes spelled "Aulaqi"), and much of the information is from the U.S. government. But some of what is "known" is only asserted. And some of the unsubstantiated assertions are critical in determining whether the killing of Awlaki satisfies what may be or should be the requirements of U.S. and international law.

Awlaki was born in New Mexico in 1971 and later educated in the United States after growing up in his father's native Yemen. He was a Muslim imam of seemingly moderate views in several cities, including the Washington, D.C., area, before adopting radical Islamist doctrines that he has espoused on the Internet for nearly a decade. He was, in no uncertain terms, someone who wished the United States ill and someone who actively encouraged others to take up jihad against the United States.

In announcing Awlaki's death, President Obama identified him as "the leader of external operations for al Qaeda in the Arabian Peninsula." In that role, Obama said, Awlaki "took the lead in planning and directing efforts to murder innocent Americans. He directed the failed attempt to blow up an airplane on Christmas Day in 2009. He directed the failed attempt to blow up U.S. cargo planes in 2010. And he repeatedly called on individuals in the United States and around the globe to kill innocent men, women and children to advance a murderous agenda."

As of this writing, the evidence to back up the most specific of those charges has not been made public. Awlaki acknowledged in an interview early last year that he knew and taught Umar Farouk Abdulmutallab, the so-called "underwear bomber" in the failed 2009 aircraft bombing. But Awlaki claimed that he did not direct Abdulmutallab to carry out the attack. The British press have reported on e-mails linking Awlaki to efforts to circumvent airport security procedures in the United Kingdom. But the evidence disclosed so far appears short of proving an operational role in the foiled October 2010 plot to place bombs aboard U.S.-bound cargo planes.

Awlaki was reported more than a year ago to have been placed on a list of terrorists targeted to be captured or killed. Representing Awlaki's father, the American Civil Liberties Union filed a federal court suit in August 2010 contesting the designation or, at the least, requiring the government to justify the decision. "Both the Constitution and international law prohibit targeted killing except as a last resort to protect against concrete, specific, and imminent threats," the ACLU argued.

The government responded by filing a document showing the procedures used for targeted drone strikes but without any specific information about Awlaki. In December, Judge John Bates dismissed the lawsuit. Bates said that Awlaki's father lacked standing to bring the action and that the suit in any event raised a political question ill suited for courts to decide.

The ACLU's arguments were just that: arguments. Neither U.S. nor international law can be said to have a settled position on the rules applicable to targeted killings outside an active combat zone. But in his role as the United Nations' special rapporteur on extrajudicial, summary or arbitrary executions, the U.S. law professor Philip Alston laid out criteria in a May 2010 report comparable to those the ACLU cited.

A targeted killing must be "required to protect life," Alston wrote in the 29-page report, with "no other means, such as capture or nonlethal incapacitation, of preventing the threat to life." In addition, a government must have reliable information and intelligence to support the targeting decision and to minimize risk to civilians. And, significantly, Alston set out detailed rules of transparency and accountability. States should lay out the claimed basis for targeted killings, the procedural rules followed and after-action procedures to monitor compliance, he said.

Benjamin Wittes, the Brookings Institution scholar who has followed the war on terror for a decade, proposed somewhat similar criteria for judging targeted killings under the Constitution's Due Process Clause. On the national security blog *Lawfare*, Wittes said the target must be "identified with a high degree of confidence" and pose "an unreasonable risk to human life" with "no option for capture." Surveying the information known about Awlaki, Wittes concludes the government's action met that test.

Wittes omitted one essential requirement from Alston's list: transparency. Many Americans, and many others around the world, have well reasoned concerns about the U.S. action. Those concerns cannot be addressed by victory statements from White House lecterns. A decent respect for the opinions of mankind demands that all the facts be laid out for Americans and the world to judge.

A year later, I was still unimpressed with the administration's explanation of its procedures for authorizing the use of drones for targeted killing of al Qaeda terrorists.

No Transparency on Drone
(*Jost on Justice*, Jan. 7, 2013)

The Obama administration has given repeated assurances that it is exceedingly careful in its expanded use of unmanned aircraft — drones — for the targeted killing of al Qaeda terrorists. Unnamed officials provided for-publication backgrounders with details of the process for identifying targets and giving the go-ahead for the kill. Defense Secretary Leon Panetta went on the record in a CBS News interview to say that only the president can give the final authorization for the kill.

The administration has also gone to some lengths to assure Americans that Justice Department and Pentagon lawyers have given the most careful consideration to the delicate issue posed by targeting a U.S. citizen allied with al Qaeda for death by drone. In the most elaborate iteration, Attorney General Eric Holder in March 2012 outlined a three-part test that must be met before a U.S. citizen is targeted; the third part itself includes a check-list of four specified conditions to meet to comply with the international law of war.

With all this ostensibly careful consideration, one would think that the administration must have a legal document that formally lays out the reasons why the law permits the government to dispense with any sort of judicial procedure or review before a targeted killing. But apparently not. At least that is the seeming conclusion from the government's position in resisting, successfully so far, lawsuits by the American Civil Liberties Union (ACLU) and *The New York Times* seeking details about the drone program, including the legal rationale relied on by the administration in carrying it out.

Between them, the ACLU and the *Times* have been invoking the federal Freedom of Information Act (FOIA) for nearly three years to force the administration to open up about the drone program. To its credit, the administration has gradually become more forthcoming about the program in speeches, interviews, and not-for-attribution backgrounders. In court, however, government lawyers have pulled out all stops to avoid being forced to turn over the actual documents about the program, including any formal legal opinions to justify it.

In a ruling last week [Jan. 2], a federal judge in New York City reluctantly sided with the government in rejecting the FOIA requests. In a 70-page opinion, U.S. District Court Judge Colleen McMahon acknowledged that "more fulsome disclosure" of information about the program "would allow for intelligent discussion and assessment of a tactic that (like torture before it) remains hotly debated." But she said that Freedom of Information Act "precedents" left her no choice but to find the requested materials covered by the act's broadly written exemptions covering national security (exemption 1), classified documents (exemption 3) and internal legal deliberations (exemption 5).

Admittedly, the ACLU and the *Times* had an uphill fight in trying to get around the first two of those exemptions covering national security and classified documents. Formal legal opinions, however, are generally not exempt under the FOIA. And the administration eventually acknowledged the existence of a joint memorandum by the Department of Defense and the Justice Department's Office of Legal Counsel (OLC) addressing the legal issue.

In seeking to keep the memo under wraps, the government argued first that it included information about intelligence sources and methods exempted under the FOIA. As McMahon noted, however, the document could have been "redacted" — that is, edited – to black out the properly classified information and the rest of the document released. But the government further argued that the memo was not a formal opinion, but was the kind of "confidential, pre-decisional, and deliberative" legal advice covered by exemption 5.

Confronted with that position, McMahon said she could not order the memo disclosed. There was "no evidence," McMahon wrote, that the government had specifically relied on the arguments made in the memo or that it had been "expressly adopted" or "incorporated by reference."

McMahon was apt in analogizing the issue to the previous dispute over the Bush administration's use of torture or torture-like tactics in interrogating al Qaeda members. Justice Department lawyers famously green-lighted the use of so-called "enhanced interrogation techniques," including waterboarding, in legal memos that came to light only after the fact — indeed, only after a new head of OLC had repudiated them. Exposed to the light of day, the legal opinions were denounced by a range of legal experts and observers as poorly reasoned.

The Obama administration's legal justifications for the drone program might or might not survive close scrutiny, but for now they are locked behind a Freedom of Information Act exemption. The ACLU and the *Times* both say they will appeal McMahon's ruling. The ACLU is asking not only for the legal memoranda, but also for the information the government used to target Anwar al-Awlaki, the U.S.-born Muslim cleric killed by a drone-fired missile in Yemen in September 2011. McMahon described the ACLU's laundry-basket FOIA request as "facially overbroad." But she clearly wanted to grant the

Times's narrower request except for the narrow reading that courts have given to the FOIA in the past.

In taking office, Obama pledged his administration to greater transparency, but freedom-of-information advocates such as the Sunlight Foundation say the administration's record has been disappointing. The administration is evidently glad to take credit for using drones to wipe out al Qaeda leaders, but unwilling to allow close scrutiny of the legal reasoning that supposedly justifies the way the program is being carried out.

With the debate over drones intensifying, and the controversy over Guantánamo still simmering, President Obama tried to get control of the issues with a major policy speech in May 2013. My attitude on his promised policies echoed President Reagan's famous admonition: "Trust, but verify."

Obama's Reset on Drones

(*Jost on Justice*, May 28, 2013)

It was billed as a major speech on national security policy. Four months after inauguration, President Obama reaffirmed his commitment to closing the Guantánamo prison camp. He promised to devise a plan for dealing with detainees who were too dangerous to release but who could not be successfully prosecuted.

The date was May 23, 2009.

Last week, almost exactly four years to the day later [May 21], Obama again vowed to close Guantánamo and promised again to devise a plan for dealing with detainees who could not be released or prosecuted. On a new issue, the president announced limits on the use of targeted drone strikes against al Qaeda and promised to look into establishing advance oversight of planned missions.

Despite the advance buildup for this second-term speech, there was less substance than met the ear. Obama said he would lift his own self-imposed moratorium on transferring Yemenis held at Guantánamo to their home country, but otherwise gave no specifics on how he would move toward closing the prison. As for drone strike oversight,

Obama mentioned two possible mechanisms — a special court or an independent oversight board within the executive branch — but raised problems with each one in the very next sentences.

The speech also appeared to fall short as political public relations. Obama did his best to sound resolute in confronting al Qaeda, but House Speaker John Boehner was among the several Republicans who criticized Obama for going soft on terrorists. Obama got some credit from the political left, but human rights-minded critics feel let down by his failure to close Guantánamo and misled by the expansion of drone strikes done with the president's full support.

Guantánamo became a more urgent issue for Obama as a hunger strike spread over the past four months to about 100 of the 166 remaining prisoners, 30 of them being force fed to keep them alive. More than half of the prisoners — 89 — are Yemenis, so Obama's decision to consider transfers back to Yemen on a case-by-case basis may help counteract the sense of desperation among prisoners held now for more than a decade. Obama also promised to designate a new senior envoy at the State and Defense departments to negotiate transfers to third countries.

Obama laid blame on Congress for imposing restrictions on detainee transfers from Guantánamo, but critics said the administration could have put more effort into meeting the mandated conditions case by case. One can also ask why Obama is only now asking the Pentagon to find a site within the United States to hold the military trials now being held at Guantanamo. As for the problem of prisoners who cannot be released or prosecuted, Obama said only that he was "confident" that it could be solved – without a hint of what the solution might be.

Far from apologizing for the drone program, Obama insisted that the strikes were legal self-defense and went on to cite its successes as the reason for now deciding to cut it back. Targeting of al Qaeda leaders and operatives has been so "effective," the president said, that the "core of al Qaeda in Afghanistan and Pakistan is on a path to defeat."

Obama acknowledged that the strikes had left civilian casualties, but instead of putting a number on the toll said simply that the government's estimates differ from those of human rights groups. Obama made a modest nod toward transparency by declassifying the deaths of four

U.S. citizens, only one of them — the al Qaeda propagandist Anwar al Awlaki — deliberately targeted.

Otherwise, the number of strikes and the resulting casualties remains classified. The New America Foundation, which maintains a database on the strikes, counts 237 strikes in Pakistan and Yemen in the Obama years (compared to 180 during Bush's two terms) with more than 3,200 people killed. Surely, most of those killed were innocent civilians, but Obama argued that more civilian casualties would have resulted if al Qaeda had been left untamed and more U.S. casualties would have resulted with boots on the ground instead of drones in the sky.

Despite those justifications, Obama now says drone strikes will be reduced in what he called "the Afghan war theater" and limited elsewhere to attacks on "al Qaeda and its associated forces" that pose "a continuing and imminent threat" to the United States. But imminence remains for the dronemasters to decide. So too the required determination that there is "a near certainty" that no civilian deaths will result. And nothing in what Obama said limits the targets to high-ranking al Qaeda leaders as opposed to rank-and-file dissidents caught up in anti-American jihadism.

Obama's progress in closing Guantánamo— or lack of progress — will be easy to measure, but the results of the reset drone program will be hard to determine as long as the strikes and their tolls remain classified. And there will be no independent oversight of the program unless the president puts aside his ambivalence about both of the suggested possibilities.

To his credit, Obama wants to get away from the Bush era mentality of an endless and boundless war on terrorism writ large. He says in effect that the country cannot remain on war footing waiting for a formal surrender from al Qaeda that will never come. "This war, like all wars, must end," he says. But Obama needs to combine strong words with strong actions to make that happen.

Two-and-a-half months after Obama's speech, New York Times *reporters Mark Mazzetti and Mark Landler wrote that there was "little public evidence of change" in the administration's drone strategy (Aug. 3). Most of the elements of the program remained in place, the reporters wrote. The administration continued to refuse to discuss specific strikes in public. And the number of strikes in Pakistan in the previous month were more than for any month since January. As for Guantánamo, two Algerian detainees were released to their home country in July, but a year later 149 prisoners remained. More than half had been cleared for release but were on hold waiting for arrangements for host countries to accept them.*

* * *

Remembering 9/11

(Jost on Justice, Sept. 5, 2011)

Walter Masterson was on a conference call in the World Trade Center's Building 5 when the first hijacked plane hit on Sept. 11, 2001. He got out of the building and, disconcerted, had to be directed by a police officer to get to safety. For the next two weeks, Masterson recalls, New Yorkers were on their best behavior. "Rudeness vanished," he says. "Everybody helped. Nobody wanted for anything."

As it was in New York, so it was in the rest of the country. Forget where you were on September 11. Remember instead how you felt for the next two weeks or so. Americans were as one in solemn mourning and steely resolve. We knew the enemy: Al Qaeda. We knew where it was: Afghanistan. We knew what to do: go to war, with might and right on our side.

Then things went wrong, terribly wrong in many respects.

At the direction of Attorney General John Ashcroft, federal agents began rounding up a total of 762 young men from the Middle East or Pakistan using immigration laws as the pretext to justify ethnic and religious profiling. Later, the Justice Department's inspector general chastised the government for holding many of the immigrants in punitive conditions, often with delayed access either to family members or lawyers. Few if any useful leads to Al Qaeda were found, but the dragnet helped justify anti-Muslim sentiment among the public at large that, sadly, persists a decade later.

Meanwhile, President Bush and Congress were rushing to imperil civil liberties with a law called the USA Patriot Act to obscure its un-American provisions. Enacted barely six weeks after 9/11, the law gave the feds carte blanche to use "national security" to justify rummaging through library records, phone calls, and e-mails with less than the probable cause standard that the Framers wrote into the Fourth Amendment. Separately, Bush issued a secret executive order expanding the government's authority under the Foreign Intelligence Surveillance Act to tap into electronic communications, even those of U.S. citizens.

A decade later, the Patriot Act has been renewed twice, admittedly with some ameliorating changes, and Bush's foreign intelligence surveillance program has been continued, again with some helpful restrictions. The government says these law enforcement tools have been essential to the war on terror, but detailed studies — notably, a new report by the Breakthrough Institute, a progressive think tank in California — have found no evidence that the controversial tactics have played any significant role in thwarting terrorist plots.

The war in Afghanistan went well: the Taliban displaced, a pro-Western democrat installed as interim leader, U.S. aid for reconstruction promised. Behind the scenes, however, the Bush White House, abetted by presidential power partisans in the vice president's office and the Justice Department, were hatching plans to put the United States on the wrong side of the law of war. "Enemy combatants" rounded up in a difficult-to-define battlefield were to be transported to the U.S. naval base at Guantanamo Bay, Cuba, chosen precisely because it was thought to be outside the reach of U.S. courts: a law-free zone.

The administration claimed the power to hold foreigners and even U.S. citizens with no hearing whatsoever. It denied any obligation to treat the Guantanamo prisoners according to the terms of the Geneva Conventions. And, most shockingly, it claimed the right to interrogate "high-value" Al Qaeda suspects in secret prisons using techniques such as forced isolation, sleep deprivation, stress positions, and waterboarding that amounted to torture.

The Justice Department unpersuasively denied that the "enhanced interrogation techniques" were torture. In any event, the department argued in an opinion later repudiated, the president had power as commander in chief to order the use of torture, laws to the contrary notwithstanding.

Then came the war on Iraq, entered into divisively on a dubious rationale supported by dubious evidence. The war drained resources from Afghanistan and made it harder to keep the support of the world's Muslim communities in the just and necessary fight against Al Qaeda. And the war drained resources from domestic needs, helping put the country into a huge fiscal hole.

There were other mistakes, perhaps more understandable. More money was spent on homeland security than necessary — $75 billion per year in state and federal spending, according to one estimate — but that can happen to well-intentioned government programs. Some 9/11 victims or survivors — first responders with serious injuries or debilitating illnesses — have had to work too hard to get compensation, but that too can happen when the government tries to dispense mass justice.

Those other mistakes, however, could have been avoided. Indeed, the other branches of government tried. The Supreme Court forced the administration to recognize the Geneva Conventions and to allow judicial review at Guantanamo. Congress outlawed the enhanced interrogation techniques — after Bush had given them up — and smoothed the edges a bit on the Patriot Act and foreign intelligence surveillance.

Apart from those changes, however, President Obama has done less than he had promised to get the United States back to its values in combating terrorism. So on this tenth anniversary we perhaps can best honor 9/11's victims by remembering how the country lost its way afterward and by vowing not to let it happen again.

5

#FirstAmendment

The Constitution won ratification by the states in 1788 despite objections that the powers given to the new national government could put Americans' liberties at risk. The Federalist supporters of the Constitution responded with what we now know as the Bill of Rights, a laundry list of rights that Americans came to take for granted. Of the 10 amendments, none is more important than the First Amendment, which protects freedom of speech and the press, freedom of religion, the right of peaceful assembly, and the right to petition the government. And none has generated more cases, or more difficult cases, for courts to consider in determining how far those freedoms extend.

#FreedomofSpeech

The First Amendment provides that Congress "shall make no law ... abridging the freedom of speech or of the press . . . ." Beginning in the 1920s, the Supreme Court ruled that the same prohibition applies to state and local governments. Free-speech claims reach the Supreme Court in many different guises. The Roberts Court has struck down on First Amendment grounds a number of federal and state laws that cover subjects as varied as campaign finance to violent video games. In one of the early free-speech cases under Chief Justice Roberts, the court had to decide how far the First Amendment rights of high school students go. The answer: not that far.

Figure of Speech
(*CQ Weekly,* Jan. 22, 2007)

School administrators around the country are punishing students for speaking out on issues ranging from abortion and homosexuality to drug use and the war in Iraq. And the Supreme Court appears poised to side with school administrators and — for no compelling reason — limit a landmark 1960s precedent aimed at safeguarding pupils' free-speech rights.

In oral arguments in March, the Juneau school board will ask the justices to uphold an Alaska high school student's 10-day suspension for unfurling a pro-drug-use banner to display as the Olympic torch relay passed by the school in 2002. The 9th Circuit Court of Appeals ruled that the suspension violated Joseph Frederick's First Amendment rights. But the school board, backed by the National School Boards Association, maintains that upholding the ruling would hinder schools' anti-drug programs and subject school administrators to damage suits in a murky area of law.

Similar cases dot dockets around the country. In Williamstown, Vt., a student went to court after he was disciplined for wearing a T-shirt identifying President Bush as "Chicken-Hawk-in-Chief" and adorned with drug and alcohol imagery. A student in Poway, Calif., challenged his suspension for wearing a T-shirt inscribed with the words "Homosexuality Is Shameful." The Alliance Defense Fund, a Christian religious liberty advocacy group, is backing the California student's cause and also has filed federal lawsuits on behalf of students in New York, Pennsylvania and Virginia who were barred from wearing anti-abortion T-shirts or distributing anti-abortion literature.

The Supreme Court established the basic precedent in 1969, when it overturned the suspensions of three Iowa teenagers who came to school wearing black armbands to protest the Vietnam War. Students do not "shed their constitutional rights . . . at the schoolhouse gate," the court observed in *Tinker v. Des Moines Independent Community School District.* In subsequent rulings, the court decided to read that precedent narrowly. In 1986, it upheld the suspension of a Washington state student for injecting "patently offensive" sexual metaphors into his speech in favor of a candidate for high school student council president. In 1988, it said schools could censor student newspapers — in the case, by spiking a story on teenage pregnancy — if the newspaper was "an integral part of the school's educational function."

In the name of preventing drug use, the court has also allowed school authorities to limit students' constitutional rights against unreasonable searches. In 1985, it upheld the search of a student's purse (marijuana was found), even though the principal lacked probable cause to believe she was carrying drugs. In 1995 and again in 2002, the court said schools may require students to submit to random drug tests as a condition of participating in varsity athletics or any other extracurricular activity.

Even in *Tinker*, the court recognized that students' free speech rights could be limited when necessary to prevent disruption or to protect the rights of other students. But Justice Abe Fortas tellingly added that open discussion — "hazardous freedom," in his words — was "the basis of our national strength."

Lower federal courts applying the Supreme Court's precedents have tended to favor students. In the Vermont case, for example, the 2nd Circuit Court of Appeals rejected the school board's view that the T-shirt's drug and alcohol images were "plainly offensive" or interfered with an "integral" school function of discouraging drug use.

On the other hand, the 9th Circuit refused to stop the Poway school board from enforcing its rule against wearing anti-gay messages. School officials had grounds to believe such displays were "injurious to gay and lesbian students and interfered with their right to learn," the court said. The student has appealed to the Supreme Court.

Given the reality of anti-gay harassment and violence in public schools, the decision is not without justification. As in the anti-abortion cases, however, the Alliance Defense Fund lawyers have grounds to complain that school authorities sometimes single out "pro-life" or "pro-family" views for censorship. Indeed, the Poway teenager wore the T-shirt on the same day that many students were observing, with the school's apparent approval, a "Day of Silence" to support gay and lesbian schoolmates.

In Juneau, Frederick's stunt — displaying for TV cameras a banner that read "Bong Hits 4 Jesus" — can easily be dismissed as sophomoric.

He muddied the case by saying the phrase was meaningless nonsense, not a pro-drug message. Still, school officials are making a far-reaching argument that the banner was "offensive" and interfered with the school's "mission" of deterring illegal drug use. Under that reasoning, the Des Moines school board might have won the *Tinker* case by claiming support for U.S. troops in Vietnam as part of its "mission."

In fact, the public schools' most important mission is to prepare students for democratic governance in a country with what the Supreme Court has called "a profound national commitment to the principle that debate on public issues should be uninhibited, robust, and wide-open." That lesson is never too early for students to learn — or for teachers and principals to teach.

Chief Justice Roberts wrote for a 5-4 majority in a decision that rejected Frederick's free-speech claim. Citing the "dangers of illegal drug use," Roberts concluded, "The First Amendment does not require schools to tolerate at school events student expression that contributes to those dangers." In the main dissent, Justice John Paul Stevens wrote, "Carving out pro-drug speech for uniquely harsh treatment . . . is inimical to the values protected by the First Amendment."

Two years later, the court considered a First Amendment defense by a Virginia man, Robert Stevens, who was convicted of selling videos depicting dog fighting and fox hunting under a federal law prohibiting "depictions of animal cruelty." I analyzed the case in advance of the Supreme Court arguments.

Protecting Animals or Speech?
(Jost on Justice, Oct. 4, 2009)

Hard cases make bad law. Consider one at the start of the Supreme Court's new term that asks the justices to choose between protecting the First Amendment and preventing cruelty to animals.

Ten years ago, Congress passed a law making the "depiction of animal cruelty" a federal crime. The act was aimed at outlawing so-called "crush videos," horrific depictions of women, often in high heels, crushing puppies, kittens, or other small animals to death. The videos were said to have been readily available on the Internet to users who, perversely, found them sexually arousing.

The law was written broadly to get over significant obstacles in enforcement. Specifically, the law prohibits creating, selling, or possessing any photograph or video in which an animal is "intentionally maimed, mutilated, tortured, wounded, or killed" if the conduct is illegal under federal law or under the law of the jurisdiction where the depiction is created, sold, or possessed.

Despite its evidently salutary purpose, the act represented a significant incursion on the First Amendment. The justices are now being asked to rule a category of speech outside the First Amendment for the first time since the court's 1982 decision, *New York v. Ferber*, upholding a state ban on child pornography. As with the child porn law, the argument is that the only way to prevent harm — to children in one case, to animals in the other — is to dry up the market by allowing the government to prosecute not only the producers of the offending material, but also the buyers.

The new act tries to acknowledge free-speech concerns. It exempts any material that has "serious religious, political, scientific, educational, journalistic, historical, or artistic value."

Ten years later, the government has prosecuted only one person under the law. Robert Stevens, a Virginia man, was indicted in 2004 for on charges of selling to undercover law enforcement agents in Pennsylvania two videos depicting dog fighting and a third showing pit bulls in a wild boar hunt. Dog fighting is illegal in all 50 states, but not in Japan, where one of the videos was made.

Stevens, who made and narrated the videos, was convicted in March 2005 by a federal jury in Pennsylvania that rejected his effort to portray the videos as a celebration of pit bulls' nobility and character. On appeal, however, the Third U.S. Circuit Court of Appeals overturned the convictions in June 2008 and found the law unconstitutional on free-speech grounds.

The appeals court said the law failed to satisfy the demanding "strict scrutiny" test. The government's interest in preventing cruelty to animals had not been shown to be compelling, the majority judges said. In addition, the statute was not narrowly tailored to further that interest; instead, the judges suggested, the government should strengthen enforcement of the underlying laws preventing cruelty to animals.

The Humane Society of the United States had cheered passage of the law and claimed success in drying up the market for crush videos — perhaps a reason for the lack of prosecutions. With the appeals court's decision, however, the society said crush videos are again readily available on the Internet. It found one site that offered 118 videos for sale at prices ranging from $20 to $100.

Media groups rallied in support of the appeals court's decision after the justices agreed to hear the government's plea to revive the law. They say the law overreaches by encompassing everything from artistic renderings of bullfights to journalistic coverage of hunting and fishing. Attacking the law is not popular, the opponents say. But their number includes one strange but powerful bedfellow: the National Rifle Association.

Conservatives like to claim that on the current Supreme Court the conservative justices are the most consistent defenders of the First Amendment. The claim depends primarily on the conservatives' recent invocation of political speech grounds to question the constitutionality of campaign finance regulations. But Justices Antonin Scalia and Anthony M. Kennedy also established their First Amendment bona fides two decades ago by joining in decisions that struck down federal and state laws banning desecration of the U.S. flag.

Handicapping the current case, *United States v. Stevens*, is difficult at best. In defending the law, the government is asking the justices to accept the broad proposition that speech can be categorically prohibited if the harm to society outweighs any benefits from the speech. That broad argument might appeal to Justice Stephen G. Breyer, who likes to take a pragmatic approach to First Amendment issues. But the court need not go that far to uphold the law. It could simply follow the "dry up the market" rationale adopted in *Ferber*.

The media groups' "slippery slope" argument may appeal to Kennedy, who has joined with liberal justices in some cases to strike down sex-related speech regulations. But Kennedy is also a moralist who, most recently, allowed his anti-drug views to overcome free-speech concerns in upholding the suspension of an Alaska student for displaying a patently harmless "Bong Hits for Jesus" banner in *Morse v. Frederick* (2006). He may find cruelty to animals at least as offensive.

The arguments are on Tuesday, Oct.5, the second day of the new term. It's a hard case. With strong arguments on both sides, the justices will need to take care to avoid making bad law.

Contrary to my expectations, justices across the ideological spectrum appeared troubled by the law during oral arguments. Six months later, Roberts led an 8-1 majority in ruling the law unconstitutional. He said the act imposed "a criminal prohibition of alarming breadth" that could apply to depictions of any illegal treatment of animals even if the conduct did amount to cruelty. Alito was the lone dissenter.

Later in the term, however, Roberts proved less receptive to a First Amendment challenge to a law that prohibited "material support" for groups designated by the U.S. government as terrorist organizations. I found the decision unpersuasive.

Trusting the Government?
(*Jost on Justice*, June 23, 2010)

Ralph Fertig has been advocating the cause of Kurdish national liberation for nearly a quarter century. But the longtime civil and human rights activist professes not to know much about the Kurdistan Workers' Party (PKK), which the United States government lists as a foreign terrorist organization.

"I don't even know who is a member of the PKK," Fertig told a radio interviewer in Februay. "I work with Kurds," Fertig explained. "I don't ask whether they're members of the PKK."

Fertig's comments came on the eve of Supreme Court arguments in his constitutional challenge to the federal law making it a crime to provide "material support," including advice or training, to officially designated foreign terrorist groups. For more than decade, Fertig has been helping the Kurds under the threat of a possible criminal prosecution under that law.

The government has not prosecuted Fertig. But in rejecting Fertig's challenge this week, the Supreme Court has given a solid green light to use of this broadly written anti-terrorism law not only against "the worst of the worst" but also in some sense against "the best of the best" — people like Fertig and groups like his Humanitarian Law Project. Fertig and others say they want to try to guide foreign organizations that use terrorism to advance their goals to turn instead to lawful advocacy and peaceful dispute resolution.

Both the Bush and Obama administrations have made the "material support" law the go-to legal weapon against suspected members or supporters of al Qaeda. The court's 6-3 decision in *Holder v. Humanitarian Law Project* (June 21) allows the government as well to prosecute human rights-minded Americans for activities that would seem to be both laudable and constitutionally protected.

For the majority, Chief Justice John G. Roberts Jr. accepted the government's different view that any "training" or "advice or assistance" to a foreign terrorist organization — even for lawful ends — is "highly likely" to inure ultimately to the benefit of its terrorist activities. Congress and the executive branch were "uniquely positioned" to make that judgment, Roberts wrote. Dissenting justices argued that the court had a more important role: to protect the First Amendment.

Up until this week, the government had fared badly in playing the anti-terrorism card at the Supreme Court. In four post-9/11 cases decided between 2004 and 2008, the justices rejected the Bush administration's claims of broad authority to detain suspected enemy combatants with limited review by the courts.

The government fared badly as well in the lower courts in defending the broad reading of the material support law. As originally enacted in 1996, the law was aimed at prohibiting the most concrete forms of aid to terrorist groups: direct financial assistance, lodging, equipment, personnel, or training. Congress substantially expanded the provision late in October 2001 — barely six weeks after the 9/11 attacks — to prohibit "expert advice or assistance" as well. That was one of the many provisions of the USA Patriot Act that got only the most cursory consideration from Congress in the post-9/11 panic.

The challenge to the law was advancing even as Congress was expanding it. A few weeks before passage of the USA Patriot Act, U.S. District Court Judge Audrey Collins issued a final ruling reaffirming her earlier decision that the law's prohibitions against providing personnel or training were "impermissibly vague." Later, in 2003, Fertig's group filed a second suit challenging the "expert advice or assistance" provision. The proceedings clearly indicated trouble for the government in defending the law as written, prompting Congress late in 2004 to narrow the definition of "training" and "expert advice or assistance." Lawmakers also added a requirement — as the Ninth Circuit appeals court had ruled necessary — that prosecutors show that a defendant had knowingly provided aid to the terrorist group.

In his opinion, Roberts cited the legislative refinements as evidence that Congress had been careful not to cross the First Amendment line. In dissent, Justice Stephen G. Breyer proposed going one step further and requiring the government to prove that a defendant knew that any training, advice, or assistance was likely to further the organization's terrorist actions, not its lawful activities. Roberts said Congress "plainly" decided not to require that kind of specific-intent proof.

Hawkish national security experts are hailing the ruling. "Terrorist organizations must be treated as pariahs and suffocated, not cultivated," former federal prosecutor National Review legal editor Andrew McCarthy writes on a *New York Times* blog. From the opposite perspective, Stephen Vladeck, a law professor at American University in Washington, warns the decision will have "a profound chilling effect on the efforts of peace-building organizations and other NGOs that seek to promote non-violent democracy building."

Much depends on whether the Justice Department makes judicious use of the law now that the high court has removed the cloud over it. In oral argument back in February, Solicitor General Elena Kagan expressly declined to speculate whether activists such as Fertig had real reason to fear prosecution under the law.

Writing in a different case earlier this year, Roberts was unwilling to trust the government's good faith alone on sensitive First Amendment questions. "We would not uphold an unconstitutional statute merely because the Government promised to use it responsibly," Roberts wrote in striking down a broadly written animal cruelty statute in *United States v. Stevens*. In the new ruling, however, the Roberts Court is willing to put the First Amendment at some risk, trusting assurance from a government that since 9/11 has proved none too trustworthy on national security matters.

"Hate speech" – speech that targets individuals or groups based on race, religion, sex, disability, or sexual orientation – poses a challenge for First Amendment advocates. The harm from such speech can be very real, and so too the impulse to punish the speaker. Yet the First Amendment protects even, perhaps especially, speech of which society disapproves. The Supreme Court dealt with an especially obnoxious instance of hate speech in 2011 and ruled, with some reluctance, in favor of the First Amendment.

Free Speech for Those Who Hate
(*Jost on Justice*, March 6, 2011)

The Westboro Baptist Church is a hate group. Its obsessively anti-gay founder, the Rev. Fred W. Phelps Sr., and Phelps' family members who make up most of the congregation of his Topeka, Kan., church are hateful in thought and deed. No truly God-loving Christian would choose the funeral of a fallen serviceman to air such hateful views as "God hates fags" or "Thank God for dead soldiers."

Yet that is what Phelps and his media-seeking followers have done some 600 times over the past 20 years. The surviving families and friends of most of those American heroes have tried to ignore the Phelpses. But Albert Snyder, who lost his 20-year-old son Marine Lance Corporal Matthew Snyder in Iraq in 2006, decided not to turn the other cheek after the Phelps clan picketed Matthew's funeral in his hometown of Westminster, Md.

Just three months later, Snyder sued Phelps and his church for what tort law calls "intentional infliction of emotional distress." Snyder explained to a federal court jury in the fall 2007 trial that he was outraged by the Phelpses' decision to turn his son's funeral into "a media circus." The jurors adopted Snyder's outrage as their own, awarding him $2.9 million in compensatory damages and $8 million in punitive damages. Judge Richard Bennett cut the award to $5 million, but like the jury he found the Phelpses' actions "so outrageous as to inflict severe emotional distress and invade the privacy of a private citizen during a time of bereavement."

Last week, a nearly unanimous U.S. Supreme Court decided that verdict could not stand. None of the nine justices evinced any respect for what the lone dissenter, Samuel A. Alito Jr., labeled the Phelpses' "malevolent verbal attack on Matthew and his family at a time of acute emotional vulnerability." Writing for the majority, however, Chief Justice John G. Roberts Jr. said that the First Amendment shielded the Phelpses from liability for their speech, however "hurtful" its impact or "negligible" its contribution to public discourse.

The March 2 ruling in *Snyder v. Phelps* was in line with free-speech precedents but somewhat at odds with the tenor of the earlier arguments in the case. Several of the justices appeared to agree with Snyder's lawyer that the Phelpses had no First Amendment protection for intruding on the funeral and targeting epithets at their son, a private citizen. Phelps' lawyer-daughter Margaret insisted, however, that the demonstration focused on matters of public concern — specifically, "why [soldiers] are dying and how God is dealing with this nation." Albert Snyder, she said, was merely saying, "I want $11 million from a little church because they came forth with some preaching I didn't like."

The nearly unanimous ruling for the Phelpses suggests that the justices came to a different view of the case after a closer examination of the facts. The placards may not have been "refined social or political commentary," Roberts wrote, but they did refer to "matters of public import," including homosexuality and public morality. And the Phelpses themselves were model First Amendment citizens in Roberts's telling. They alerted local authorities to their plans and fully complied with police guidance on where to stage their picketing, some 1,000 feet from the church. There was "no shouting, profanity, or violence."

On those facts, the Phelpses could not be punished except for the content of their message — and that, Roberts said, the First Amendment forbids. Speech on a matter of public concern, he wrote, "cannot be restricted simply because it is upsetting or arouses contempt."

Alito came to an opposite conclusion mainly by treating some of the Phelpses' placards — for example, "You're Going to Hell" — as a personal attack on Matthew Snyder, with the evident but false insinuation that he was gay. Alito also relied in part on a video posted later on the church's Web site that claimed the Snyder parents had taught Matthew to be "an idolater" by raising him as a Catholic. Roberts said the video was out of the case because Snyder's lawyer had not raised it in asking the justices to review the decision.

Roberts stressed that the decision was narrow, but a narrow decision can still be a landmark. The court has not always been friendly toward free speech. The court upheld criminal convictions of anti-war activists and anarchists in the early 20th century, of communists in mid-century. Those decisions are today remembered as much for their dissents as for their majority opinions.

It was in another dissent that the great justice Oliver Wendell Holmes Jr. set out the principle that the former *New York Times* columnist Anthony Lewis used in 2007 as the title for his so-called "biography of the First Amendment." Rosika Schwimmer, a Hungarian-born pacifist, had been denied U.S. citizenship because she refused to promise to take up arms in defense of her to-be-adopted country. The court in *Schwimmer v. United States* (1929) ruled against her, 6-3.

In his dissent, Holmes acknowledged that Schwimmer's views "might excite popular prejudice," but he extolled what he called "the principle of free thought — not free thought for those who agree with us but freedom for the thought that we hate." It is a measure of progress that eight decades later, the Phelpses benefit from that principle, however hateful their thought and deed may be.

#FreedomofPress

The New York Times *published a full-page advertisement on March 29, 1960, sponsored by the Committee to Defend Martin Luther King and the Struggle for Freedom in the South. The advertisement, critical of the conduct of police in Montgomery, Alabama, contained a few minor factual errors. Louis Sullivan, Montgomery's police commissioner, filed a libel suit against the Times and four of the ministers responsible for placing the ad, including King's lieutenant at the Southern Christian Leadership Conference, the Rev. Ralph Abernathy. Alabama courts* awarded Sullivan $500,000 in damages from the Times and the ministers even though he was not named in the advertisement. The Supreme Court threw out the award in an historic decision, New York Times Co. v. Sullivan *(1964), that stands fifty years later as an essential bulwark of a free press in the United States. Even so, the 50th anniversary celebration included a dissenting view from none other than Justice Antonin Scalia.*

Celebrating Times v. Sullivan
(*Jost on Justice*, April 20, 2014)

When the Supreme Court struck down so-called "aggregate" campaign contribution limits earlier this month [April 2], Chief Justice John G. Roberts Jr. cast the decision as in line with a long series of free-speech rulings. "If the First Amendment protects flag burning, funeral protests, and Nazi parades — despite the profound offense such spectacles cause — it surely protects political campaign speech despite popular opposition," Roberts wrote.

Justice Antonin Scalia was not on the court at the time of the Nazi parade decision (*National Socialist Party v. Village of Skokie*, 1977), but he joined in the two other earlier decisions: *Texas v. Johnson*, 1989; and *Snyder v. Phelps*, 2011. Indeed, Scalia often boasts of his vote in the flag-burning case to prove his fidelity to originalist constitutional principles.

Scalia's devotion to freedom of speech, however, has its limits. He draws the line at a landmark decision being celebrated this year on the occasion of its fiftieth anniversary: *New York Times v. Sullivan*. The court's 1964 decision established the now famous rule that a public official cannot recover damages for libel unless he or she proves that the alleged defamation was made with knowledge that it was false or with reckless disregard as to its truth or falsity.

Appearing in a joint interview with Justice Ruth Bader Ginsburg on "The Kalb Report" [April 17], Scalia volunteered his disagreement with the decision. "It's wrong," Scalia said. "You cannot sue anybody for libel unless you can prove he knew it was a lie," Scalia declaimed. The Framers "would have been appalled" by the ruling. The court "was revising the Constitution," he continued, not interpreting it.

– 154 –

Ginsburg quietly demurred. If the Founding Fathers had been around in the 1960s, they would have approved of the decision, she said. Today, she added, the ruling is "well accepted."

Indeed, the precedent is quite secure: no justice has called in a published opinion for reconsidering the ruling since Chief Justice Warren E. Burger and Justice Byron R. White did in separate opinions in a 1985 decision, *Dun & Bradstreet, Inc. v. Greenmoss Builders, Inc.* But Scalia's was not the only dissenting voice heard during the 50th anniversary celebration. Writing for *Bloomberg View* last month [March 27], Harvard law professor Cass Sunstein echoed the complaint heard often from public officials that the ruling has left them with no protection against slanderous lies, especially from the news media.

Far from promoting democracy, Sunstein opined, the ruling has actually disserved self-government. "Talk show hosts, bloggers and users of social media can spread ugly falsehoods in an instant—exposing citizens to lies that may well cause them to look on their leaders with unjustified suspicion," he wrote. The decision, he continued, "can claim at least some responsibility for adding to a climate of distrust and political polarization in the U.S."

With those complaints in mind, it is well to recall the case itself. The *Times* was called to answer in an Alabama courtroom, along with four leaders of Martin Luther King's Southern Christian Leadership Conference, for an advertisement the civil rights group had placed in the newspaper in 1960. Montgomery police commissioner L.B. Sullivan was not named in the ad, but sued for libel on the theory that the criticism of "police" with minor factual discrepancies defamed him personally.

Sullivan won six-figure judgments against the *Times* and the civil rights leaders — serious financial penalties for the newspaper, not to mention the civil rights leaders. The Alabama Supreme Court affirmed the judgments, blinking at Sullivan's implausible theory of the case.

Unanimously, the Supreme Court reversed the decision and went further to order Sullivan's suit dismissed altogether. Justice William J. Brennan Jr. rightly noted that Sullivan's theory would have allowed libel suits for any criticism of government. And he surely captured the Founding Fathers' spirit when he said the First Amendment reflects "a national commitment to the principle that debate on public issues should be robust, uninhibited, and wide open and that it may well include vehement, caustic, and sometimes unpleasantly sharp attacks on government and public officials."

Despite the rhetorical flourish, Brennan actually crafted a compromise of sorts: the so-called "actual malice" test allows a public official to win a libel case by meeting the demanding burden of proof. Three justices — Hugo Black, William O. Douglas, and Arthur J. Goldberg — would have gone further and blocked libel suits by public officials for anything relating to their official duties.

The court fractured three years later in imposing the same burden of proof on public figures in libel cases. Over the years, the court has limited the impact of that decision by narrowing somewhat the definition of public figures. Still, it is undeniably true that libel cases are daunting for public official and public figure plaintiffs these days.

Importantly, this free-speech protection for libel defendants extends not just to the institutional press, but to anyone — including the bloggers and social media users that Sunstein referenced. As Roberts acknowledged in the campaign contributions case, freedom of speech does come at a cost. But public officials and public figures know how to defend themselves in public debate without the chilling effect of haling their critics into court. Fifty years out, *Times v. Sullivan* rightly deserves its place in the pantheon of First Amendment landmarks.

The Supreme Court may have reduced the threat to press freedom from libel suits, but it opened the door to another threat with its ruling in Branzburg v. Hayes *(1972) rejecting a reporter's privilege for confidential sources. James Risen, a* New York Times *reporter, sought to claim a privilege to avoid disclosing the source for his critical account of a botched CIA operation aimed at disrupting Iran's nuclear program. The Obama administration disappointed journalists and other free-press advocates by supporting the threat to jail Risen for defying the subpoena. Here is my account, written after a divided federal appeals court upheld a contempt citation against Risen.*

Reporter Bound for Jail?
(*Jost on Justice*, July 22, 2013)

James Risen may need to start packing a toothbrush and overnight bag because the Pulitzer Prize-winning reporter and author is headed to jail barring an unlikely change of heart by either the government or the federal judiciary.

Risen, who covers national security for the *New York Times,* got the bad news on Friday [July 20] that the federal appeals court in Richmond, Va., had upheld the government's effort to force him to testify in the prosecution of an alleged CIA leaker. The government believes that ex-CIA agent Jeffrey Sterling leaked classified materials to Risen to use in his book *State of War* to recount a botched CIA operation a decade ago aimed at disrupting Iran's nuclear program.

Risen has fought the subpoena, claiming a reporter's privilege to protect confidential sources. Judge Leonie Brinkema, who is presiding over Sterling's now-held-in-abeyance trial in federal district court in Alexandria, Va., ruled in July 2011 that Risen did not have to testify about any confidential sources. On Friday, however, the Fourth U.S. Circuit Court of Appeals reversed Brinkema's ruling in a split decision by a three-judge panel.

For the majority, Chief Judge William Traxler found no reporter's privilege under either the First Amendment or federal common law. In a sharp dissent, Judge Roger Gregory argued that the government does not actually need Risen's testimony and that forcing him to testify would undermine freedom of the press in general and the ability of the press in particular to hold the government accountable on national security issues.

The ruling against Risen reflects the confluence of three unfavorable trends for reporters. Federal courts, starting with the Supreme Court in 1972, have been unreceptive to claims of a journalist privilege to refuse to disclose confidential sources. States have passed reporter shield laws, but they have been only partly effective and Congress has not acted on a federal shield law at all. And, most recently, the Obama administration has aggressively gone after government leakers, charging 11 people so far, including Sterling, with violating the federal Espionage Act and facing the risk of long prison sentences.

The Supreme Court started things going downhill for reporters with its 1972 decision in *Branzburg v. Hayes* that rejected a reporter's privilege to protect confidential sources in three consolidated cases that involved reporting on marijuana users and black militants. Writing for the 5-4 majority, Justice Byron R. White, no fan of the press, said courts were entitled to testimony from reporters just like from anyone else. White disregarded such common law privileges as husband-wife, attorney-client, doctor-patient, and priest-penitent. Justice Lewis F. Powell Jr. added what has been labeled an "enigmatic" concurrence that seemed to recognize a limited privilege even while joining White's majority opinion.

The Supreme Court has not revisited the issue. But Congress in 1975 approved a new provision for the Federal Rules of Evidence, Rule 501, that explicitly gives federal courts the authority to create new privileges. In 1996 the Supreme Court cited that provision in recognizing for the first time a psychotherapist privilege in federal courts (*Jaffee v. Redmond*).

Free press advocates use that precedent to argue for a federal common law privilege for journalists. But the argument failed before the D.C. Circuit in the case eight years ago that led to the jailing of *New York Times* reporter Judith Miller. And the Fourth Circuit panel rejected it as well in last week's decision in Risen's case. "[N]either Rule 501 nor *Jaffee* overrules *Branzburg* or undermines its reasoning," Traxler wrote for the majority.

Risen's case illustrates the heightened danger for reporters when the government decides to prosecute leakers themselves. In *Branzburg*, the reporters argued in part that the government did not need their testimony to prosecute the drug users or black militants for any crimes they may have committed. In the leak cases, however, the leak is the crime itself and the reporter may very well be a direct eyewitness.

As Traxler wrote, Risen "can provide the *only* first-hand account of the commission of a serious crime. . . ." (Risen has been granted immunity, so he cannot claim the Fifth Amendment privilege against self-incrimination.) In his dissent, Gregory disagreed, noting the circumstantial evidence the government has against Sterling, including records of telephone calls and e-mails between him and Risen. But Traxler says the government is entitled to the best evidence available: Risen's own testimony about his sources.

The Obama administration is quite serious about going after government leakers, as documented in a thorough story in the *Times* on Sunday by reporter Sharon LaFraniere. "It is good to hang an admiral once in a while," Dennis Blair, Obama's first national director of intelligence and a former Navy man, is quoted as saying. He and Attorney General Eric Holder fashioned an anti-leak crackdown that filtered down to courtroom prosecutors.

Obama has turned aside criticism that the crackdown goes against his campaign promises for greater transparency. New Justice Department guidelines issued this month in response to media criticism seem to offer little help to Risen or others in like circumstances.

Risen and his lawyers are promising to appeal up to the Supreme Court if necessary. And Risen has indicated he will go to jail rather than comply with the subpoena. In his dissent, Gregory said the newsworthiness of Risen's reporting outweighs any benefit to law enforcement from his testimony. Traxler brushed the argument aside, apparently willing to take the risk that reporters will find it that much more difficult to tell the public what the government does not want it to know about U.S. intelligence agencies.

Risen appealed the ruling to the Supreme Court, but the justices declined to hear the case. In the end, however, Risen avoided jail after the government decided not to call him as a witness in Sterling's trial; Risen made clear in a so-called "offer of proof" outside the jury's presence that he would not identify Sterling as a source if forced to testify.

Meanwhile, the administration was contending with a leak of exponentially greater magnitude: an uncountable number of National Security Agency (NSA) files downloaded and then leaked by a former NSA technician, Edward Snowden. I wrote twice, both times acknowledging Snowden's character flaws but praising him for provoking a needed debate over the government's telephone surveillance program.

Needed Debate on Surveillance

(Jost on Justice, June 16, 2013)

Edward Snowden lied about his salary: $122,000 per year, not $200,000. He probably puffed up some of the other things he has said over the past week. He violated federal law by disclosing classified information. And he forfeited the status of hero by fleeing the country instead of staying in the United States to face the consequences of his civil disobedience.

Journalists, however, do not have the luxury of dealing only with sources who are pure of heart and noble in motive. Sources typically come with axes to grind and flaws to conceal. Snowden and his flaws are part of the story of the last two weeks, but the real story is what he has disclosed: government monitoring of telephone calls and e-mails wider than previously understood with supposed privacy safeguards even more secret than the surveillance itself.

Snowden, who will turn 30 on Friday [June 21], unmasked himself last week as the source of the extraordinary disclosures about the super-secret surveillance by the super-secret National Security Agency (NSA) published a few days earlier in the British newspaper *The Guardian* and then in *The Washington Post*. The story of the leak is both mundane — Did this low-level NSA contractor really walk out of Booz Allen with all these documents on a thumb drive? — and tawdry. The computer geek high-school dropout apparently played blogger and *Guardian* contributor Glenn Greenwald and the *Post* alumnus Barton Gellman against each other to maximize the media splash.

Putting Snowden to the side, here is what Americans know now that they did not know before, based in part on a three-page fact-sheet by the Brennan Center for Justice:

* The NSA has been secretly collecting phone records of millions of Americans since 2006 under orders issued by the super-secret Foreign Intelligence Surveillance Court (FISC) at the request of the FBI under the supposed authority of section 215 of the post-9/11 USA PATRIOT Act. Snowden disclosed one such court order issued to Verizon; Gellman reports in the *Post* today [June 16] that the court has issued similar orders for other large phone companies, including Bell South and AT&T.

* The NSA has also obtained what the Brennan Center calls "unprecedented access" to data processed by nine leading U.S. internet companies, including Google, Facebook, Skype, and Apple, thanks to a computer network named PRISM. Stories about the program prompted James Clapper, the director of national intelligence, to put out an extraordinary three-page fact-sheet that stresses that the program is aimed at foreign targets and is carried out under orders issued by the FISC.

Clapper's reassurances in the fact sheet and elsewhere must be considered in the light of what went before: his outright denial before the Senate Intelligence Committee in March that the NSA was collecting "any type of data at all on millions of Americans." Clapper now calls his reply — "No, sir. Not wittingly" — "the least untruthful" answer he could have given. Sen. Ron Wyden, the Oregon Democrat and surveillance critic who posed the question, avoids calling the answer a lie. Instead, Wyden says merely that Americans are entitled to "straight answers to direct questions" about domestic surveillance.

Wyden and fellow Democrat Mark Udall of Colorado have been raising alarms about the surveillance program for a while from their handcuffed positions as Intelligence Committee members bound by the committee's secrecy rules. They are skunks at the garden party, however. Democratic Chair Dianne Feinstein of California and Republican vice chair Saxbe Chambliss of Georgia have taken to the microphones and news programs ever since the first disclosures to insist that the surveillance program is as effective and necessary as it is legal and constitutional.

The efficacy of congressional oversight is further undermined by the number of senators and representatives who have professed surprise at the scope of the surveillance programs in the past two weeks. As one example, Rep. James Sensenbrenner, Republican of Wisconsin and one of the authors of the PATRIOT Act, says the telephone monitoring goes beyond what the law authorizes. "How can every call that every American makes or receives be relevant to a specific investigation?" Sensenbrenner asked in an op-ed in *The Guardian*.

In Gellman's telling, the validity of the orders turns on the Foreign Intelligence Surveillance Court's pivotal decision on March 24, 2006, to expand the "business records" that the government could obtain if "relevant" to a particular terrorism investigation. "Henceforth, the court ruled, it would define the relevant business records as the entirety of a telephone company's call database," Gellman explains. The substance and the legal reasoning of that order, however, are secret — just like virtually everything the court does.

That secrecy casts doubt on the claimed efficacy of judicial oversight of the surveillance programs. So too does the composition of the court. As I was first to point out, all but one of the court's 11 members are Republican-appointed judges, selected in secret by Chief Justice John G. Roberts Jr., himself a Republican appointee who in eight terms has consistently voted for the government in national security cases. It is no surprise that the government has an all-but-perfect record before the court.

President Obama says he welcomes the debate over the surveillance programs even as the Justice Department is studying what charges to bring against Snowden. Whatever happens to Snowden, that debate should continue.

With Snowden effectively in exile in Russia, I argued for granting him clemency.

Clemency for Edward Snowden
(*Jost on Justice,* Jan. 5, 2014)

Developing story: The National Security Agency (NSA) is hard at work on a so-called quantum computer that could break nearly every kind of encryption used to protect digitized personal, business, and government records around the world.

That's how *The Washington Post* reported the news in a front-page story last week [Jan. 3], based not on an NSA press release — as if there were such a thing — but on documents provided by the NSA's wayward former contractor, Edward Snowden.

The $79.7 million research program could have "revolutionary implications" for the NSA's intelligence gathering, the *Post* reported – not to mention the effects on privacy-protecting efforts of 21st century individuals, businesses, and governments. But the classified program was all hush-hush, except for speculation among physicists and computer scientists, until the *Post*'s Steven Rich and Barton Gellman mined some details from documents leaked by Snowden.

Snowden, now in a sort of exile in Russia, has been a divisive figure ever since he unmasked himself as the source for stories in the British newspaper The Guardian and the Post on the NSA's vacuuming up of bulk telephone records. The government has charged him with espionage, and some national security hawks call him a traitor. But many critics of broad government surveillance view him as a whistleblower, hero, and patriot.

The debate over Snowden has intensified since an NSA official suggested and *The New York Times* editorially endorsed the idea of granting him some sort of amnesty or clemency. The idea seems destined to go nowhere, at least not anytime soon, but Snowden's contribution to understanding and debating the government's overly broad surveillance programs warrants something other than long prison time or lifetime banishment.

As the *Times* reported in a news story [Jan. 4], Richard Ledgett, head of an NSA task force assessing the damage from Snowden's disclosures, floated the idea of a deal — amnesty for "assurances" against any more revelations — in an interview aired on the CBS program *60 Minutes* [Dec. 15]. "My personal view is, yes, it's worth having a conversation about," said Ledgett, who is in line to become the secret agency's second-in-command.

The *Times* forcefully advocated clemency or a plea bargain in a long editorial [Jan. 2] that editorial page editor Andrew Rosenthal said had been in the making for weeks. The *Times* editorial listed "substantially reduced punishment" as one possible outcome for Snowden. Still, Rosenthal conceded to the *Times*'s public editor Margaret Sullivan that the newspaper's stance might be "beyond what is realistic."

Reaction over the next few days confirmed Rosenthal's assessment. Even some critics of the intelligence establishment disagreed. Fred Kaplan, who writes on foreign policy for *Slate*, opened a long column [Jan. 3] by criticizing the government's surveillance program but argued against amnesty for Snowden because of his disclosure of other, legitimate intelligence-gathering activities.

Richard Clarke, the former White House counterterrorism adviser best known for his criticism of the government's pre-9/11 failures on al Qaeda, also came down against amnesty for Snowden. "In any outcome here, he's going to serve time," Clarke, currently one of five members of a White House-appointed task force reviewing the surveillance program, told the *Times*'s White House correspondent Peter Baker.

Baker said two other members of the group also voiced opposition to amnesty for Snowden, including Geoffrey Stone, a professor at the University of Chicago Law School and longtime critic of government secrecy. "'Even if Snowden's benefit outweighed his costs, you don't want to encourage people to make this decision for themselves," Stone said. As for the White House and Justice Department, Baker said Ledgett's suggestion had been met with "stony opposition."

In principle, the critics of any amnesty have a sound point, but principle often bows to reality in criminal justice. The NSA's interest in cutting a deal with Snowden suggests that the agency sees a possible net gain in a plea bargain. And whatever the government's interest, a just outcome in Snowden's case must also take into account the real public benefit of his actions.

The NSA's collection of telephone records raises profound issues of how best to serve both national security and individual liberty, but those issues received far too little attention from policymakers in Congress or the executive branch before Snowden's disclosures. Only now has it been learned that the super-secret Foreign Intelligence Surveillance Court upbraided the NSA for some operations of the program. And only now has there been full, public litigation over the legality of the program and a quasi-independent executive branch review of possible changes.

Justice would not have been well served 40 years ago if the Pentagon Papers leaker Daniel Ellsberg had gone to prison. He was spared prison thanks to the illegal break-in at his psychiatrist's office committed under President Richard M. Nixon, who himself was spared prison for political rather than legal reasons. In the decade since 9/11, there has been little accountability for executive branch officials and personnel for possible crimes in the so-called war on terror.

Edward Snowden is a flawed figure, to be sure, guilty of deception and self-aggrandizement. But the public benefits of his actions outweigh the proven harm to the government's intelligence-gathering interests. Snowden may or may not want to return to the United States, but a deal that limits his possible punishment would serve the ends of justice.

#FreedomofReligion

The First Amendment's two religion clauses – prohibiting a government establishment of religion but protecting an individual's freedom to exercise the religion of his or her choice – require a careful calibration of government actions affecting persons or institutions of faith. The original Constitution includes a seemingly straightforward prohibition against the use of any "religious test" for an office in the national government.

The United States' purported history of religious tolerance and pluralism is belied to some extent by its actual history: the long dominance of Protestant Christians in politics, culture, and society, combined with periodic outbreaks of anti-Catholic, anti-Semitic, and, most recently, anti-Muslim prejudice. I took exception when Glenn Beck, a hero of the religious right, questioned President Obama's religious views.

"No Religious Test"
(*Jost on Justice*, Aug. 31, 2010)

. . . but no religious Test shall ever be required as a Qualification to any Office or public Trust under the United States."
(U.S. Constitution, Art. VI, cl. 3)

The Framers could hardly have been clearer, but political history has made short shrift of their effort to create what in 21st-century parlance would be called a non-sectarian state. Over more than two centuries now, every president of the United States has been a Christian — and as a practical matter required to profess as much.

Still, nothing in American history provides a precedent for the extraordinary episode over the past weekend [Aug. 28-29] in which a radio and television commentator with no known theological training went on national television to depict the sitting president as a bad Christian. For that is what Americans who did not spend Sunday morning in church got if they watched and listened to Glenn Beck attack President Obama for what Beck called the president's devotion to "liberation theology."

In Beck's telling (on "Fox News Sunday," under relatively friendly questioning from his fellow Fox-man, Chris Wallace), Obama is wrong about how to achieve salvation. Beck says that instead of seeing salvation as requiring an individual relationship with God, the president views salvation through the collectivist lens of "liberation theology."

"You see, it's all about victims and victimhood; oppressors and the oppressed; reparations, not repentance; collectivism, not individual salvation," Beck said. "I don't know what that is, other than it's not Muslim, it's not Christian. It's a perversion of the gospel of Jesus Christ as most Christians know it."

Perversely, Beck's critique of Obama's supposed religious views came by way of an apology for his previous description of Obama as a "racist" with a "deep-seated hatred of white culture." So, now, instead of seeking to estrange Obama from his followers on the unacceptable basis of race, Beck chooses religion instead. And he did so in the context of the widely shared view among Republicans and conservatives that Obama is actually a Muslim.

Beck's religion-based attack came one day after he presided over his self-styled "Restoring Honor" rally in Washington, which drew an impressive if not overwhelming crowd stretching from the steps of the Lincoln Memorial to the Washington Monument. The three hours of speeches were largely clear of political divisiveness, but in their overt Christianity — to the exclusion of other faiths — they carried the taint of sectarianism.

It is worth recalling that for 170 years, it was a recognized fact of political life that the president must also be a Protestant: no Catholics need apply. John F. Kennedy broke that barrier, but only after satisfying a "religious test" that he would not take his Catholicism into the Oval Office when making political decisions.

The country today is more religiously pluralistic and in some ways more religiously tolerant than ever before. Joe Lieberman's religion was of course remarked when Al Gore selected him as the Democratic nominee for vice president in 2000 and the first Jew ever to run on a national ticket of a major party. But Lieberman's religion never amounted to an issue in the campaign.

The country's religious pluralism definitely has its limits. Could a Jew be elected president today — or in your lifetime? The odds are no better than 50-50. Can a Muslim be elected to Congress without controversy? No, as Rep. Keith Ellison, the Minnesota Democrat, learned when he took the oath by swearing on a Koran instead of the Christian Bible.

And one need go no further than the pages of the week's newspapers to know that religious divisiveness is spiking these days. Exhibit No. 1: the debate over the proposed Islamic center to be built in lower Manhattan, a few blocks from "Ground Zero." Even if one grants the particular sensitivities of some Americans to siting a mosque — one of the planned uses of the center — so near to the epicenter of the Sept. 11 attacks, there is also exhibit No. 2: the apparent torching of construction equipment at the site of a planned mosque in Murfreesboro, a town in Tennessee hundreds of miles from New York City.

Beck's understanding of "restoring honor" to America had no room for an appeal for tolerance for those who do not share his Christian faith, no room for denouncing the acts of intolerance and even violence against Muslim Americans. As a Mormon, Beck should know better. Mormons themselves were and still are depicted as un-Christian by many Christians, who see them as worshiping a false savior other than Jesus.

Beck's rally was at the same site, and on the same date, as the historic "March on Washington for Jobs and Freedom" in 1963. Among the great anthems of the civil rights movement was "We Shall Overcome" with one of its refrains celebrating "black and white together." On the dais that day, and in the audience, Christians and Jews were conspicuously united in a cause truly dedicated to "restoring honor" in the United States.

Sadly, Beck's rally did not appeal to that unifying sentiment. There would have been honor indeed had he done so, but little real honor in its absence.

Can the government provide funds for church-affiliated schools? The Establishment Clause seemingly says no, but advocates of sectarian education have come up with a variety of schemes to get around it. In one such plan, Arizona gave taxpayers the chance to get a one-for-one tax credit for contributions to an organization that awarded scholarships to students in parochial schools. Some Arizona taxpayers objected, but the Supreme Court threw the case out.

Religious Neutrality
(*Jost on Justice*, April 11, 2011)

A riddle, attributed to Abraham Lincoln: How many legs does a horse have if you call the tail a leg? Answer: Four. Because a tail is a tail no matter what you call it.

The Supreme Court confronted its own version of this riddle last week (April 4). Does a government subsidy to religious schools possibly violate separation of church and state if you call it a tax credit instead? In a 5-4 decision, the court said no. But the answer is as wrong as calling a horse's tail a leg.

The court's conservative majority reached for that wrong answer in an activist move to protect government aid to religion from taxpayer suits despite a 43-year-old precedent permitting them, *Flast v. Cohen* (1968). As Justice Elena Kagan explained in a powerful dissent, the new ruling "devastates" what is often the most practical legal vehicle for enforcing the Constitution's guarantee of religious neutrality in government policy.

The ruling in *Arizona Christian School Tuition Organization v. Winn* turns aside an Establishment Clause challenge to an Arizona tax-credit system that funnels government money to religious schools as surely as if the government wrote the check instead of an individual taxpayer. The Arizona law, enacted in 1997, gives a participating state taxpayer a dollar-for-dollar credit of up to $500 for individuals or $1,000 for married couples for contributions to specially established "school tuition organizations" or STOs.

Those STOs provide tuition grants to students attending qualified private schools in the state. To qualify, schools cannot discriminate on the basis of race, color, national origin, handicap, or familial status. But schools can discriminate on the basis of religion.

The largest STOs, such as the Arizona Christian School Tuition Organization, limit their aid to students attending religious schools. So, much of the $350 million in tax revenue that the state has forgone over the past decade has subsidized schooling for which eligible students were excluded on the basis of religion.

That is not the American way of public education. A group of Arizona taxpayers raised that argument in a federal court suit contending that the tax-credit scheme operates to provide an impermissible government subsidy for religious discrimination. The state disagrees. It contends the program operates as neutrally as a school voucher program of the sort that the Supreme Court upheld, in another 5-4 decision, back in 2000 (*Zelman v. Simmons-Harris*).

In ruling on that question, a three-judge panel of the Ninth U.S. Circuit Court of Appeals found the program unconstitutionally skewed toward religious schools. The full court refused to rehear the case en banc, with eight judges dissenting.

The Supreme Court chose instead to rule on another issue: standing. Significantly, *none* of the appeals court judges on either side questioned the taxpayers' basis for challenging the program. Writing for the Supreme Court's conservative bloc, however, Justice Anthony M. Kennedy concluded that the plaintiff taxpayers had suffered no injury because none of *their* money went to religious schools.

The tax credit is "not tantamount to a religious tax," Kennedy wrote. "When Arizona taxpayers choose to contribute to STOs," he explained, "they spend their own money, not money the State has collected from respondents or from other taxpayers."

Kagan ably demonstrates the error in Kennedy's conclusion. At tax time, Arizonans calculate their tax payment and, if they choose, can then decide to write two checks: one to a student tuition organization and the other, for the balance, to the state.

The tax credit is "costless" to the individual taxpayer, Kagan explains. "It comes out of what she otherwise would be legally obligated to pay the State — hence, out of public resources." In fact, the STO's "capitalize on this aspect of the tax credit," Kagan notes. One STO advertises that the tax credit "won't cost you a dime."

As an original question, perhaps reasonable people can disagree on how to classify this system. But, as detailed in Kagan's opinion, the Supreme Court and lower federal courts have ruled on any number of Establishment Clause challenges to tax credits or deductions without ever questioning taxpayers' standing to bring the suits.

In oral argument, the government — which oddly sided with the state on the standing issue — conceded as much. In answer to a question from Kagan, Acting Solicitor General Neal Katyal agreed that under the government's position, the Supreme Court erred in five cases by ruling on the merits instead of dismissing them for lack of standing.

Five precedents is a lot to disapprove at one time, even for the Roberts Court. Kennedy argued that taxpayers in those other cases may have had standing on other grounds and, in any event, standing may not have been questioned. Kagan rightly notes that the court is obliged to consider standing on its own whether or not raised by the parties.

Kennedy says and Kagan agrees that other individuals may have standing to challenge Arizona's program. Opponents may try to mount a new case. But taxpayer suits are both a practical and a logical means to enforce the rule against government establishment of religion because the right to religious neutrality, as Kagan explains, in fact belongs to all of us.

"State sponsorship of religion sometimes harms individuals only (but this 'only' is no small matter) in their capacity as contributing members of our national community," Kagan writes. In those cases, she says, "our Constitution's guarantee of religious neutrality still should be enforced."

·

Can someone refuse to obey a law because of religious objections?
In general, the answer is no. But two family-owned companies brought

religious-exercise claims to the Supreme Court seeking an exemption from a requirement under President Obama's health care reform to provide contraceptive coverage in employee health benefit plans. In advance of Supreme Court arguments, I analyzed the novel proposition that secular, for-profit corporations had religious rights. Even if they did, I suggested that the government's interest in providing access to contraception would take precedence over any religious objections to the requirement.

Religion, Contraception, and Law
(*Jost on Justice*, Sept. 23, 2013)

When an Amish farmer claimed religious objections to paying Social Security taxes for his employees back in the 1980s, the Supreme Court had little difficulty in ruling against him. "When followers of a particular sect enter into commercial activity as a matter of choice," Chief Justice Warren E. Burger wrote for a unanimous court in *United States v. Lee* (1982), "the limits they accept on their own conduct as a matter of conscience and faith are not to be superimposed on the statutory schemes that are binding on others in that activity."

Three decades later, the same issue is before the Supreme Court, but in a very different political context. The government program at issue in the current cases is not Social Security — a long established and popular success — but one provision in President Obama's Affordable Care Act, which is new and unpopular. And the religious belief at issue is not the idiosyncratic Amish opposition to government assistance, but the widely shared opposition among religious conservatives to contraception, especially the so-called Plan B emergency contraceptive, which some view as a drug to induce an abortion.

The legal context has also changed. Under a law passed by Congress in 1993 — the Religious Freedom Restoration Act (RFRA) — the federal government cannot abridge a person's free exercise of religion except to serve a compelling government interest in the least restrictive manner possible — the so-called "strict scrutiny" test.

Despite the change in law, however, make no mistake: the cases that reached the court last week are politically driven and the outcome as likely as not to be determined by political as much as by legal considerations. Congress had sound reasons to require employers to include free coverage of contraceptives in their employee health plans. Those reasons would satisfy the strict-scrutiny test but for the political opposition to the Affordable Care Act found not only among politicians and the public but also within the federal judiciary, including at the Supreme Court.

The two cases before the court both involve companies formed as closely held corporations by families whose members are opposed to abortion and to emergency contraception on religious grounds. The Mennonite Kahn family in Lancaster County, Pa., own a woodworking company, Conestoga Wood Specialities, with about 950 employees. David Green and his family, evangelical Christians, own (through a trust arrangement) the Oklahoma-based Hobby Lobby Stores, a chain of some 500 arts and crafts marts with 13,000 employees all told.

The corporate status of the two companies raises a preliminary but potentially determinative issue that has divided the federal courts of appeals to rule on these cases so far: Does a secular, for-profit corporation have a constitutionally protected right to free exercise of religion? In the Conestoga case, the Third U.S. Circuit Court of Appeals said no. The free exercise right is "purely personal," the court ruled in a 2-1 decision. The Sixth Circuit agreed in a decision issued last week [Sept. 17]. In the Hobby Lobby case, however, the Tenth U.S. Circuit Court of Appeals cited precedents recognizing free-exercise rights for churches organized as corporations and found no basis for treating for-profit corporations differently.

The government and the administration's supporters in the legal blogosphere are investing a lot of capital on this issue. Corporations, they note, do not enjoy all of the protections listed in the Bill of Rights. A corporation, for example, has no Fifth Amendment privilege against self-incrimination. But the five justices who found a broad right of political speech for corporations in the Citizens United case may see no reason not to recognize a corporation's right to religious expression as well, especially since all five have been sensitive to free exercise claims in other contexts.

So the administration needs to invest equally in defending the contraception mandate on the merits if the court agrees to hear the case (as seems likely) after considering the separate petitions filed by Conestoga and by the government in the Hobby Lobby case. And on the merits the Supreme Court's reasoning in rejecting the Amish farmer's case 30 years ago directly applies to the current issue.

The tax system could not function, Burger wrote, if people could challenge it because tax payments were spent in a manner that violated their religious beliefs. Given the importance of maintaining a sound tax system, he concluded, "religious belief in conflict with the payment of taxes affords no basis for resisting the tax."

In enacting the Affordable Care Act, Congress and the president decided that the government has a strong interest as well in a health care system that, among other things, ensures adequate insurance coverage for preventive services, including contraception. Increased access to contraceptive services is important, the government argues in the Hobby Lobby case, because lack of contraceptive use can have "negative health consequences for both women and children." The government also has a separate interest in ensuring equal access to health care for women, who pay more than men out of pocket for health care.

Accommodating the Kahns, the Greens, and others like them would deny the employees of their companies the benefits of this government policy. It would also invite other exceptions, the government notes — for example, religious-based objections to immunizations. These are strong legal arguments, but they may not be enough for the five Roberts Court justices who have already shown themselves to be deeply skeptical of the Affordable Care Act's major premises.

The court's eventual 5-4 decision, issued on June 30 as the term ended, upheld the two companies' claims under RFRA. Alito reasoned for the majority that the government could ensure access to contraception without requiring the companies themselves to provide the coverage. In a dissenting opinion, Ginsburg argued that the ruling opened the door for employers to object to other medical procedures and even to general civil rights laws against discrimination. In his opinion, Alito dismissed Ginsburg's fears as unrealistic.

In the meantime, the court had favored religious interests in another case by allowing state and local governments to open official proceedings with prayers even if the invocations were predominantly Christian and sectarian in nature. I agreed with Kagan in dissent that the ruling went against the principle of religious neutrality envisioned in the Constitution.

Passing on Legislative Prayer
(*Jost on Justice*, May 11, 2014)

Rajan Zed wore a traditional Indian kurta adorned with a gold scarf as he stood at the front of the U.S. Senate chambers on July 12, 2007, to deliver the opening prayer for the day's session. Before the Hindu priest could begin, however, Sen. Bob Casey had to gavel three times for order and Capitol police officers had to remove and arrest three Christian activists who were protesting from the galleries.

The Reno, Nevada, priest had been invited to deliver the invocation by his home state senator, Majority Leader Harry Reid. When news of his selection got out, however, the American Family Association, a fundamentalist Christian organization, sent out "an action alert" to protest.

"This goes against all history and all tradition of our country," the group's president Tim Wildmon said in the message, according to the account in the Capitol Hill newspaper *Roll Call*. "This fella does not even believe in one god as the Constitution and Declaration of Independence speak of."

With order restored, Zed delivered his prayer. Reid spoke from the floor afterward to thank him. "It speaks well of our country that someone representing the faith of about a billion people comes here and can speak in communication with our heavenly father regarding peace," Reid said.

Later the same year, the small suburban town of Greece, New York, had its own controversy over the issue of legislative prayer. Two of the town's non-Christian residents objected to the unvarying succession of Christian ministers invited to open the Board of Supervisors' monthly meetings, many of them with prayers explicitly invoking Christian doctrines.

After Susan Galloway and Linda Stephens objected, the board allowed a Jewish layman, a Baha'i leader, and a Wiccan priestess to open meetings. But a Christian minister opened another of the sessions with a prayer that criticized "the "ignorant minority" who had objected to the sectarian invocations.

Expect more of these unedifying — and, one might say, unchristian — episodes thanks to the Supreme Court's decision last week [May 5] allowing sectarian, legislative prayers with only the slightest hint of judicial review to help instill religious tolerance. In a 5-4 decision, *Town of Greece v. Galloway*, the court found nothing by way of an Establishment Clause violation in Greece's practice of turning over the official dais to Christian ministers to pray in sectarian terms before citizens gathered for the secular business of municipal government.

In the main opinion, Justice Anthony M. Kennedy invoked historical tradition dating from the First Congress. The practice of legislative prayer, with what Kennedy called Christian "vocabulary," was "accepted by the Framers" and "has withstood the critical scrutiny of time and political change."

For the dissenters, Justice Elena Kagan invoked a different tradition, a promise in the Constitution to treat believers of every faith alike. As citizens performing duties or seeking benefits of citizenship, Kagan wrote, every American "does so not as an adherent to one or other another religion, but simply as an American."

The dissenters — significantly, the three Jewish justices and the liberal Catholic Sonia Sotomayor — conceded the constitutionality of legislative prayer, but wanted only to require "religious neutrality," in Kagan's phrasing: accommodation for prayer givers of all faiths and all in nonsectarian terms only.

In his opinion, Kennedy was more worried about the rights of the government-invited prayer-givers than those of the public audiences. Rules about the content of legislative prayer, he said, would amount to "a form of government entanglement with religion that is far more troublesome than the current approach."

Years earlier, Kennedy had had no problem with a different kind of government entanglement in a First Amendment context. He joined the 5-4 majority in *Rust v. Sullivan* (1991) in upholding a law telling federally funded family planning clinics that they could not counsel clients about whether to seek an abortion.

In the prayer case, Kennedy cautioned that there might be a constitutional problem with "a pattern" of invocations that either "denigrate" other religions, "threaten damnation," or "preach conversion." By finding no such pattern in Greece, however, Kennedy signaled clearly that lower courts should not look hard for any violations.

Among the other four justices in the majority — significantly, all of them Catholic — Justice Clarence Thomas went along, but only after reiterating his view that the prohibition against government establishment of religion does not apply to state and local governments at all. Thomas was not even sure about its meaning for the federal government. The First Amendment, he said, "probably" prohibits a national establishment of religion.

Among the many commentators pro and con on the issue, George Will reflected the view of many supporters of government-sponsored prayer by criticizing those who object for having "a thin skin." On the other side, such columnists as E.J. Dionne Jr. and Ruth Marcus criticized the court's majority for a lack of "empathy" toward the nation's non-Christians.

In her dissent, Kagan dropped a footnote invoking George Washington, Thomas Jefferson, and James Madison in warning that the government's aligning itself with any particular sect or creed was inevitably divisive. As Kagan noted, the nation was overwhelmingly Christian at the time and far more religiously diverse today. The sight of a Hindu priest delivering a prayer in the Senate chamber produced the kind of acrimony that Washington warned against two centuries earlier. With an Establishment Clause pass from the Supreme Court, one can expect only more such acrimony in the future.

6

#GayRights

The gay rights revolution began not with the Stonewall riot in 1969 but earlier, with the organization of gay rights groups in the 1950s and the peaceful picketing and protests of the 1960s. Much of the credit for those early developments goes to an American hero who was long celebrated by the LGBT community but gained wider public recognition only in the later years of his life.

Frank Kameny (1925-2011)
(Jost on Justice, Oct. 17, 2011)

For all their undoubted bravery, the men and women who waged the battle for civil rights for black Americans in the 1950s and '60s were not alone in their struggles. They had behind them and on their side black civil rights organizations, black churches, some white liberals in churches and synagogues, some sympathetic coverage in the news media, and, as early as *Brown v. Board of Education*, the federal government.

Frank Kameny, who died last week (Oct. 11) at the age of 86, had virtually no one behind him or on his side when he began fighting for civil rights for gay Americans like himself in the late 1950s. Back then, homosexuals were all but alone, deemed either immoral or mentally ill or both, presumed unfit for government service, politically powerless, and invisible in information or entertainment media.

Kameny did as much as to change that, probably more, than any other single person. Speakers at a program last week sponsored by the Rainbow History Project of Washington, D.C., rightly remembered him as having laid the philosophical basis for the gay rights movement. Kameny led the legal fight to remove homosexuality as the basis for disqualification from working for the federal government. He led the successful effort to get the American Psychiatric Association to stop classifying homosexuality as a mental illness. And he coined the phrase, "Gay is good," which over time gave gays and lesbians self-esteem and self-confidence and eventually helped change society's views of homosexuality as well.

Kameny, a World War II veteran and Harvard-trained astronomer, started the fight out of necessity after having been fired from his job as an astronomer with the U.S. Army's Map Service. (It is commonly reported that Kameny was arrested for cruising in Washington's Lafayette Park, but in his later appeal Kameny attributed his dismissal to his truthful disclosure on an employment form of a prior arrest in San Francisco on a baseless charge that was later expunged.) He fought his dismissal all the way to the U.S. Supreme Court, representing himself — on his own — in a strongly argued plea that his personal life had nothing to do with his government service. The justices refused to hear the case. (The 1961 petition is available as part of the Rainbow History Project's Frank Kameny pages.)

In the same year, Kameny founded one of the first gay rights organizations, the Mattachine Society of Washington. There were other organizations of the same name founded in the 1950s in Los Angeles and San Francisco. (Mattacino was a character in Italian theater, a court jester of sorts.) The Washington organization was independent, however, both in form and spirit. Unlike the California organizations, Kameny resolved to be as public as possible in advocating for the rights of gays and lesbians.

It was in that spirit that Kameny led the first gay rights picketing in front of the White House on April 17, 1965 — four years before the raid on the Stonewall bar in New York City that is often treated as the beginning of the gay rights movement. The demonstration drew no news coverage except a brief mention in Washington's *Afro American* newspaper, but the placards that Kameny and his dozen or so allies carried have now been turned over along with Kameny's papers to the Library of Congress. Six years later, in 1971, Kameny ran for the District of Columbia's non-voting seat in the House of Representatives. He was the first openly gay person to seek federal office in the United States.

Kameny was equally bold in challenging the psychiatric establishment to remove homosexuality from its authoritative Diagnostic and Statistical Manual of Mental Disorders (the so-called DSM). As speakers at the Rainbow History program recalled, Kameny led a small band of gay guerrillas into the APA's annual meeting at a Washington, D.C., hotel, stormed the stage, and lectured the startled psychiatrists that they were all wrong about homosexuality.

Along with public advocacy, Kameny and the Mattachine Society also functioned as a self-help organization for gays and lesbians. A friend recalled to me having called the group's hot line for medical advice after having his first same-sex experience. The society published a pamphlet with advice about what to do if arrested on sex-related charges. And Kameny provided his apartment as a way station for visiting gay activists.

The APA delisted homosexuality in 1973. Two years later, the U.S. Civil Service Commission decided that homosexuality was no longer. Eventually, the District of Columbia police retreated from targeting gays for arrests for consensual sex. And in 2003, the Supreme Court ruled, in *Lawrence v. Texas,* that an individual's "intimate relationships" were of no concern to the government, at least as far as criminal law was concerned.

Kameny lived long enough to be recognized as a gay rights hero. The obituary in *The New York Times* and the appreciation on the CBS program "Sunday Morning" included pictures of Kameny with President Obama in the White House, four decades after he picketed outside its gates. Kameny recognized the changes, but he was also unchanged in his determination. He was not satisfied that Congress has yet to make it illegal to discriminate in the workplace on the basis of sexual orientation. He was not satisfied that marriage equality remains a goal, not a fact. But he could take some pride in having accomplished to some extent the goal set out in the initial charter of the Mattachine Society of Washington: "to secure for homosexuals the right to life, liberty, and the pursuit of happiness."

#Don'tAskDon'tTell

Long before my own coming out, I recognized the need to eliminate discrimination against homosexuals. In a review of Randy Shilts's book Conduct Unbecoming, *I wrote critically about the military's policy of discharging homosexual service members. President Clinton failed in his effort to eliminate the policy; Congress instead enacted the "don't ask, don't tell" policy, which protected closeted military service members but called for discharging anyone who was open about his or her homosexuality. As a candidate for president in 2008, Barack Obama promised to repeal the policy if elected. My first column on the issue sought to hold him to that promise.*

Power of Presidential Pen
(*Jost on Justice*, Oct. 8, 2009)

John F. Kennedy promised during his 1960 presidential campaign to end racial discrimination in federally assisted housing "with the stroke of a pen," but the author of *Profiles in Courage* waited almost two years to issue the promised executive order.

Bill Clinton promised during his 1992 campaign to end discrimination against gays in the military, but in office he backed away from an executive order and gave Congress running room to write discrimination into law with the "don't ask, don't tell" policy.

Fifteen years later, Barack Obama campaigned on a promise to repeal "don't ask, don't tell" if elected. But the White House and Congress have put gays in the military on a back burner along with other gay rights issues until the economy is revived, health care reformed, and Afghanistan made safe for democracy.

As a result, some in the gay rights community are calling for Obama to end the discrimination against gay and lesbian service members with the stroke of his presidential pen. Specifically, they believe Obama can and should stop any enforcement of "don't ask, don't tell" under a statutory provision authorizing the commander in chief to issue a "stop loss" executive order during what is recognized as an official military emergency.

With two wars ongoing and manpower needs pressing, advocates for gay service members point out that the policy has cost the military more than 13,000 service members since its inception. Among those discharged are at least 59 Arabic linguists, trained by the military at considerable expense and vitally needed for intelligence-gathering and analysis in combating al Qaeda and other anti-American Islamist groups.

In the first place, Congress passed the law establishing the policy on the basis of anecdote and opinion instead of research and evidence. The Pentagon submitted a 15-page report by its Military Working Group that consisted mostly of compilations of anti-gay attitudes by senior military officers. The Pentagon succeeded in mostly burying a more scientific, 500-page study by the RAND Corporation that said sexual orientation was "not germane" to military service and predicted a non-discrimination policy could be implemented effectively with proper leadership.

Whatever plausibility the military's concerns might have had in 1993, they are refuted by the evidence since then from the 24 countries that now allow military service by out gay men and lesbians, according to Nathaniel Frank, a senior researcher with the Palm Center at the University of California-Santa Barbara. As Frank writes in his argumentative but well documented book *Unfriendly Fire*, none of those countries — including such U.S. allies as Britain, Canada, and Israel — has seen any impairment to unit cohesion, recruitment, or fighting capability.

Within the U.S. military, "don't ask, don't tell" has hurt rather than helped unit cohesion. For gay service members, the policy fosters suspicions of their colleagues and diminishes military comradeship at a time when more and more straight service members have no problem interacting with gays. But for homophobic service members, the policy contributes to a climate that encourages anti-gay harassment and ignores it when it occurs.

One thing has changed since 1993: public opinion. Most Americans opposed the idea of gays in the military in 1993. Today, various polls show upwards of 75 percent of Americans favor allowing gays to serve openly in the military. The most recent Gallup poll found majority support even among self-identified conservatives, Republicans and churchgoers.

Despite the compelling evidence and the favorable shift in public attitudes, the White House says Obama cannot act on his own because "don't ask, don't tell" is statutory law, not an executive order. Frank and fellow researchers at the Palm Center disagree. They point to a provision in the law (10 U.S.C. § 12305) that allows the president to suspend separations from the military during any period of national emergency, such as now, in which members of a reserve component are serving involuntarily on active duty.

The White House is reportedly unconvinced of the legal argument and concerned about the political fallout. The risks are not slight. A preemptive presidential action could antagonize both Congress and the military leadership. "If you stick your finger in the eyes of [Defense Secretary Robert] Gates and [Joint Chiefs of Staff Chairman] Mike Mullen, I'm not sure how far that gets you," says Aubrey Sarvis, executive director of Servicemembers Defense Legal Network.

Sarvis says he would favor the executive order approach only if Obama simultaneously pushes the issue on Capitol Hill. Frank and his colleagues say the executive order might cost Obama less political capital in the end. And they also expect that allowing gays to serve openly would prove to all but the unpersuadable that an enlightened policy enhances military readiness at no cost to unit cohesion or recruitment.

Sixty years ago, President Harry Truman ended racial segregation "with the stroke of a pen." Military leaders were opposed — and later dragged their feet in implementing the new policy — but Truman reminded them that he was commander in chief. History vindicates his decision. Obama, facing a less treacherous political terrain, might consider whether history would similarly look with favor on a similar exercise of presidential courage today.

Obama decided against eliminating "don't ask, don't tell" by executive order, but he did put White House muscle behind the effort to get Congress to repeal it in a lame-duck session after the November 2010 elections. The House approved the measure 250-175 on Dec. 15; the Senate followed suit, 65-31, on Dec. 18. As enacted, the law provided that the policy would be repealed if, after a Pentagon study, the president, secretary of Defense, and chairman of the Joint Chiefs of Staff certified that the repeal would not adversely affect military readiness. Despite the waiting period, gay rights advocates began celebrating even as they waited for Obama to sign the measure into law.

Land of the Free

(*Jost on Justice*, Dec. 20, 2010)

The Gay Men's Chorus of Washington was all set Saturday night [Dec. 18] for its seasonal frolic "Men in Tights: A Pink Nutcracker." But artistic director Jeff Buhrman wanted to begin on a serious note.

A few hours earlier, the U.S. Senate had completed congressional action on a bill to repeal the "don't ask, don't tell" policy on gays in the military. In honor of the occasion, Buhrman asked the audience at George Washington University's Lisner Auditorium to stand and join in singing "The Star-Spangled Banner."

It was an "emotional moment," one friend later commented on Facebook, to hear so many gay and lesbian Americans join in a celebration of their patriotism. When younger, my friend wrote, "I'd have been so proud to have served my country openly as a gay man. Instead, I had to serve with a portable closet by my side to hide in."

Not yet but soon, thousands of gay men and lesbians already in the military and many others eager to join will be legally free to make up their own minds whether to stay in or come out of the closet. The hard-fought, down-to-the-wire victory gives Gay America something to celebrate this holiday season. Overall, however, both President Obama and the Democratic-controlled Congress get only middling grades for advancing LGBT rights.

Obama took office amid much optimism among LGBT Americans and their straight allies. He had campaigned on a platform that included repealing "don't ask, don't tell" as well as the Defense of Marriage Act (DOMA), the 1996 law that prohibits federal marital benefits for same-sex couples. He also backed the Employment Non-Discrimination Act (ENDA) to prohibit job discrimination on the basis of sexual orientation. And he favored amending the federal hate crimes law to include offenses aimed at gays or lesbians.

With the Democratic-controlled Congress about to yield to divided government on Capitol Hill, only two of those items have been approved. Neither has yielded concrete results.

The Matthew Shepard and James Byrd Jr. Hate Crimes Prevention Act became law in October 2009. But despite the recent flurry of news about gay-bashing and gay-bullying, the Justice Department has yet to invoke the law against any anti-gay offense.

The "don't ask, don't tell" repeal itself provides that the 1993 law remains on the book for now until the Pentagon can prepare new regulations and training. Then the president, secretary of defense, and chairman of the Joint Chiefs of Staff all have to certify to Congress that repeal is "consistent with the standards of military readiness, military effectiveness, unit cohesion, and recruiting and retention of the Armed Forces." Until then, openly gay or lesbian service members are theoretically subject to discharge.

Gay rights organizations had high hopes for the job-discrimination bill as Obama and Congress started work in 2009. But the bill fell victim to other priorities, in particular health-care reform. As for repealing DOMA, the issue never made it past the starting gate in Congress.

In their last-ditch effort to keep "don't ask, don't tell" on the book, Senate Republicans echoed anti-gay organizations in depicting repeal as a political payoff by the Democrats to "the homosexual lobby." True, gay political organizations are predominantly Democratic. That is hardly a surprise given the Republican Party's stout opposition to gay rights measures.

For many gay and lesbian Americans, however, the issues are not political, but personal. Consider, for example, Lisa Howe, fired earlier this month as women's soccer coach at Belmont University in Nashville, Tenn., after she told her team that she and her partner are expecting a child. Howe had previously kept her sexual orientation private, but thought she could share her good news with the team. ENDA might have allowed her to keep her job.

With DOMA on the books, many same-sex couples are paying more in taxes or receiving less in federal benefits than their straight-sex counterparts even in the five states and the District of Columbia where gays and lesbians supposedly enjoy equal marriage rights. A federal judge in Massachusetts ruled the law unconstitutional on equal protection grounds this summer, but the Obama administration is continuing to claim that it is obliged to defend the law in court.

Similarly, the administration had been defending "don't ask, don't tell" in court even as it was urging Congress to repeal the law. A federal judge in Riverside, Calif., ruled the law unconstitutional earlier this fall and went so far as to block its enforcement. The administration rushed to a federal appeals court to overturn the injunction. With the law still on the books, it will be interesting to see whether the case continues or is put on hold.

With Obama set to sign the "don't ask, don't tell" repeal on Wednesday [Dec. 22], gay rights leaders are emphasizing that much has been accomplished and that much remains to be done. At least on Saturday night, however, hundreds of Washingtonians were proud to join the Gay Men's Chorus as they raised their voices to sing of a rainbow flag that waves "o'er the land of the free … and the home of the brave."

#MarriageEquality

Early in the 1970s, a gay Minnesota couple took their effort to be legally married all the way to the U.S. Supreme Court. The justices in 1972 rejected their appeal "for the lack of a substantial federal question." When a new case, out of Hawaii, hit the news in the 1990s, the backlash was immediate and widespread. States started passing laws to prohibit same-sex couples from marrying; Congress followed in 1996 with a law, the Defense of Marriage Act (DOMA), that explicitly gave states the right to refuse to recognize same-sex marriages from other states. The law also defined marriage for purposes of federal law as consisting of one man and one woman; that meant that if any state was to recognize same-sex marriages, the couples would be ineligible for marriage-based federal benefits.

DOMA had no actual impact before 2004, when Massachusetts became the first state to recognize marriage rights for gay and lesbian couples. The ruling by the Massachusetts Supreme Judicial Court encouraged gay couples in other states to go to court with similar cases. But the next few state courts to rule on the issue upheld the challenged laws that denied marriage rights to same-sex couples. I found those decisions unpersuasive.

Judicial Lapses of Logic
(*CQ Weekly*, Aug. 14, 2006)

A few years back, the city of Cincinnati tried to reduce on-street litter by prohibiting the distribution of "commercial handbills" from sidewalk news racks. The city allowed the coin-operated news racks to remain, however, on the theory that people were more likely to discard free commercial shoppers than bought-and-paid-for newspapers.

The policy seemed sensible, but not sensible enough for the Supreme Court, which turned its attention to the commercial publishers' First Amendment rights. The justices in 1993 ruled the policy unconstitutional on the ground that Cincinnati had failed to show a "reasonable fit" between its anti-litter goal and the selective enforcement scheme adopted to further the goal.

The decision illustrates in an unremarkable way the courts' well-established role in critically examining the rationality of legislative or executive branch policies that affect constitutional rights. As important as the First Amendment is to our society, one might think that courts would be at least as rigorous in scrutinizing the basis of laws affecting more personal liberty interests, including the right to select a life partner.

Last month, however, the highest courts in two states — New York and Washington — were far less than rigorous in finding a "rational basis" for laws denying same-sex couples the right to marriage. The two blue-state rulings — which leave Massachusetts alone in recognizing marriage for same-sex couples — have forced gay rights supporters to reconsider litigation as a strategy for achieving marriage equality for gay men and lesbians.

The judicial setbacks for gay rights supporters reinforce a growing body of thought among liberals against using courts instead of legislative bodies to establish new civil rights and liberties. Jeffrey Rosen, a professor at George Washington University Law School and frequent legal commentator, provides the most extended recent version of this thesis in his new book, *The Most Democratic Branch: How the Courts Serve America.*

Rosen argues that courts can reliably safeguard individual rights only if they already are recognized for the most part by a "constitutional consensus" among Congress, the president, and the public. In his view, *Brown v. Board of Education* survived because the public was ready to bury racial segregation. *Roe v. Wade* became a battleground because Americans were not — and still are not — ready to accept what opponents call "abortion on demand."

Rosen cites the Massachusetts decision on gay marriage along with *Roe* as examples of "judicial unilateralism." He calls instead for "judicial restraint," which he depicts as a "venerable tradition" under siege from activists of the left and the right. The New York and Washington decisions on gay marriage, however, represent restraint at the expense of reason. The two grounds that both courts cited as providing a rational basis for limiting marriage to opposite-sex couples fall apart under even the slightest degree of critical scrutiny.

Most provocatively, the courts argued that legislators had good reason for limiting marriage to opposite-sex couples because they are all too prone to producing babies "by accident or impulse." For the sake of these casually conceived children, the courts reasoned, legislatures give opposite-sex couples an incentive to stay together: marriage, with its attendant legal and financial benefits.

Gay couples with children don't need the same incentive to stay together, both courts reasoned, because they have to think and work harder before they can have kids. As any number of gay commentators remarked, the courts in effect said that gay couples — far from being instinctively promiscuous — are so virtuous that they don't need the binding ties of marriage, but opposite-sex couples do.

In addition, the New York and Washington courts both said that legislators could have believed that children fare better in families with both a mother and a father as role models. Neither court had research to prove the point: There is none. Instead, as the New York court said in the main opinion, the supposed advantage was a "common sense premise" supported by "intuition and experience."

Whatever quibbles one might raise about each of the points, both courts were guilty of an overriding lapse of logic. The issue in both cases was not whether marriage for opposite-sex couples is a good thing, but whether legislators had some reason — other than ignorance or prejudice — to deny those benefits to same-sex couples. As Chief Judge Judith Kaye wrote in dissent in the New York case, "There are enough marriage licenses to go around for everyone."

Far from being under siege, judicial restraint appears to be very much in vogue these days — endorsed by no less a figure than Chief Justice John G. Roberts Jr. Despite Rosen's reconstruction of history, however, the United States would have fewer freedoms and less justice today if courts always had waited for a constitutional consensus before safeguarding individual rights. And, when restraint does no more than provide cover for societal prejudice, courts dishonor their proper role by going along.

Gay marriage advocates pressed their case in courts and in state legislatures. The California Supreme Court ruled in favor of gay marriage in May 2008, but voters overturned the decision in November by approving a ballot measure known as Proposition 8. The tide began to turn for gay rights advocates in 2009 with a ruling by the Iowa Supreme Court and legislative victories in Vermont, New Hampshire, and the District of Columbia. Meanwhile, lawyers with Gay and Lesbian Advocates and Defenders (GLAD), the public interest law firm that had litigated the Massachusetts marriage-equality case, went to federal court to challenge DOMA as unconstitutional. I wrote on the case while it was pending before a federal judge in Boston.

DOMA's "Insult" to Gay Couples
(*Jost on Justice*, May 17, 2010)

Keith Toney got a new passport last summer. Usually, no big deal. But Keith had to join a federal court lawsuit before the State Department agreed to issue a passport in his legal name.

The problem? Keith took the surname of his longtime partner Al Toney after they were married in Massachusetts in March 2004. Keith had no problems changing his driver's license, credit cards, and so forth. But when he tried to renew his passport in 2005, the State Department told him that the Defense of Marriage Act (DOMA) — which prohibits any federal recognition of same-sex marriages — prevented it from issuing a passport in his legally recognized marital name.

Over the next four years, Keith managed as best he could when he and Al traveled to Costa Rica, where they own property. He got used to carrying his marriage license and a news article with him to help explain — sometimes across the Spanish-English language barrier — why his passport bore a different name from the rest of his identification. But he never got used to the fact that the government was forcing him to carry a document that no longer represented his real identity. "It was an insult," he recalls today.

To put their anger to good use, Keith and Al signed on to the legal attack on DOMA that was tried earlier this month (May 6) before a federal judge in Boston. Along with other same-sex couples all legally married in Massachusetts, the Toneys argued that the federal government is violating the Constitution's Equal Protection Clause by denying them the same privileges and benefits that it extends to other legally married couples in the Bay State and everywhere else in the country.

The State Department finally relented last year by agreeing to accept Keith's marriage license as evidence of a change of name — one of several gay-friendly actions taken under Secretary of State Hillary Rodham Clinton. After five years, the department even waived the usual name-change fee and delivered the new passport within two days of a specially arranged interview.

The other plaintiffs in the case, *Gill v. Office of Personnel Management*, are not so lucky. Their complaints about the second-class status of their marriages are unanswered, at least, not yet. But attorneys for Gay and Lesbian Advocates and Defenders (GLAD), the Boston-based legal center that filed the suit, were professing cautious optimism after the 90-minute hearing before Senior U.S. District Court Judge Joseph Tauro.

For his part, Justice Department attorney Scott Simpson was in the awkward position of defending a law that the Obama administration says it wants to repeal. "This presidential administration disagrees with DOMA as a matter of policy," Simpson said, according to news accounts of the hearing. "But that does not affect its constitutionality."

As with Keith Toney's problem, the stakes in the case for the 17 remaining plaintiffs — seven couples and three men whose husbands died — sound more like the product of bureaucratic snafus than the stuff of constitutional litigation. Lead plaintiff Nancy Gill has worked for the U.S. Postal Service for more than 20 years, but cannot provide the same benefits to her spouse, Marcelle Letourneau, that other married workers provide to theirs. Other couples cannot file joint federal income tax returns. The three "widowers" — including Dean Hara, husband of the late congressman, Gerry Studds — have been denied Social Security survivor benefits.

Congress passed DOMA in 1996 in an effort to thwart any progress toward gay marriage in the states. The House committee report on the bill said its purpose was to "express moral disapproval of homosexuality." One section provides that no state is obliged to recognize same-sex marriages recognized in another state. The Massachusetts plaintiffs are challenging a second provision that defines marriage for federal law purposes as between one man and one woman.

In defending the law today, the Obama administration has expressly disavowed many of the lawmakers' motives behind its enactment. Whatever the political reasons, the concession may also be sound legal strategy. The Supreme Court's 1996 decision striking down an anti-gay initiative in Colorado, *Romer v. Evans*, held that anti-gay animus cannot be used to justify a law, even under the most relaxed constitutional scrutiny.

Instead, the government now argues the law preserves the status quo while states debate marriage rights for gays and lesbians. In court,

GLAD attorney Mary Bonauto answered that the law actually "upended" the status quo by superseding the states' traditional prerogative to define marriage.

Tauro encouraged the plaintiffs' side by vigorously challenging Simpson on the point. "When did it become a federal matter — the definition of marriage?" Tauro asked. Massachusetts will be making a similar federalism-style argument later this month (May 26) in its separate legal action to strike down the law.

Tauro gave no indication when he will rule, but the Toneys — who watched the hearing along with the other plaintiffs from the jury box in Tauro's courtroom — were optimistic afterward. "The judge was very respectful," said Keith "We personally feel it went very well."

"We're hopeful people anyway," Al added. "It would be kind of sad to go through life not being hopeful. The other way is pretty grim."

Judge Tauro ruled DOMA unconstitutional in a decision issued in early July 2010. In the meantime, two same-sex couples in California had gone to federal court in an effort to overturn the state's gay-marriage ban, Proposition 8. The case was litigated by a seemingly unlikely team of nationally prominent lawyers: Theodore Olson, a conservative Republican, and David Boies, a liberal Democrat, who had famously opposed each other in the 2000 presidential election contest, Bush v. Gore. Olson and Boies made their case with compelling testimony from the four plaintiffs backed up by evidence from experts debunking the arguments against recognizing gay marriage. As I wrote in my column, Judge Vaughn Walker relied on that evidence in his decision ruling Proposition 8 unconstitutional.

Facts on Gay Marriage
(*Jost on Justice*, Aug. 6, 2010)

When future Supreme Court justice Louis Brandeis was defending early in the 20th century the constitutionality of an Oregon law limiting hours of laundry workers, he adopted a then unheard of legal strategy. Brandeis filled his brief to the Supreme Court not with legal abstractions, but with documented facts showing the adverse health and social effects of long hours on laundry workers, virtually all of them women.

This first ever "Brandeis brief," recently displayed at the court by the curator's office, revolutionized Supreme Court practice. Today, advocates and judges alike emphasize facts, not legal abstractions, as a matter of course in constitutional litigation.

Federal judge Vaughn Walker understood this mode of constitutional adjudication in his precedent-making decision on Aug. 4 to strike down Proposition 8, the voter-approved initiative in California denying marriage rights to same-sex couples. The guts of his 136-page ruling in *Perry v. Schwarzenegger* consists of 50 pages of "findings of fact," carefully annotated to testimony from the 2½- week trial. Those findings point ineluctably to one conclusion: Prop. 8 has no purpose or effect other than the impermissible goals of denying gay men and lesbians the liberty to define their own life relationships and demoting them to second-class status — legally, socially, and economically.

Those findings make it difficult, but not impossible, for a higher court to reverse Walker's ruling. But they are aimed directly at the Supreme Court justice whose vote is essential to a victory for gay rights advocates in the case: Anthony M. Kennedy.

Twice before, Kennedy has written and cast a pivotal vote in decisions striking down anti-gay enactments. In *Lawrence v. Texas* (2003), Kennedy concluded for a five-justice majority that a Texas law criminalizing gay sex infringed a protected liberty interest in defining one's intimate relationships. Eight years earlier, in *Romer v. Evans* (1995), Kennedy led a 6-3 majority in concluding that a Colorado initiative forbidding passage of anti-gay discrimination laws was an animus-motivated enactment aimed solely at shutting gays and lesbians out of the political process.

In his ruling, Walker began with a series of numbered findings of fact demonstrating the obvious and undisputed benefits of marriage. "Material benefits, legal protections, and social support resulting from marriage," he wrote, "increase wealth and improve psychological well-being for married spouses" (FF39). Those benefits accrue as well to the children of married spouses (FF41).

Domestic partnerships are not the same, Walker found. They are not recognized by the federal or many state governments (FF52) and in any event do not provide the same benefits or cultural status as marriage (FF53). But same-sex couples are "identical" in all relevant aspects to opposite-sex couples in their ability to form "successful marital unions" (FF48). And "marrying a person of the opposite sex," Walker notes, "is an unrealistic option for gay and lesbian individuals" (FF51).

Significantly, Walker notes that California law encourages gays and lesbians to become parents through adoption, foster parenting, or assistive reproductive technology; about 18 percent of same-sex couples in the state are, in fact, raising children (FF 49). Children of same-sex parents benefit when their parents can marry (FF56), and children raised by same-sex parents are as likely to be "healthy, successful and well-adjusted" as those raised by opposite-sex parents (FF70). That finding, Walker adds, is accepted by psychologists as "beyond serious debate."

What about the threat to "traditional marriage," to use Prop. 8 supporters' phrasing? "Permitting same-sex couples to marry," Walker writes, "will not affect the number of opposite-sex couples who marry, divorce, cohabit, have children outside of marriage or otherwise affect the stability of opposite-sex marriages" (FF54).

What then does Prop. 8 accomplish? The measure, Walker writes, "places the force of law behind stigmas against gays and lesbians" — bluntly, that they are "not as good as heterosexuals" and their relationships "do not deserve the full recognition of society" (FF58). It reserves for heterosexual couples "the most socially valued form of relationship" (FF60) while it "increases costs and decreases wealth" of same-sex couples (FF66), domestic partner status notwithstanding.

Set against the acknowledged "long history of discrimination" against gays and lesbians (FF75), the Prop. 8 campaign relied on false "stereotypes" about gays and lesbians (FF80) and unfounded fears that children exposed to the concept of same-sex marriage could become gay or lesbian as a result (FF79). And, once enacted, the measure "results in frequent reminders for gays and lesbians in committed long-term relationships that their relationships are not as highly valued as opposite-sex relationships" (FF68).

Against that backdrop, Walker proceeds to find that none of the proffered justifications for Prop. 8 — preserving tradition, moving slowly on social change, preferencing opposite-sex parenting, or protecting freedom of opponents of same-sex marriage — pass constitutional muster. The measure has no "rational basis," he concludes, but serves merely to "enshrine" in law the purported superiority of heterosexual to same-sex couples.

The ruling is a testament not only to the litigation strategy of the plaintiffs' strange bedfellow lawyers, liberal David Boies and conservative Theodore Olson, but also to the factual vacuum of the Prop. 8 campaign. Just one day later, Robert George, a Princeton professor and leading gay marriage opponent, was vowing that his side — out-litigated at trial — would be presenting new information for appeals courts to consider. For now, however, Walker's fact-heavy decision makes the most compelling of cases to date for recognizing marriage rights for same-sex couples.

President Obama disappointed gay rights advocates by refusing to endorse marriage rights for same-sex couples until May 2012. His position on the issue, both he and his press secretary said time after time, was "evolving." In the meantime, however, Obama and his attorney general, Eric Holder, made the momentous decision early in 2011 that the government would no longer defend DOMA in court. In my column, I emphasized the importance of the government's conclusion that laws that discriminate on the basis of sexual orientation are constitutionally suspect and should be subject to some form of "heightened scrutiny" by courts.

Challenging Anti-Gay Discrimination
(*Jost on Justice*, March 28, 2011)

The Supreme Court struck a major blow for racial justice in 1954 when it outlawed racial segregation in public schools. But *Brown v. Board of Education* said nothing about legally enforced racial segregation in other public services or in public facilities.

Even so, the principle that discrimination on the basis of race violates the Equal Protection Clause was evidently just as applicable to segregation in public parks, golf courses, and swimming pools, as federal judges in the South quickly ruled. When those cases reached the Supreme Court, the justices summarily affirmed the rulings without comment.

As the episode illustrates, a new legal principle cannot be neatly confined to the case at hand. In a rule-of-law society, precedents have consequences; rulings have legs. So it was with the Supreme Court's first blow against racial segregation. And so it may be with the federal government's first direct challenge to legally enforced discrimination against gays and lesbians.

In deciding not to defend the constitutionality of the Defense of Marriage Act (DOMA), the Obama administration adopted for the first time the view that laws based on sexual orientation are constitutionally suspect and cannot be upheld without surviving some unspecified measure of "heightened scrutiny." Attorney General Eric Holder listed four factors in his letter explaining why courts should be "suspicious" of laws based on sexual orientation.

Holder cited first "the significant history of purposeful discrimination" against gays and lesbians. He pointed next to the "growing consensus" that sexual orientation, like race, is an immutable characteristic and the "growing acknowledgment" that sexual orientation has no bearing on an individual's ability to contribute to society. And, despite gains in recent years, he noted that gays and lesbians generally have had "limited political power" as a minority in society.

No court, federal or state, has yet to hold that laws based on sexual orientation are constitutionally suspect. Courts that have upheld bans on gay marriage have applied the relaxed "rational relationship" test. Courts that have struck down bans on gay marriage have hinted that a stricter test might be appropriate but have ended by saying that laws denying marriage rights to gays and lesbians have no rational basis because they serve no legitimate government purpose.

The DOMA case is pending before the federal appeals court in New York, but even before a ruling the Justice Department's position is being extended into other matters. In a preliminary ruling last week [March

22], an immigration judge in New York City cited the government's position in the DOMA case in allowing an Argentine woman a chance to challenge her deportation because she and her U.S. citizen wife were legally married in Connecticut in August. And a few days earlier [March 17], the Justice Department itself applied heightened scrutiny to governmental conduct based on sexual orientation in accusing the New Orleans Police Department of "bias-based profiling" against LGBT individuals.

In the immigration case, first reported in the *Gay City News*, Monica Alcota, who came to the United States 10 years ago, is claiming she is entitled to permanent residency status because of her marriage to Cristina Ojeda, a U.S. citizen — just as she would be if she were in a heterosexual marriage. Immigration judge Terry Bain allowed Alcota to petition the U.S. Citizenship and Immigration Services (USCIS) to be recognized as Ojeda's spouse.

The doubts about deporting foreign spouses in same-sex marriages with U.S. citizens may be shared by immigration officials. Newsweek/ The Daily Beast reported last week [March 25] that the directors of the Washington and Baltimore immigration offices have put deportation proceedings in such cases on hold pending further consideration of DOMA's validity.

The Justice Department's report on the New Orleans Police Department accused the force of "a pattern or practice of discriminatory policing" against, among others, African Americans, Latinos, and LGBT persons. As reporter Chris Geidner wrote last week [March 23] in the gay Washington publication *Metro Weekly*, the findings of discrimination against LGBT individuals were not only "notable on their own," but also significant because of the constitutional standard used to judge the department's treatment of LGBT individuals. Heightened scrutiny of discrimination by law enforcement on the basis of sexual orientation and gender identity was justified, the report stated, by "many factors . . . including a long history of animus and deeply-rooted stereotypes about lesbian, gay, bisexual, and transgender ("LGBT'") individuals."

For now, these developments are merely embryonic. To date, no one in the LGBT community has won vindication of any legal right because of the government's position. But the Justice Department carries a big stick in federal courts. In *Brown*, the government sided with the plaintiffs and against the segregated school districts. The government's support for desegregation over the next two decades helped stiffen the court's resolve on the issue. Conversely, President Eisenhower's failure to immediately endorse *Brown* gave segregationists room to mount resistance to the ruling.

The U.S. government did not participate in the Supreme Court's most important gay rights ruling: *Lawrence v. Texas* (2005), which struck down state anti-sodomy laws. President Obama, who is reported to have been personally involved in the decision on DOMA, has for the first time put the government's significant clout on the side of constitutionalizing gay rights. The next move is up to the courts.

The Obama administration's decision to join same-sex couples in challenging DOMA must have helped give judges confidence in ruling the law unconstitutional. The First U.S. Circuit Court of Appeals, ruling in the Massachusetts, found DOMA unconstitutional late in May 2012. In October, the Second Circuit ruled to the same effect in a case brought by a New York widow, Edith Windsor, who had to pay $363,000 in federal estate taxes after her wife's death – a tax that a surviving spouse in an opposite-sex marriage would not have had to pay. Windsor's case would be the one to reach the Supreme Court for the justices to rule on the law.

Offense Against Marriage Act
(*Jost on Justice*, Oct. 21, 2012)

The federal Defense of Marriage Act (DOMA) is all but dead. Seven federal courts have ruled it unconstitutional, and Supreme Court watchers have a growing consensus that at least five justices will agree before the court's current term ends next June.

Yet Congress passed this anti-gay marriage law by overwhelming, bipartisan majorities in 1996, and a Democratic president who had support from many gay leaders and gay rights advocates signed it into law. Back then, opponents raised constitutional doubts mainly about the provision — section 2 — that no state was required to recognize same-sex marriages from another state. Some of the opponents said merely that the provision was unnecessary since states have historically had the discretion to determine whether to recognize marriages from other states.

Far less attention was paid to the provision, section 3, that defined marriage for purposes of federal law as the union of one man and one woman. The federal government had never before established a national definition for marriage, but to many people it seemed unsurprising that the government would have that authority. And the provision seemed to have no immediate impact since no state at the time granted marriage rights to gay or lesbian couples.

Things are different today. The harm that the law imposes is now tangible and concrete. Thousands of same-sex couples are legally married in the United States. Six states and the District of Columbia allow same-sex couples to marry; so do Canada, the United States' neighbor to the north, and nine other countries at latest count. At least one state, Maryland, recognizes same-sex marriages from other jurisdictions; and Maryland is one of three states — Maine and Washington are the others — that have measures on the Nov. 6 ballot to legalize same-sex marriages.

These legal developments unmask the federal law for what it is: not a defense of marriage, but an offense against marriage. Congress approved the law in 1996 for reasons that seemed self-evident: preserving traditional marriages, protecting kids and promoting morality. Today, the law is recognized as denying legally married gay and lesbian couples benefits — financial and otherwise — matter-of-factly extended to opposite-sex couples living in the same state, even on the same block.

Edith Windsor, the DOMA victim in the most recent federal court decision, was hit with a $363,000 estate tax bill after her wife, Thea Spyer, died in 2009. Windsor and Spyer, New York residents, had married in Canada two years earlier; New York recognized same-sex marriages from other jurisdictions even before the state legislature voted to approve gay marriage in June 2011.

In opposite-sex marriages, a spouse's estate passes to his or her surviving spouse without incurring federal tax liability. But under DOMA, Windsor was not eligible for that same, uncontroversial tax benefit. The plaintiffs in other DOMA challenges have suffered similar, if less dramatic, financial disadvantages. The widower of former congressman Gerry Studds was denied Social Security survivors benefits. Several current or former federal employees have been prevented from extending health insurance or retirement to their spouses.

In ruling for Windsor last week [Oct. 18], the New York-based Second U.S. Circuit Court of Appeals held that laws that single gays and lesbians out for unfavorable treatment are subject to heightened constitutional scrutiny. The majority in the 2-1 decision cited the history of discrimination against gays and their lack of political power to prevent legally sanctioned discrimination.

Having raised the bar a bit, the court then rejected all of the rationales offered by lawyers for House Republicans to uphold the law. (The Obama administration no longer defends the law.) The court said the law did not help maintain a uniform definition of marriage, protect the federal treasury, preserve a traditional understanding of marriage or encourage responsible procreation.

The case, *Windsor v. United States*, is viewed as the best of four cases pending before the Supreme Court for the justices to use to resolve the issue. One reason: Justice Elena Kagan, the former solicitor general, may be disqualified from the other cases, but not from this one. The justices have the cases ready for conference early next month. The Second Circuit must have been aware of that schedule as it rushed its decision out only three weeks after argument.

When the case is argued, the challengers will certainly face combative questions from Justice Antonin Scalia. The court's guardian of constitutional originalism will undoubtedly contend that a provision adopted in 1868 — the Fourteenth Amendment's Equal Protection Clause — was not intended or understood to say anything about gay marriage.

Scalia will be right on that point, but irrelevant. Despite Scalia's protests, the Constitution is in fact a living document for an ever-changing country and its people. None of the Fourteenth Amendment's framers would have understood it to prohibit discrimination on the basis of sex, but the Supreme Court decisions from the 1970s applying the Equal Protection Clause for that purpose are now well established.

The pivotal vote in the DOMA case likely rests with Justice Anthony M. Kennedy. When he led the court in striking down anti-sodomy laws in 2003, Kennedy made clear his view that the Constitution protects gay and straight people alike. "As the Constitution endures," Kennedy wrote, "persons in every generation can invoke its principles in their search for greater freedom." Weighed against those principles, DOMA seems doomed.

Political developments outside the Supreme Court also were trending toward marriage equality. After suffering an uninterrupted string of defeats by state voters stretching back to the 1990s, gay rights advocates won victories in four states on Nov. 6, 2012. Voters in Maine, Maryland, and Washington approved laws to recognize marriage rights for same-sex couples, while Minnesota voters rejected a constitutional amendment to bar gay couples from marrying.

"Tipping Point" on Gay Marriage?

(*Jost on Justice*, Nov. 7, 2012)

> *As Maine goes, so goes the nation.*
> — Traditional political adage

The press release hit e-mail boxes shortly before midnight on election night (Nov. 6): "Mainers Approve Marriage for Same-Sex Couples; First Time Freedom to Marry Passed in Ballot Measure." For gay rights advocates, the vote in Maine broke a string of 31 consecutive defeats in statewide voting on marriage equality. By the next morning, however, they could claim a four-state winning streak, as voters in Maryland and Washington state also approved measures to recognize same-sex marriages and Minnesotans rejected a measure to ban same-sex marriage in the state.

Voting in all four states was close, but not razor-thin. The gay marriage proposals won with 53 percent in Maine, 52 percent in Maryland and Washington. In Minnesota, the constitutional amendment to define marriage as the union of one man and one woman failed with a little under 48 percent of the vote.

The margins were far smaller than the 2-to-1 majorities that gay marriage opponents typically gained in their string of victories dating from 1998 in Alaska and Hawaii. Still, a win is a win, however close, whether in baseball or politics. Gay rights organizations were trumpeting the results even as gays and lesbians around the country were hailing the victories as a watershed event. "The word tipping point comes to mind," Ian McCann, a gay journalist in Dallas, posted on his Facebook page.

LGBT Americans had other grounds for celebrating. Tammy Baldwin, a Democrat, will become the first openly LGBT member of the Senate in January after defeating her Republican opponent, popular former governor Tommy Thompson, by a 5 percent-plus margin. Baldwin's House seat was won by another openly gay Democrat, Mark Pocan. Mark Takano, a Japanese American, became the first openly gay person of color to be elected to Congress by winning a House seat in California. In all, the Gay and Lesbian Victory Fund counts six openly gay members of the U.S. House and seven candidates who won election as the first or the only out members of their state legislatures. "This was a breathtaking leap forward," said Chuck Wolfe, president and CEO of the fund.

Gays and lesbians were also celebrating President Obama's re-election. Obama had disappointed the LGBT community in his first two years in office by moving slowly on repealing the military's "don't ask, don't tell" policy and failing to get behind a federal bill to ban anti-gay discrimination. But he solidified support after signing the "don't ask, don't tell" repealer in December 2010 and then again when he endorsed marriage equality for same-sex couples in May 2012.

More important than any individual race or ballot measure, gay marriage appears to have achieved majority support nationwide, according to several recent polls, and with that support appears to be receding as a political wedge issue. Republican strategists used anti-gay marriage amendments in 2004 to help drive the GOP base to the poll. The tactic may or may not have helped George W. Bush carry Ohio and with it win re-election, but regardless there was little evidence in the 2012 balloting that support for gay marriage carried a political cost. At the head of the ticket, Republican Mitt Romney said he opposed gay marriage but did not highlight the issue.

The victories in Maryland and Washington came after state legislatures voted to recognize same-sex marriages; in both states, Democratic governors pushed the measures through Democratic-controlled legislatures, but won only thanks to a handful of votes from Republican lawmakers backing the party lines. Opponents forced referendums on the measures, professing confidence that voters would reject the laws; they were wrong.

Once the newly approved laws take effect, gay marriage will be legal in nine states — Connecticut, Iowa, Maine, Maryland, Massachusetts, New Hampshire, New York, Vermont, Washington — plus the District of Columbia. Of those 10 jurisdictions, elected lawmakers voted their approval in eight — all but Iowa and Massachusetts. Opponents can no longer blame activist judges alone for "redefining" marriage; the change is now coming through the political process.

The argument over the litigation strategy versus the political strategy has simmered within the LGBT community. Those who favored going to courts argued for boldly claiming constitutional rights now, not later; those who stressed the political route warned of a backlash that could harm, not help, the cause. From the perspective of 2012, it appears that both sides can claim vindication. Without litigation, the issue would never have risen to the top of the national agenda. Without victories in legislatures and at the ballot box, favorable court rulings will be hard to win and — as in California, with Proposition 8 — at risk of reversal.

The wall of anti-gay marriage constitutional amendments, adopted in most red and a handful of blue states, now poses a daunting obstacle for marriage equality advocates. Reversing them through the political process is out of the question today, and perhaps for the foreseeable future. For that reason, the focus of attention must inevitably shift to the Supreme Court, which could decide to hear the constitutional challenge to Proposition 8 later this term. As Mr. Dooley wisely observed, the Supreme Court reads the election returns. It remains to be seen whether the justices will look to Maine as a bellwether on this issue.

The DOMA and Proposition 8 cases gave the Supreme Court its first opportunity to consider marriage rights for same-sex couples since the justices' curt dismissal of the issue back in 1972. The court's 5-4 ruling in United States v. Windsor found DOMA unconstitutional. The decision by a different 5-4 majority in Hollingsworth v. Perry represented a victory of sorts for gay marriage advocates. The court dismissed the effort by supporters of the initiative to reinstate the measure after lower courts had struck it down. The ruling left unsettled the constitutionality of other state gay-marriage bans, but in California it cleared the way for wedding bells to ring for same-sex couples.

Gay Weddings Busting Out

(*Jost on Justice*, June 30, 2013)

The weddings were hastily arranged, with little time to notify friends and family before the happy couples rushed to city hall. There was no music nor flowers except for the corsages worn by the men and a bouquet carried by one of the women. But what the weddings lacked in trappings was more than made up for in high drama and heartfelt celebration.

Kris Perry and Sandy Stier and Paul Katami and Jeff Zarrillo, both couples together for more than a decade, had to go to the U.S. Supreme Court to win the right to get married in their home state of California. Twice, the people of their state had voted that they could not wed: in 2000 and then again in 2008. They sued in federal court for the right to marry against strong doubts that they could win and fears that a loss would set their cause back.

The path to marriage was cleared by an ambiguous ruling from the Supreme Court on Wednesday [June 26] and a sudden decision by the Ninth U.S. Circuit Court of Appeals on Friday afternoon to lift the judicial order that had kept them in legal limbo despite two lower-court victories.

With all that, government officials enlisted to perform the ceremony — California Attorney General Kamala Harris in San Francisco and Mayor Antonio Villaraigosa in Los Angeles — naturally emphasized the long struggle as the couples prepared to exchange vows. "Today, their wait is finally over," Harris said as TV cameras captured the scene with Perry and Stier before her. Some 90 minutes later, Villaraigosa echoed the point with Katami and Zarrillo beaming before him. "Today, your wait is finally over," he said.

For all of the excitement of the week, however, the wait is not over for most of the gay and lesbian couples in the United States. Two Supreme Court decisions pushed the fight for marriage equality ahead by only a couple of steps and only by the narrowest of margins.

The court's 5-4 decision in *United States v. Windsor* to strike down the federal Defense of Marriage Act took the federal government out of the business of discriminating against legally married same-sex couples. But it has no direct impact on the laws now in 36 states that bar gay and lesbian couples from being wed. In *Hollingsworth v. Perry*, a different 5-4 majority allowed California's Proposition 8 to die at the hands of a now-retired, gay-partnered federal judge in San Francisco. But the justices made no comment on the plea by the lawyers for the two couples to constitutionalize marriage rights for gays and lesbians nationwide.

The court's rhetoric in *Windsor* may set the stage for that to happen, but not in the immediate future. In his opinion for the majority, Justice Anthony M. Kennedy based the decision on federalism grounds. DOMA, he said, departed from the federal government's traditional deference to the states on marriage law. New York or any other state, he reasoned, was free to decide on its own whether to grant legal recognition to same-sex couples.

In reaching that conclusion, Kennedy emphasized that a state's decision to allow same-sex couples to marry "conferred upon them a dignity and status of immense import." Kennedy rejected DOMA without even acknowledging the possible reasons for Congress to have enacted it. "[N]o legitimate purpose," he wrote, "overcomes the purpose and effect to disparage and injure those whom the State, through its marriage laws, sought to protect in personhood and dignity.

For good measure, Kennedy forcefully rejected the argument from opponents that gay marriage is bad for the kids. To the contrary, Kennedy explained, barring gay or lesbian couples from getting married "humiliates the tens of thousands of children now being raised by same-sex couples" and makes it hard for them to understand "the integrity and closeness of their own family."

The court's four liberal justices — Ginsburg, Breyer, Sotomayor, and Kagan — joined Kennedy's opinion with no further comment. In an appearance at the Aspen Institute on Saturday, however, Kagan hinted at the ruling's potential impact by suggesting that in her view moral disapproval is no adequate basis for legislation at either the federal or state level.

The DOMA ruling leaves a host of issues for government and private lawyers to work out — chiefly, how to define the federal rights of the gay and lesbian couples who live in or move to states that do not recognize their marriages. Federal law traditionally defines marriage based on where a couple lives, not where they came from. After having urged the court to strike down DOMA, the Obama administration must now work through a web of laws and regulations to make federal benefits a reality for legally married same-sex couples.

In California, gay marriage opponents tried to gum up the works by asking the Supreme Court on Saturday to override the Ninth Circuit's action to allow same-sex weddings to proceed. Kennedy, supervising justice for the circuit, rejected the move on Sunday. The brief skirmish left California bursting with gay pride and scores of couples pledging to love and comfort, have and hold, honor and respect, for the rest of their lives. "I don't know about you," Villaraigosa said as he ended the ceremony for Paul and Jeff, "but I got goose bumps."

Six months later, I noted that marriage equality remained a work in progress and that, with any advances blocked in red states, courts were to be the next battlegrounds. I suggested that judges who read the Supreme Court's decision on DOMA faithfully could do nothing else but strike down the bans on same-sex marriage.

Courts Next on Marriage Equality
(*Jost on Justice*, Dec. 15, 2013)

The past year has been very, very good for marriage equality for gay and lesbian couples in the United States. In a 13-month period (November through November), the number of states recognizing marriage rights for same-sex couples more than doubled from six (plus the District of Columbia) to 16; the number of people living in marriage equality states more than tripled from about 35 million to 118 million.

But hold the applause. Despite that progress for gay rights supporters, somewhat more than 60 percent of Americans still live in states where same-sex couples cannot marry. And the barriers to marriage equality in almost all of those 34 states are formidable. All but a few have Republican-controlled legislatures and Republican governors, and the Republican Party has yet to get the memo that most Americans now support marriage rights for gay and lesbian couples.

In addition, most of those states have constitutional amendments defining marriage as "one man and one woman," provisions that cannot be repealed by simple legislation. Voters approved most of those anti-gay measures in the decade from the mid-1990s through 2004 while gay marriage supporters were focusing mostly on court cases.

Gay marriage was terra incognita for the voters at that time. As of November 2004, Adam and Steve could get married in only one state: Massachusetts. It was easy for anti-gay groups to depict this uncharted terrain as hostile to traditional marriage, unhealthy for children, and unsettling for public morality. Through 2004, all the amendments but one (Oregon's) won approval with more than 60 percent of the votes cast.

Since Massachusetts, gay marriage supporters have turned to and succeeded in the political sphere. Along with the District of Columbia, 12 states have decided to allow same-sex marriages by legislation, not by judicial fiat. That number includes Maine, Maryland, and Washington, where voters last year rejected referenda aimed at overturning the legislative enactments. And it includes five more states that enacted same-sex marriage legislation since November 2012: Minnesota, Rhode Island, Delaware, Hawaii, and Illinois.

The political route, however, appears now to be, if not at a dead end, at the start of a steep incline. So attention turns to the courts, which yielded two of the state victories in the past year. Most significantly, the Supreme Court in late June greenlighted gay marriage in California by leaving on the books a lower federal court decision that struck down the state's anti-gay marriage initiative Proposition 8 (*Hollingsworth v. Perry*).

On the same day, the court struck down the federal Defense of Marriage Act (DOMA), which barred federal marriage-based benefits to same-sex couples even if legally married in their home states. The ruling in *United States v. Windsor* provided the basis for a New Jersey trial-level court three months later to strike down the state's ban on same-sex marriage. The court reasoned that New Jersey's law, by denying federal benefits to same-sex couples, violated the state constitution's own equal protection requirements. Advised that the New Jersey Supreme Court would likely affirm the decision, Gov. Chris Christie decided the state would not appeal.

Gay marriage supporters sense another possible victory in New Mexico, where the state supreme court heard arguments on the issue on Oct. 23. News accounts viewed the questions from the justices as favoring the gay marriage advocates. Meanwhile, marriage equality supporters in Oregon say they have enough signatures to qualify a proposal to repeal the state's gay marriage ban for the November 2014 ballot.

Meanwhile, federal court suits are pending in 17 states, including Oregon, aimed at judicially overturning gay marriage bans, according to a compilation by the national advocacy group Freedom to Marry. One other federal court suit, in Tennessee, is limited to seeking to force the state to recognize same-sex marriages from other states. These suits are pending in federal courts in some of the reddest of the red states, such as Arkansas, Mississippi, Oklahoma, and South Carolina. A comparable suit is pending in state court in Colorado. Some suits are far along— notably, those in Nevada and Michigan; others have just been filed.

In all of these cases, the Supreme Court's decision in *Windsor* is potentially powerful support for gay marriage advocates. Admittedly, Justice Anthony M. Kennedy took care in his opinion for the 5-4 majority to acknowledge the states' "unquestioned authority" over marriage law. In the critical passages, however, Kennedy said that the federal government's refusal to recognize same-sex marriages places those couples "in an unstable position," burdens their lives "in visible and public ways," and "humiliates tens of thousands of children now being raised by same-sex couples."

Suppose, for a moment, that you are a federal judge, with those passages before you, trying to write a decision upholding a state's ban on same-sex marriages. What arguments are still open to you? Harm to traditional marriage? Harm to children? Harm to society? In the first cases after Massachusetts, state high courts in New York and Washington accepted those arguments, in closely divided decisions. Now, almost a decade later, they fail, by experience as well as logic.

Opponents of gay marriage are losing in the court of public opinion and being pushed back in political forums. With so many suits pending, federal courts may not all agree. But the arc of history is bending toward marriage equality. And the Supreme Court's ultimate role in this litigation may only be to ratify a consensus that Americans have already accepted.

Within the week this column appeared, the New Mexico Supreme Court and a federal district court judge in Utah struck down those states' bans on gay marriage. I read the news while on vacation; it was stunning to learn that my prediction was proving so quickly to be well-founded.

Over the next six months, more than two dozen courts followed suit: mostly federal but a few state courts as well. Then in summer 2014, three federal appeals courts — the Tenth Circuit in the Utah and Oklahoma cases, the Fourth Circuit in a Virginia case, and the Seventh Circuit in cases from Indiana and Wisconsin —ruled gay marriage bans unconstitutional.

The issue seemed destined for a showdown at the Supreme Court, probably in the 2014-2015 term. The justices surprised most observers by declining in October 2014 to take up the states' appeals from the circuit court decisions. In November, however, the Sixth Circuit upheld anti-gay marriage provisions in four states: Kentucky, Michigan, Ohio, and Tennessee. The justices agreed to hear the plaintiffs' appeals with arguments in late April 2015 and a decision by the end of June.

In the meantime, an unseemly credit-taking controversy had arisen from a history of the Proposition 8 case written by an experienced reporter who had been granted exclusive access to the plaintiffs and their lawyers from the early days of the case.

Heroes of Marriage Equality
(*Jost on Justice*, May 18, 2014)

Richard Kluger opened his magisterial history of the struggle for racial equality in education, *Simple Justice*, by telling the story of poor black families in backwater Clarendon County, S.C., protesting for school bus transportation for their children. The NAACP Legal Defense Fund turned the grassroots protest into a court case, *Briggs v. Elliott*, which predated by a year the case now memorialized in history as *Brown v. Board of Education.*

Jo Becker opens her book on "the fight for marriage equality" with the story of Chad Griffin, a well-to-do, well-connected political and public relations consultant in chi-chi West Hollywood, Calif. Becker, an award-winning journalist, embedded herself in Griffin's camp for four years to chronicle what she hoped would be a landmark Supreme Court ruling for gay marriage.

Unfortunately for Becker and her book, *Forcing the Spring*, the Supreme Court did not use Griffin's built-from-the-top-down case to outlaw marriage discrimination against gay and lesbian couples in one judicial blow. Undeterred, she opens her book, however, by likening Griffin to civil rights heroine Rosa Parks and depicting Griffin's decision to challenge California's 2008 ban on gay marriage, Proposition 8, as the beginning of the marriage equality revolution.

The movement for marriage equality for same-sex couples actually marked a 10-year anniversary last week. The first legally sanctioned marriages of gay and lesbian couples in the United States were officiated in Massachusetts on May 17, 2004, thanks to a ruling six months earlier by the state's highest court. In its 4-3 ruling in *Goodridge v. Dep't of Public Health* (2003), the Supreme Judicial Court of Massachusetts said same-sex couples had a right under the state's constitution to the legal benefits of civil marriage and gave the Massachusetts legislature 180 days to pass a law consistent with its ruling. When the state Senate asked whether civil unions for same-sex couples would suffice, the court said no — setting the stage for marriages to begin when the 180-day deadline expired.

Becker's book includes no index entry for Goodridge and only slight references to the lead attorney, Mary Bonauto, who had been litigating gay marriage cases in New England states for several years by then. Bonauto and her colleagues at the Boston-based Gay and Lesbian Advocates and Defenders went on to win the first lower court ruling to strike down the federal Defense of Marriage Act (DOMA), which barred federal marriage-based benefits for legally married same-sex couples.

Bonauto appears for the first time in Becker's book at page 280. Becker uses her only to commend the federal court trial that Griffin's dream team of strange bedfellow lawyers — conservative Republican Theodore Olson and liberal Democrat David Boies — put together to challenge Proposition 8.

Another of the heroes given short shrift in Becker's account is Evan Wolfson, who can rightly be called the intellectual father of the marriage equality movement and its most important political tactician. As a student at Harvard Law School, Wolfson wrote a 140-page thesis, "Same-Sex Marriage and Morality: The Human Rights Vision of the Constitution," one of the earliest arguments for recognizing marriage rights for gay and lesbian couples.

Wolfson went on to head the national marriage project at Lambda Legal Defense and Education Fund from 1989 to 2001 before founding Freedom to Marry as a stand-alone lobbying and election-oriented organization. Becker notes this history, but calls Freedom to Marry's strategy "plodding." Wolfson appears mainly as one of the established gay rights leaders who warned against Griffin's go-for-broke federal court strategy.

The more serious slights in Becker's book, however, are the countless gay men, lesbians, and straight allies who had been working on the marriage issue for years before Griffin came on to the scene. The plaintiffs in the early marriage cases took some risks in agreeing to be identified with a cause that was then politically unpopular and legally uncharted. The recruited plaintiffs in the Prop 8 case — Paul Katami and Jeff Zarrillo and Kris Perry and Sandy Stier — sacrificed some privacy and suffered some harassment, but they had no real fear of backlash in their gay-friendly communities in Los Angeles and the San Francisco Bay area.

Becker also credits Griffin, and Griffin alone, with marriage equality's first electoral victories: the pro-gay marriage votes in November 2012 in Maine, Maryland, Minnesota, and Washington. In Becker's telling, it was Griffin's decision, as president of the national Human Rights Campaign, to funnel money to those states that turned the tide. Freedom to Marry's role goes mostly unmentioned — and the same for the in-state organizers and political foot soldiers.

At the Supreme Court, Becker treats the Prop 8 case as the main attraction and the DOMA case the justices agreed to hear, *United States v. Windsor*, as sideshow. When the Prop 8 case is dismissed without a ruling, Griffin nevertheless manufactures the iconic photo op of the four California plaintiffs emerging arm in arm, along with Griffin and Boies, at the top of the Supreme Court steps. And Becker gives Olson the credit for the expansive language that Justice Anthony M. Kennedy included in Windsor in striking down DOMA — language cited in the unbroken string of pro-gay marriage rulings since.

Marriage equality remains a work in progress. Becker has told a good, if partly misleading, story. The history of the fight for marriage equality is yet to be written.

7

#CivilRights

The Supreme Court outlawed racial segregation in public schools in 1954, the year that I entered first grade in my home town of Nashville, Tennessee. The school system slow-walked its way to integration; when I graduated from junior high school eight years later, my school still had no African American students. And the private high school that I attended also had no African American students until years after my graduation. I wrote an editorial for the school newspaper calling for the admission of black students; it was initially spiked but then published after I wrote another editorial criticizing the censorship.

Issues of racial justice have continued to be important for me throughout my career. Here is what I wrote on the 50th anniversary of Brown v. Board of Education *in a review for* Legal Times *of two excellent histories of the case. One highlights the plaintiffs and lawyers who shaped the litigation; the other examines broader social and political changes that helped shape the Supreme Court's eventual decision.*

Brown v. Board After 50-Years
(Legal Times, May 3, 2004)

From Jim Crow to Civil Rights: The Supreme Court and the Struggle for Racial Equality. By Michael J. Klarman. Oxford University Press, New York.

Simple Justice: The History of Brown v. Board of Education and Black America's Struggle for Equality. By Richard Kluger. Vintage, New York.

The fiftieth anniversary of *Brown v. Board of Education* has brought forth an outpouring of books examining the Supreme Court's landmark decision to outlaw racial segregation in public education from all angles. For students of history, two of the most interesting tell the story of the decision — how it came about when it did —in strikingly different ways.

Richard Kluger's magisterial history of the Brown litigation, published in 1976 and now reissued with a new final chapter, tells the story in mythic terms. Kluger starts his story — a decade in the writing — with African American parents who braved white power establishments in segregationist bastions to demand better education for their children.

Their causes were taken up by a band of civil rights lawyers, spearheaded by the indomitable and indefatigable Thurgood Marshall. They fashioned and executed a legal strategy that forced a fractious Supreme Court to confront the contradictions of separate but equal. And, by a fortunate coincidence, the court pondered long enough to allow the arrival of a new chief justice, Earl Warren, endowed with the political skills to win the wavering justices' assent to a unanimous decision.

Michael Klarman tells the story of *Brown* only as a small part of the history of race law from the birth and entrenchment of segregation through the first decade of its supposed demise. Klarman, a professor at the University of Virginia Law School [*update*: now at Harvard] who also spent a decade on his book, deals hardly at all with personalities. Indeed, he completely passes over the litigants in *Brown*. Instead, Klarman sees Supreme Court decision-making as largely determined by broad social, economic and political conditions.

Klarman posits that justices make decisions along two axes — one legal, one political — whose relative importance varies from case to case and justice to justice. In the indeterminate area of constitutional law, Klarman thinks the political typically dominates. So the meaning of the

Fourteenth Amendment necessarily depends on events and conditions outside the court. Kluger seems to proceed instead from the view that in constitutional law — as in public policy — some decisions are right, and some are wrong.

Thus, Kluger and Klarman differ in recounting the court's 1896 ruling in *Plessy v. Ferguson* to uphold racial segregation in public accommodations. Kluger depictcs the court's decision — resting on the premise that separate but equal in no way consigned Negroes to an inferior status — as willfully callous and stupid, not to mention legally erroneous. Klarman, on the other hand, thinks the court could have done nothing else. Post-Reconstruction white supremacy was a fact, Klarman says, that the court had no power to stand against even if the justices had wanted to.

Klarman views the demise of segregation as a gradual and inexorable process resulting from a constellation of factors. The migration of blacks to better-paying jobs in the North created a political constituency there for improving race relations. It also led to some relaxation of the strictures of segregation in the South that created breathing space for blacks to petition for redress of their grievances. He also notes the importance of the founding of the National Association for the Advancement of Colored People in 1909 and its legal arm, the NAACP Legal Defense and Educational Fund, three decades later in 1940.

Kluger puts the Legal Defense Fund in the foreground, external conditions in the background. Marshall was tapped by Charles Houston, dean of Howard Law School, to tackle segregation as a full-time mission. Marshall then traveled throughout the South and Border States in the 1940s to organize anti-segregation litigation, heedless of personal dangers and undeterred by the odds against him. With a core of half a dozen lawyers, the Legal Defense Fund assembled a solid evidentiary and legal case against segregated schools.

By this time, Klarman emphasizes, other outside forces were undermining segregation too. The dislocation of World War II engendered increased restiveness among African Americans, especially among black veterans who fought for democracy in Europe and the Pacific only to return to second-class citizenship in the United States. Some in white America also saw the contradiction. In any event, racial segregation was a liability in seeking international favor in the emerging Cold War with the Soviet Union.

Kluger tells the story of each of the four *Brown* cases in detail — from trial to Supreme Court argument in December 1952 and reargument in December 1953. Klarman skips straight to the justices' deliberations. His deterministic thesis seems to point to the conclusion that the court was bound to outlaw segregation, but he must account for the justices' initial, splintered vote — with two justices in favor of upholding segregation and three, including Chief Justice Fred M. Vinson, wavering. Vinson's death paved the way for Warren's appointment.

The rest is history. Separate but equal has no place in public education, Warren declared from the bench on May 17, 1954. A year later, however, the court said school districts need not desegregate immediately, nor by a fixed date, but "with all deliberate speed." Kluger closed his book originally with Marshall's confident prediction in 1955 that southerners "would get tired of having Negro lawyers beating 'em every day in court." Klarman carries the story forward through a decade of massive resistance and foot-dragging. By 1964, only 2 percent of black pupils were attending desegregated schools in the South.

Klarman says that with little political support—President Eisenhower was conspicuously silent — the court had no choice but to lie low. Only when external conditions changed — chiefly because of the national indignation over the televised abuse of civil rights demonstrators — did Presidents Kennedy and Johnson and Congress lend support to the court. But, as Kluger says in his new chapter, political conditions changed back, beginning in the 1970s. Today, he says, much of white America thinks the racial issue solved. Black America, meanwhile, is split between a middle- and upper class that enjoys relative comfort despite the always-present consciousness of being part of a minority and an underclass that lives in "a vicious cycle of ghetto existence."

Together, Klarman and Kluger point to a single lesson. To borrow the astrologers' axiom, history impels, but it does not compel. *Brown* may or may not have been impossible years earlier, but it resulted eventually from a combination of historical conditions and personal efforts. At present, the political will to provide equal education for all students — white, black and brown too — may seem lacking. But the future is in our hands, not yet in history's.

In a companion piece, I reviewed two other books, both by African American law professors and both critical of the contemporary status of education for minority pupils.

Hold the Celebration
(*Legal Times*, May 3, 2004)

Charles J. Ogletree, Jr. *All Deliberate Speed: Reflections on the First Half Century of* Brown v. Board of Education. Norton, New York.

Sheryll Cashin. *The Failures of Integration: How Race and Class Are Undermining the American Dream*, Public Affairs, New York.

Hold the celebrations for *Brown v. Board of Education*. After 50 years of court-ordered desegregation, public schools for blacks (and Latinos) have gone from "separate but equal" in law to increasingly separate and demonstrably unequal in fact over the past 15 years.

That's the message of two prominent African American law school professors: Harvard's Charles Ogletree and Georgetown's Sheryll Cashin. In books written for *Brown*'s 50th anniversary, Ogletree and Cashin both cite the evidence of "resegregation" over the past 15 years — a trend fostered by the Rehnquist Court's hands-off attitude toward local school policies.

Black and Latino pupils are more likely today to be attending racially or ethnically identifiable schools than in the late 1980s. These "black" and "Latino" schools typically have fewer resources than "white" schools — as Cashin demonstrates by a close comparison of Wilson High School in Washington, one of the city's best, with the far better equipped Whitman High School in suburban Bethesda, Md.

Neither Ogletree or Cashin is giving up on integration, but they both depict the ambivalent views in black America on the issue. Both see merit in the growing number of charter schools designed by blacks for blacks — the consequences for racial separatism notwithstanding.

More broadly, both professors want white America to pay down its debt to black America. Cashin wants a serious federal commitment to a program of social justice, but admits she got nowhere with the issue as a policy adviser in the Clinton White House. Ogletree is a prominent advocate for reparations — for example, as attorney for plaintiffs in a suit seeking compensation for the Tulsa race riot of 1921. Both are hopeful but realistic about white America's likely response.

#RacialJustice

The Roberts Court took on the issue of racial integration in public schools in a pair of cases from Seattle and Louisville-Jefferson County, Kentucky, in Roberts's second term as chief justice. The 5-4 decision in Parents Involved in Community Schools v. Seattle School District No. 1 *(2007) prohibits local school boards from using race in pupil assignments in order to promote diversity in individual schools. Roberts wrote for a plurality of four justices, with Kennedy providing the fifth vote in a concurring opinion that left school boards some options for trying to break down de facto segregation. Breyer spoke for the four liberal dissenters in a long and forceful opinion that he summarized from the bench; I used Breyer's dissent to discuss the early signs of the Roberts Court's willingness to upset established precedents.*

Agents of Change
(*CQ Weekly*, July 16, 2007)

From the bench on the final day of this Supreme Court term, Stephen G. Breyer offered a stinging dissent in the case limiting local school board power to adopt racial mixing policies — but the barb also summed up moderate and liberal frustration at the court's behavior during the preceding nine months. "It's not often in law," the justice said, "that so few have changed so much so quickly."

Breyer was referring directly to the conservative majority of his colleagues, which solidified during the year under Chief Justice John G. Roberts Jr. But his remark applies as much to George W. Bush and his judicial-nomination advisers, who in just 24 months shifted the court markedly to the right because of their choices of Roberts and Samuel A. Alito Jr.

Bush's success in securing the court's conservative ideology for the next decade or longer — no matter who succeeds him — seems likely to stand as one of his hallmark second-term accomplishments, all the more remarkable given the historic narrowness of his two elections.

But as president, Bush has consistently acted as though empowered by a popular mandate to remake the federal judiciary to satisfy the conservatives who are his political base. Roberts and Alito were screened to suit them. (His failed choice, Harriet Miers, notably was not.) Both reached the court with less than impressive Senate support: Only two chief justices were confirmed with more "no" votes than the 22 cast against Roberts, and no successful nominee in more than a century has won less support from the opposition party than Alito, who received just four Democrats' votes.

At his hearings Roberts extolled the virtues of judicial modesty and the benefits of unanimous decisions, and his first term's results appeared to match those views with more unanimous rulings and fewer 5-4 decisions than in the recent past. But his second term saw the highest share of one-vote decisions in the court's history — 35 percent, or 24 of the 68 argued cases.

With Roberts and Alito voting the same way on all but five cases in the past year, the court cut a wider swath through established law than happened in the first two terms of the previous three chief justices. *Brown v. Board of Education* came in 1954, Earl Warren's first term, but his court's signature decisions on criminal law, reapportionment and free speech all came in the 1960s. The Warren Burger Court never did more than trim those precedents. And the court under William H. Rehnquist did not start its marked turn to the right until its third term.

By contrast, the first full year with Bush's two justices on the court has upset decades of case law. Its school decision unsettles precedents since the 1960s upholding race-conscious pupil assignment policies to promote racial mixing. Its ruling upholding the federal ban on "partial birth" abortions contradicts a requirement, first laid down in 1973, that any abortion regulation include a health exception for the woman. And it effectively gutted one of the two major provisions in the McCain-Feingold campaign finance law, just four years after the court upheld the statute.

In those cases, Roberts and Alito said they were following precedents even while emasculating them. In two others, they joined majorities to explicitly overturn precedents. One, from the 1960s, had created an excuse for missing deadlines for appeals in "unique circumstances." The other, from 1911, had prevented manufacturers from dictating minimum retail prices for their products; that ruling will likely mean higher consumer costs.

In other ways, business interests that are another big part of the GOP base fared especially well in the past year. Ruling after ruling limited the legal remedies for workers, consumers, investors or taxpayers against wrongs committed by employers, manufacturers, corporate executives or government contractors. Bush's faith-based initiative also got a measure of legal immunity with a ruling making it difficult for anyone to challenge the government's largess to religious groups on grounds of separation of church and state.

This rightward shift is likely to be long-lasting. Roberts is 52, and Alito is 57, so both can be expected to serve two decades or more. Clarence Thomas is 59. Only Antonin Scalia and the swing voter, Anthony M. Kennedy, are older than 70, but both seem in good health and to relish their jobs. And so the justices most likely to leave soon are in the liberal bloc. At 87, John Paul Stevens is inevitably near the end of his tenure. Ruth Bader Ginsburg, a cancer survivor, is 74. David H. Souter is only 67 but has been on the job 17 years, and Thomas Goldstein of the well-regarded *SCOTUSblog* speculates that Souter may gladly give up his robes to return to New Hampshire.

Conservatives are eager to capitalize on what Bush has wrought. They want to overturn *Roe v. Wade*, bar all racial preferences in higher education and limit congressional power vis-à-vis the states. All are ideas without great popular support, and in a legislative forum compromise would be necessary to change course on each. At the Supreme Court, however, counting to five is all it takes to change "so much so quickly."

The Supreme Court upheld the limited use of racial preferences in public colleges and universities in a pair of decisions in 2003 from the University of Michigan: Grutter v. Bollinger *and* Gratz v. Bollinger. Justice O'Connor's majority opinion in Grutter *upheld the law school's admissions policies because race was one part of a "holistic" evaluation of each individual applicant; Chief Justice Rehnquist's opinion in* Gratz *struck down the undergraduate college's policies because black and Hispanic applicants were given a large numerical bonus that virtually guaranteed their admission.*

The Roberts Court took on the issue in a case from the University of Texas nearly a decade later. As indicated in my column in advance of arguments, supporters of affirmative action feared that the case, Fisher v. University of Texas, *could lead to a decision prohibiting even the limited use of race in admissions policies to help promote racial and ethnic diversity. In advance of the arguments, I wrote about the history of the Fourteenth Amendment to refute the arguments by Justices Scalia and Thomas among others that it completely prohibited any governmental preferences for disadvantaged minorities.*

History and Affirmative Action
(*Jost on Justice*, Aug. 27, 2012)

Supreme Court justices were hopelessly divided after the first round of arguments in the landmark school desegregation case *Brown v. Board of Education* (1954). To gather more information — and buy some time — they asked opposing attorneys for a new round of briefs and arguments on what the authors of the post-Civil War Fourteenth Amendment thought about the issue.

Despite the extensive research and argument, Chief Justice Earl Warren wrote in the eventual opinion that the history was "inconclusive" on the issue before the justices. So Warren went on to analyze the constitutionality of "separate but equal" in the context of public education in the United States in the mid-twentieth century.

The 21st century Court is now preparing to hear a new case in October on the issue of race-conscious affirmative action policies in higher education (*Fisher v. University of Texas*). The justices have been presented stacks and stacks of friend-of-the-court briefs addressing the issues from every possible perspective, including historical. Once again, the history is ambiguous and to some extent inconclusive. But those justices – think, Antonin Scalia and Clarence Thomas – who view original meaning as the touchstone of constitutional interpretation will be hard pressed to find a complete prohibition on governmental use of racial preferences in the history of the Fourteenth Amendment.

Inconveniently for Scalia's and Thomas's declared opposition to racial preferences, the same Congress that approved the Fourteenth Amendment in June 1866 also voted one month later to extend the life of a government agency set up to provide special aid to newly freed slaves. The Freedmen's Bureau provided clothing, food, and other necessities to former slaves as well as to white Union sympathizers who had fled the South during the Civil War.

Congress originally created the bureau in March 1865 with Abraham Lincoln in the White House and the Civil War about to end. As set out in a brief filed by lawyers with the Constitutional Accountability Project, a progressive Washington advocacy group, the law directed the bureau to provide open-ended assistance to the former slaves but aid to "loyal refugees" only to the extent "necessary to enable them . . . to become self-supporting citizens." The law also authorized the agency to acquire property abandoned in the South for schools for the former slaves.

Congress originally established the Freedmen's Bureau for one year. In 1866, with the former southerner Andrew Johnson in the White House, Congress voted to extend the bureau's life for two years. Johnson vetoed the measure, but Congress overrode the veto in July 1866 by votes of 104-33 in the House and 33-12 in the Senate — substantially more than the two-thirds majority needed.

Opponents in Congress specifically criticized the preferential treatment for the freed slaves. One member said the law treated the freedmen not as equal but superior, "in opposition to the plain spirit of the Constitution." In vetoing the bill, Johnson criticized it as "class legislation." Supporters in Congress answered the criticism by saying the preferential aid was needed to "break down discrimination between whites and blacks."

The bureau was hampered by opposition by unreconstructed southerners and was eventually allowed to fade out of existence after 1871 as northerners' support for reconstruction faded. Opponents of affirmative action today can cite that history to argue that the bureau was viewed as a temporary measure that would no longer be needed once former slaves got on their feet.

Even at the time, however, some supporters recognized the need for longer term measures. "The effects of ages of slavery are not to be removed in a day, by a mere legislative vote," the Rev. William Weston Patton, a white abolitionist, said in a speech in 1877 at Howard University, the historically black college established by the Freedmen's Bureau and named for its first commissioner, Army general Oliver Howard.

Supporters of Reconstruction could not have imagined the new roadblocks that the country would erect to true equality for African Americans. The federal government turned a blind eye as legal, political, and social barriers went up, in the North as well as in the South. The Supreme Court played its ignominious part by striking down the law prohibiting racial discrimination in public accommodations and upholding racial segregation in public education on the legal fiction of separate but equal.

The march toward real racial equality resumed with *Brown* and continued with civil rights legislation in the 1960s and with the growth of affirmative action policies in the 1970s aimed at improving African Americans' opportunities in higher education. Those admissions policies met resistance immediately. Twice, the court has narrowly approved limited consideration of race by state universities: *Regents v. Bakke* (1978); *Grutter v. Bollinger* (2003). In casting the decisive vote in *Grutter*, however, Justice Sandra Day O'Connor voiced the expectation that racial preferences would no longer be needed in another 25 years.

Impatience is no basis for constitutional adjudication, however. The Roberts Court should carefully consider the role of elite public colleges and universities in the United States today and the actual impact of race-conscious admissions on opportunities for racial and ethnic minorities and on the legitimate goal of student diversity. In weighing that evidence, the justices should recognize that the constitutional insistence on equal protection was not written to prevent the government from enacting policies to break down the barriers to actual equality.

Writing again before oral arguments, I argued that the critics' "impatience" with the continuation of racial preferences had no historical justification.

Affirmative Action Showdown
(*Jost on Justice*, Oct. 8, 2012)

When the Supreme Court pulled the plug on an ambitious school desegregation plan for Kansas City in 1995, Justice Ruth Bader Ginsburg complained in dissent that the retreat was both "too swift and too soon" (*Missouri v. Jenkins*). Much the same could be said about the growing discontent among the American public and among many experts about the efforts to use race-conscious admissions policies in order to increase racial and ethnic diversity in U.S. colleges and graduate schools.

The latest manifestation of this supposed re-examination of racial preferences came last week [Oct. 4] in a report by the Century Foundation written by Richard Kahlenberg, a longtime advocate of using socioeconomic status instead of race or ethnicity to increase diversity in higher education. In presenting the report at the progressive think tank's Washington office, Kahlenberg bluntly warned that race-based affirmative action "is likely on its way out" — unpopular with the public and under challenge in legislatures, at the ballot box, and in the courts.

The discontent is fed further by the new book, *Mismatch: How Affirmative Action Hurts Student It's Intended to Help, and Why Universities Won't Admit It*, by UCLA law professor Richard Sander and legal affairs journalist Stuart Taylor Jr. The book elaborates on Sander's empirical research over the past decade that he says shows many beneficiaries of racial preferences fare badly in college or law school, doomed to failure because they are competing with academically superior classmates.

The publication of the report and the book were both timed to coincide with the Supreme Court's oral arguments on Wednesday [Oct. 10] in the latest showdown on affirmative action, *Fisher v. University of Texas*. The justices are being asked to invalidate UT's use of race as part of what administrators describe as a "holistic" evaluation of applicants for about one-fifth of the slots in each year's entering first-year class.

The Fifth U.S. Circuit Court of Appeals upheld UT's policies, saying that they conformed to the criteria set out by the court nine years ago in a University of Michigan case, *Grutter v. Bollinger* (2003). Attorneys representing Abigail Fisher, an unsuccessful white applicant for admission in 2008, argue that UT's policies go beyond the limited use of race allowed under *Grutter*. Alternatively, they urge the court to overrule *Grutter* and severely limit or completely prohibit consideration of race in college and university admissions.

The case can be handicapped easily: Justice Sandra Day O'Connor, who authored the majority opinion in *Grutter*, has been succeeded by Samuel A. Alito Jr., a hard-edged conservative who has cast decisive votes against race-conscious policies in two major decisions since his appointment in 2006. For many court-watchers, the only question in the case is not *whether* but *how far* the court will go in limiting race-conscious admissions policies.

Institutionally, however, the court is not supposed to change course simply because of a change in personnel. So the justices need to closely examine UT's policies, as they have evolved during two decades' worth of litigation, along with the densely statistical debate waged in friend-of-the-court briefs about the overall impact of racial preferences. On both counts, the evidence is less than clear-cut and the interpretations by opposing sides in sharp conflict.

For UT, the pivotal question will be whether the university had good reason to re-introduce some consideration of race after *Grutter* since it was already using an ostensibly race-neutral mechanism to boost enrollment of African American and Hispanic applicants. The state's "Top Ten Percent" law, passed in 1997, guarantees students in the top 10 percent of their high school graduating classes a slot at UT's flagship campus in Austin. With black and Latino students concentrated in racially identifiable schools, the law increases their enrollment, but not enough to satisfy the school. Today, blacks comprise about 4.5 percent of UT's student body, Hispanics 16.9 percent; both figures are below the proportions for the state's population overall.

Justices on both sides may cite the broader policy debate to help make their case. Conservatives will surely cite the supposed costs of racial preferences — stereotyping and stigmatizing minority students — along with Sander's claimed proof of "mismatch." The statistical argument goes far beyond what can be elaborated in a weekly column, but it can be said at least that Sander's conclusion is disputed and, if valid, merely shows the need for universities to follow through with well designed and well resourced academic support for affirmative-action admits.

As for the alleged stigmatization, Sander and Taylor are selective in quoting prominent African Americans as critics of racial preferences, including Supreme Court Justice Clarence Thomas, who has famously described his indignation at bearing "the taint of racial preference." They do not note that the court's only Hispanic justice, Sonia Sotomayor, proudly counts herself as "an affirmative action baby," apparently unaware of any taint due to her status.

The University of Texas admitted its first African American student in 1950, only after a unanimous Supreme Court decision forced it to do so (*Sweatt v. Painter*). Sixty years later, the Austin campus is by no means a model of racial harmony, as seen in a recent report of "bleach ballooning" incidents directed at African American students and fraternity parties with anti-immigrant themes. Admissions policies aimed at making the campus more diverse, on paper and in practice, deserve respectful consideration from a Supreme Court dedicated to equal justice under law.

The court's eventual decision proved to be anticlimactic. By a 7-1 vote (with Justice Kagan recused), the court sent the case back to the Fifth Circuit with instructions that race-based admissions policies could be upheld only if narrowly tailored to promote diversity and no race-neutral alternative was sufficient for that purpose. On remand, the Fifth Circuit again upheld UT's policies, in another split decision. Fisher again asked the Supreme Court to overrule the appeals court's decision; the case was pending as of September 2014.

In the meantime, the court had dealt supporters of affirmative action a partial setback by upholding the right of states to prohibit any use of race or ethnicity in college admissions. The decision upheld a Michigan initiative, adopted by voters three years after the court's ruling in Grutter. Opponents of the initiative argued that the measure went against a doctrine, dating from a Supreme Court decision in the late 1960s, that prohibited laws imposing a special political burden on racial minorities. I wrote about that doctrine in advance of the arguments in Schuette v. Coalition to Defend Affirmative Action and again after the court's 6-2 decision upholding the Michigan measure.

Rights Precedent at Risk
(*Jost at Justice*, Oct. 13, 2013)

When the Akron, Ohio, city council enacted a fair housing ordinance in 1968, opponents drafted and won voter approval of a charter amendment prohibiting adoption of any such law unless approved by a majority of voters. The Supreme Court cried foul. With only one justice dissenting, the court held in *Hunter v. Erickson* (1969) that the Equal Protection Clause prohibits a change in the political process that imposes "special burdens on racial and religious minorities . . . by making it more difficult for them to secure legislation on their behalf."

A decade later, voters in Washington state approved a ballot measure, Initiative 350, that effectively prohibited school districts from using busing for purposes of racial integration while allowing it for any of several other educational policies. Again, the court cried foul, this time by a 5-4 vote. For the majority, Justice Harry A. Blackmun wrote in *Washington v. Seattle School Dist. No. 1* (1982) that the initiative "creates a constitutionally-suspect racial classification and radically restructures the political process," amounting to "a major reordering of the state's educational decisionmaking process."

Together, the cases establish what is called the political restructuring doctrine, a rule unfamiliar even to many legal experts because so rarely invoked. But the federal appeals court in Cincinnati invoked it last year in striking down a Michigan ballot measure that bars racial preferences in state and local government policies, including admissions at public colleges and universities.

The state has appealed that decision to the Supreme Court, which is set to hear arguments in the case this week [Oct. 15]. Supreme Court handicappers are predicting that the decision in *Schuette v. Coalition to Defend Affirmative Action* will significantly limit or possibly even overturn a doctrine that, however infrequently used, is viewed by traditional civil rights groups as a logical and necessary part of equal protection law.

Michigan became one of the major battlegrounds in the war over race-conscious admissions policies in the late 1990s. The anti-racial preference group Center for Individual Rights filed separate challenges against admissions policies at the University of Michigan's flagship undergraduate college in Ann Arbor and the university's law school. In separate cases, the Supreme Court upheld the limited use of race in the law school's admissions policies (*Grutter v. Bollinger*) but ruled out the substantial numerical preferences for minority applicants at the undergraduate college (*Gratz v. Bollinger*).

Taking its cue from *Grutter*, the university revamped undergraduate admissions policies to allow the use of race as one among other factors. Opponents responded by qualifying what they entitled the Michigan Civil Rights Initiative for the statewide ballot in November 2006. The measure prohibits discrimination or "preferential treatment" in public employment, government contracts, or public education on the basis of race, sex, color, ethnicity, or national origin. The measure won approval with 58 percent of the vote: two-thirds of white voters voted for it; 90 percent of black voters voted no.

Complex litigation that spanned six years culminated in a fiercely fought, 8-7 decision by the full Sixth U.S. Circuit Court of Appeals in November 2012 striking down the measure. Opponents argued that the measure imposed a political burden on advocates of race-based preferences not imposed on supporters of other admissions preferences, for example for children of wealthy donors or alumni. The measure "undermines the Equal Protection Clause's guarantee that all citizens ought to have equal access to the tools of political change," the majority wrote.

In appealing that decision to the Supreme Court, the state's attorney general, Bill Schuette, depicts the initiative as an unexceptional guarantee of civil rights. "It is curious to say that a law that bars discriminating on the basis of race or sex violates the Equal Protection Clause by discriminating on the basis of race or sex," the brief filed by Schuette's office states.

Mark Rosenbaum, legal director for the American Civil Liberties Union of Southern California and attorney for one set of plaintiffs in the case, calls that depiction of the initiative misleading. The initiative's prohibition against discrimination is gratuitous, he notes, since it is already illegal for state or local governments to discriminate on the basis of race or the other factors. The effect of the initiative, Rosenbaum stresses, is to prohibit race-conscious admissions policies that would be lawful under *Grutter* — and to set up an effectively insurmountable political obstacle for advocates of such policies.

Rosenbaum emphasizes that the case is not about affirmative action as such, but the opposing briefs by Schuette and by the pro-affirmative action coalition rehash the debate over race-conscious admissions at length and with heat. The conservative majority on the Roberts Court are no great fans of affirmative action, and the five justices are not seen as likely fans of the political restructuring doctrine either. Tellingly, Justice Anthony M. Kennedy did not rely on it in the opinion he wrote in *Romer v. Evans* (1996) striking down an analogous anti-gay rights initiative in Colorado.

The Michigan measure is a verbatim copy of a California ballot initiative, Proposition 209, adopted in 1996 and upheld by the Ninth U.S. Circuit Court of Appeals. The Supreme Court left that ruling standing. Supporters of race-based admissions policies fear — and their opponents hope — that a Supreme Court ruling to reinstate the Michigan measure will encourage other states to follow suit in prohibiting racial preferences in university admissions. That could be a decisive turning point in a war that traditional civil rights groups already seem to be losing.

Retreat on Racial Justice

(*Jost on Justice*, April 27, 2014)

A year ago, the Supreme Court gutted a law passed overwhelmingly by Congress aimed at preventing states from reducing voting rights for racial and ethnic minorities. The 5-4 decision in *Shelby County v. Holder*, written by Chief Justice John G. Roberts Jr., blinked at the contemporary evidence of racial discrimination in voting and paused only briefly before overriding the decision of the political branches to extend the Voting Rights Act through 2031.

Now, the Roberts Court has given states another free pass to reduce the political rights of racial and ethnic minorities, in the face of its own precedents. This time, justices in the majority paid great obeisance to the political process — in this case, a decision not by Congress but the voters of Michigan to prohibit public colleges and universities from using racial preferences in admissions.

The 6-2 decision in *Schuette v. Coalition to Defend Affirmative Action* [April 22] upheld a state constitutional amendment approved by 58 percent of Michigan voters in 2006. The amendment did not merely override the decision by the University of Michigan's elected Board of Overseers to retain limited racial preferences in admissions. It took away the university's power ever to consider reinstituting racial preferences, even though the school's more common legacy preferences for children of alumni was left untouched.

The ruling came as no surprise. The Roberts Court conservatives have already shown themselves to be no fans of the remedies previously approved by the Supreme Court to promote racial diversity in K-12 public schools or in state colleges and universities. A 5-4 decision written by Roberts in 2007 limited the ability of public schools to make race-based assignments to ensure diversity in K-12 education (*Parents Involved in Community Schools v. Seattle School District No. 1*).

Conservatives clearly had the upper hand in last year's 7-1 decision, *Fisher v. University of Texas*, that made it measurably harder for state universities to justify racial preferences in admissions. Liberal justices, other than Ruth Bader Ginsburg, went along, quite possibly out of relief that the majority had stopped short of overruling the precedents that allow racial preferences.

The unifying theme in these decisions is the conservative justices' seeming belief that the rights of racial and ethnic minorities no longer need special guardianship from the Supreme Court. And that is the background needed to understand the impassioned dissent in last week's case from Justice Sonia Sotomayor. The court's first Latina justice openly credits affirmative action with allowing her to rise from a housing project in the Bronx through two Ivy League schools to reach the nation's highest court.

Sotomayor attacks at the outset the majority's belief in the sanctity of the political process. "Without checks, democratically approved legislation can oppress minority groups," she writes. "For that reason, our Constitution places limits on what a majority of the people can do."

In prior cases, the court itself had recognized that risk. In 1969 the court struck down an Akron, Ohio, ballot measure that barred the enactment of fair housing legislation except with voter approval (*Hunter v. Erickson*). Thirteen years later, it threw out a Washington state constitutional amendment that would have prevented the use of busing to achieve racial balance in public schools (*Washington v. Seattle School Dist. No. 1*, 1982).

In both cases, the court held that the Equal Protection Clause prohibits a restructuring of the political process designed to make it harder for minorities to obtain government action in their behalf. Opponents of Michigan's amendment relied on this so-called political process doctrine in challenging the measure in federal court. The federal appeals court for Michigan divided bitterly in the case, but the 8-7 majority applied the Supreme Court's precedents in ruling the measure unconstitutional.

In upholding the amendment instead, Justice Anthony M. Kennedy wrote in the controlling opinion that the measure was not designed to inflict injury on minorities. Michigan's minority voters did not see it that way: exit polls indicated that 86 percent of African Americans and 69 percent of Hispanics voted against it.

Kennedy suggested that voters were simply acting to prohibit a practice — racial preferences — that itself was a source of racial resentment and hostilities. The same could have been said of the anti-fair housing and anti-busing measures that a previous Supreme Court had struck down. In any event, the number of minority applicants admitted to the University of Michigan has declined since the amendment was adopted, as Sotomayor noted in her dissent.

In distinguishing but not overruling those prior cases, Kennedy wrote only for himself, Roberts, and Justice Samuel A. Alito Jr. Conservatives Antonin Scalia and Clarence Thomas more candidly called for overruling the cases entirely. In her dissent, Sotomayor aptly said that the decision "effectively discards those precedents." The logic of the decision, she wrote, "embraces majority rule without an important constitutional limit."

Sotomayor continued with a personal *cri de coeur* over her colleagues' seeming blindness to race-based realities in the United States today. "Race matters," she writes, listing the kinds of slights regularly experienced by African Americans and Hispanics. The court's ruling operates on the premise that legal rules recognizing that reality serve only to reinforce it. The history of equal protection law teaches the different lesson that the law, over time, can help society root out racial discrimination. But the Supreme Court is pulling back before the task is complete.

#WomensRights

As a high school student, I was introduced to liberal political thought through the pages of The New Republic, *well before the magazine's evolution into an eclectic mix of neoliberal and neoconservative reportage and commentary. Thinking back on those times, I vaguely recall skipping over many, perhaps most, of the articles about "women's rights." I evolved over time as I learned of the historic discrimination against women, in this country and abroad, on matters political, social, economic, and cultural.*

Today, as proud father of a feminist, college-graduate daughter, I count myself a feminist as well. Even so, I see from reviewing my columns that I have written on those issues only infrequently. Here are two, beginning with an article on abortion rights in advance of the Supreme Court's arguments on the federal law banning so-called 'partial birth" abortions.

Just the Facts, Please
(*CQ Weekly*, Nov. 20, 2006)

Everybody's entitled to his opinion, it is said, but not to his own facts. Congress, however, decided to make up its facts when it wrote a law in 2003 banning a procedure that opponents call "partial-birth abortion."

Now the Supreme Court is considering the constitutionality of the law in a case that will turn in part on real facts — as found by judges — instead of made-up facts as found by members of Congress playing to political constituencies. And the case will provide a key test of whether the court's newest members, Chief Justice John G. Roberts Jr. and Justice Samuel A. Alito Jr., will decide this case on the basis of the law and the facts — as they promised during their confirmation hearings — and not on the basis of their personal political views.

The debate over the sort of abortion at issue, now more than a decade old, has been misleading from the start. In medical terms, the procedure is actually called a "dilation and extraction," D&X, or sometimes an "intact dilation and evacuation," or intact D&E. The procedure calls for the woman's cervix to be dilated, the fetus to be brought partly out of the vaginal canal and the skull to be punctured to allow for complete removal of the fetus.

Despite the term coined by anti-abortion groups, the procedure entails no "partial birth" — at least, not when performed in the second trimester of a pregnancy. At that point, a fetus is not viable: It cannot live outside the womb. When pressed, even anti-abortion groups concede that banning the procedure while allowing other abortion techniques would not increase the number of live births.

Without doubt, the procedure is controversial within the medical community. Doctors who use the technique say removing a fetus largely intact instead of dismembering it in the womb is safer for the woman because it involves less instrumentation inside her body. Other doctors say the procedure is not safe, in part because it may increase the incidence of preterm deliveries in later pregnancies.

Many doctors, however, simply recoil at the procedure for the same reasons that anti-abortion groups cite: It sounds gruesome. But when the Supreme Court struck down a Nebraska law banning the procedure six years ago, Justice John Paul Stevens aptly said that it was "irrational" to ban one procedure while allowing other, "equally gruesome" abortion techniques.

That 5-4 decision held the Nebraska law unconstitutional because it did not permit the use of the procedure to protect the woman's health. *Roe v. Wade,* the Supreme Court's landmark 1973 abortion rights decision, established that any regulation of abortion — even during a pregnancy's final trimester — must allow such a health exception. Throughout more than three decades, that bedrock principle has remained unchanged.

Congress, however, still wanted to ban the procedure. Since lawmakers may not change a constitutional ruling by the Supreme Court, they did the next best thing: They tried to change the facts. The federal ban, passed in 2003, opens with 28 paragraphs of "factual findings" aimed directly at defying the court's ruling.

Most broadly, Congress got around the need for a health exception by "finding" that the banned procedure was "never" medically necessary and was not "safe." It found a "consensus" within the medical community against the procedure. It went so far as to say that the procedure is not taught in medical schools.

Each of those statements is simply wrong — as U.S. District Court Judge Richard Kopf of Lincoln, Neb., found at the start of an exhaustive, 474-page decision in September 2004 that found the law unconstitutional. Kopf said the record before Congress itself, along with the later evidence in the court case, showed the procedure to be necessary in some circumstances, safe and recognized by a "substantial body" of medical opinion.

Kopf's ruling, upheld by the federal appeals court in St. Louis, was one of two cases the justices agreed to use to decide the constitutionality of the federal ban. Defending the law during arguments Nov. 8, Solicitor General Paul Clement acknowledged that some of the congressional findings were unsupported.

All eyes were on Justice Anthony M. Kennedy during the arguments. He had voted to uphold the Nebraska law, but in the new cases he closely questioned lawyers on both sides about the claimed need for the procedure. Many saw his questions as leaving an opening for him to change his vote from the previous case. Roberts was also an active questioner, with some of his comments seemingly aimed at finding a basis for upholding the law. Alito said nothing and was seen frequently staring off into space.

Anti-abortion groups are counting Roberts and Alito as votes to uphold the law and hoping to hold Kennedy's from the prior ruling. Applying Supreme Court precedent to the proven facts in this case, however, points inexorably to striking down the federal statute. Upholding it would mean that Congress could intrude on the court's constitutional authority and — for Roberts and Alito — send a distressing signal that they did not leave their political agendas behind when they donned their justices' robes.

The court upheld the law in a 5-4 decision written by Kennedy with a forceful dissent by Ginsburg, who with O'Connor's retirement was then the only woman on the court. In his opinion, Kennedy concluded that the law "does not on its face impose a substantial obstacle" to late-term, previability abortions. He also said Congress had legitimate interests in enacting the law: promoting respect for human life and, in a controversial passage, minimizing women's regrets about the procedure afterward. In her dissent, Ginsburg took special exception to Kennedy's unsubstantiated adoption of what she called the "anti-abortion shibboleth" that women frequently experience regret and remorse after the procedure. She said the ruling "cannot be understood as anything other than an effort to chip away at a right declared again and again by this Court" and expressed the hope that the decision would be overruled in time.

Four years later, Ginsburg had two women as colleagues: Sotomayor and Kagan. As I wrote in a column in the middle of the 2010-2011 term, however, the three female justices were not enough to ensure a favorable reception on issues of women's rights.

Women of the Court

(*Jost on Justice*, Jan. 17, 2011)

Sandra Day O'Connor, retired Supreme Court justice, could not contain her delight as she recalled her recent visit to her former courtroom.

"It was absolutely incredible," O'Connor said in a Dec. 13 program at the Kennedy Library in Boston. "On the far right was a woman. Boom, boom, boom. Near the middle was a woman. On the far left was a woman. Three of them. Now think of it. It was incredible."

O'Connor, the first woman to serve on the nation's highest court, had good reason to think that Americans' "image" of the court "has to change a little bit" with three female justices: Ruth Bader Ginsburg, Sonia Sotomayor, and Elena Kagan. But image is only part of the struggle for equal rights and equal opportunities for women. Court decisions on women's issues are part of the struggle too.

On that score, women's rights advocates have as much cause for concern as for celebration today, in the sixth year of the Roberts Court. The conservative majority fortified with the appointments of John G. Roberts Jr. as chief justice in September 2005 and Samuel A. Alito Jr. as O'Connor's successor early in 2006 has shown no special awareness of the history of discrimination against women in law and society.

"It's been very disappointing," says Marcia Greenberger, co-president of the National Women's Law Center. "We have lost ground as a result of a number of narrowly divided decisions."

Women's rights advocates were given additional cause for concern this month with published statements from Justice Antonin Scalia questioning the line of decisions since the 1970s that rely on the Fourteenth Amendment's Equal Protection Clause to establish constitutional limits on sex discrimination. In an interview in *California Lawyer*, the monthly magazine of the California state bar, Scalia repeated his oft-stated contention that the amendment does not prohibit sex discrimination at all. "Nobody ever thought that's what it meant," Scalia said. "Nobody ever voted for that."

Scalia is unlikely to find a majority to reverse those decisions, but his vote — along with that of his originalist fellow traveler, Clarence

Thomas — could help limit future decisions scrutinizing sex-based distinctions in the law. Roberts and Alito seem unlikely to overturn prior rulings, but their records ever since their days in the Reagan administration reflect no special solicitude for gender equality.

In her list of unfavorable decisions, Greenberger starts with two, both from the first full term of the Roberts-Alito Court. In *Gonzales v. Carhart*, the court in April 2007 upheld a federal ban on the procedure that opponents have provocatively labeled "partial-birth abortions." The 5-4 majority upheld the law even though it included no exception for procedures deemed necessary to protect the woman's health. The court had required a health exception to any abortion regulations ever since *Roe v. Wade* first established a qualified right to abortion in 1973.

A little over a month later, the court in *Ledbetter v. Goodyear Tire and Rubber Co.* blocked an Alabama woman from collecting several years' worth of back pay for what a jury found to have been illegal sex discrimination. The alleged pay discrepancies dated back beyond the normal 180-day period for bringing a job discrimination claim under the federal Civil Rights Act, but Ledbetter argued they continued to affect her present salary. The 5-4 majority rejected the argument, adopting what Ginsburg called in her dissent a "cramped" interpretation that Congress overruled by statute two years later.

Ginsburg, then the only woman on the court, emphasized her discontent with both decisions by reading her dissents from the bench. In the abortion case, Ginsburg faulted the majority (in an opinion by Justice Anthony M. Kennedy) for adopting what she called an "antiabortion shibboleth" that women suffer depression and a loss of self-esteem after an abortion. In his opinion, Kennedy conceded there were "no reliable data" to measure the supposed phenomenon.

Greenberger acknowledges that the Roberts Court has had a mixed record in post-*Ledebetter* civil rights cases, with some helping plaintiffs, including women, others not. A series of rulings strengthening protections against retaliation for complaining about discrimination includes one brought by a Nashville woman, who accused her supervisor of sexual harassment during an internal investigation of a complaint by a coworker (*Crawford v. Metropolitan Government of Nashville and Davidson County*, 2008). On the other hand, women who often enter or re-enter the workforce at an advanced age after raising a family may be particularly disadvantaged by a decision raising the burden of proof for plaintiffs under the Age Discrimination in Employment Act (*Gross v. FBL Financial Services*, 2009)

Like *Ledbetter*, *Gross* hurt civil rights plaintiffs without regard to gender. But as long as women do not enjoy equal rights in the workplace or elsewhere, their advance will be hampered by rulings that limit the force of laws aimed at prohibiting sex discrimination. Three female justices represent an advance for women, but grouped together in the court's liberal bloc they need at least one vote from men in a conservative bloc that has shown less than strong interest in women's equality up till now.

Three years later, the three female justices, along with their male ally Breyer, were on the losing end of a 5-4 decision that allowed some employers to claim a religious exemption from covering all federally approved contraceptives in their employee health plans. The end-of-term decision in Burwell v. Hobby Lobby Stores, Inc. *(2014) is discussed in the First Amendment chapter as a religious-freedom ruling, but Ginsburg emphasized its impact on women in her dissenting opinion. The ruling, she said, "would deny legions of women who do not hold their employers' beliefs access to contraceptive coverage that the [law] would otherwise secure." A month later, Ginsburg remarked in an interview with Yahoo's Katie Couric that the five male justices who formed the majority in the case did not understand the ramifications of the decision. "I am ever hopeful that if the Court has a blind spot today," Ginsburg went on to say, "its eyes will be open tomorrow."*

8

#CriminalJustice

The popular lawyer television shows when I was coming of age celebrated not prosecutors but defense attorneys. Perry Mason always managed to clear his wrongly accused clients; E. G. Marshall and Robert Reed took on unpopular causes on the short-lived series The Defenders *(1961-1965). That was the popular-culture backdrop for the Supreme Court's long overdue ruling in 1963 that indigent criminal defendants are entitled to a lawyer even if they cannot afford one. As with so many other criminal justice reforms initiated in the 1960s, the promise of the decision has been only partly fulfilled.*

Gideon's Unfulfilled Promise
(*Jost on Justice*, April 14, 2013)

Clarence Earl Gideon revolutionized the criminal justice system with a handwritten petition to the U.S. Supreme Court complaining about the state's refusal to appoint a lawyer for him when he was tried and convicted in Florida in 1961 of breaking into a pool room. Gideon's victory did not end, however, with the Supreme Court's decision on March 18, 1963, requiring the government to provide public defenders for indigent defendants in felony cases. Gideon himself benefited from the decision in a retrial five months later when, represented this time by a lawyer, he was found not guilty.

The 50th anniversary of the court's unanimous decision in *Gideon v. Wainwright* is a fitting time both for celebration and for rededication to making the promise of *Gideon* reality. The Sixth Amendment right to counsel that *Gideon* and later cases safeguards exists in far too many cases only on paper, not in reality. Public defenders — overworked, underpaid, underresourced — give far too many defendants only the semblance of legal representation in a criminal justice system where the prosecution still has most of the cards.

That is the central message of a 24-page report released last week [April 9] by the Brennan Center for Justice that describes the promise of *Gideon* as "unrealized." Brennan Center attorneys Thomas Giovanni and Roopa Patel aptly depict *Gideon* as an "unfunded mandate" — a directive from the Supreme Court that state and local governments fail to adequately fund.

The need for legal representation for the poor is if anything greater than it was in Gideon's day. A half-century of tough-on-crime legislation has made the United States a global leader in incarceration. U.S. prisons held about 217,000 people in 1963; the prison population has increased since then more than tenfold to 2.3 million. "We live in an era of mass incarceration," Giovanni and Patel write.

The unwinnable war on drugs is one of the major reasons why U.S. prisons are filled to capacity and beyond. Almost half the people in federal prisons are there for drug offenses, but only a small fraction of those are serving time for serious drug trafficking. In state prisons, nearly half of the inmates are behind bars for nonviolent offenses, including a fair share of drug-related convictions.

Tough sentencing laws give federal and state prosecutors more leverage in plea bargaining than they had a half century ago. Prosecutors who charge to the max hold draconian sentences over a defendant's head in plea negotiations. Any number of defendants risk a decade or more in prison if they turn down a plea offer and insist on going to trial.

Against the well-armed prosecutor, indigent defendants typically have a public defender with far too many cases to give any of them the attention they deserve. As Giovanni and Patel note, the American Bar Association recommends that public defenders carry a caseload of 150 felonies or 400 misdemeanors per year. The average public defender's load is considerably higher. In New Orleans, for example, defenders handled on average 19,000 cases in 2009 — seven minutes per case.

For many indigent defendants, this is assembly-line injustice. In the mine-run of cases, public defenders have little to review the evidence or conduct an investigation — indeed, they have barely enough time to interview their clients.

Federal public defenders are on average better qualified and better resourced than their state and local counterparts. But the current budget sequestration is having some impact. The federal defenders representing Suleiman Abu Ghaith, Osama bin Laden's son-in-law and alleged al Qaida spokesman, in his conspiracy trial in federal court in New York City have asked that the case be delayed until January because of the five-week furlough imposed on the office to absorb the budget cut.

The federal government does offer grants to supplement state and local spending on public defenders under the 20-year-old Justice Assistance Grant program. States have discretion on how to allocate the money: $287 million in 2012. Most of the money — 60 percent in 2012 — went to law enforcement. Combined, prosecutor and defenders offices got less than $16 million, and prosecutors got the lion's share: $13.8 million versus only $1.9 million for defenders. Giovanni and Patel note that many defender offices are unaware they can apply for grants under the program.

The Brennan Center report offers three "common sense reforms" to improve the country's system of public defense. One step is to reduce the number of defendants put into the assembly line by reclassifying many petty offenses into non-jailable civil infractions or legalizing the conduct altogether.

The two other steps focus directly on defender offices. The report naturally calls for more funding not only from the usual sources — state and local budgets and federal grants — but also from "unlikely sources," such as the private bar. The report suggests that more law firms follow example of some in Atlanta and New York City of sending associates to externships in public service organizations, including defender offices. The report also specifically calls for more funding for training public defenders and for hiring social workers for defender offices.

Political, fiscal, and financial realities militate against all these recommendations. Law-and-order sentiment remains strong; governments at all levels are financially strapped; and private law firms are themselves financially pinched. But the Supreme Court's historic step in *Gideon* deserves better today than to be honored more in the breach than in the observance.

#Police

The Warren Court's criminal justice revolution was embodied most dramatically by its ruling in Miranda v. Arizona *(1965) requiring police to inform suspects of their rights before any custodial interrogation. Chief Justice Earl Warren, a district attorney in Oakland a quarter-century earlier, said the ruling was necessary to protect suspects from psychological coercion by police. Dissenting justices warned the decision would handcuff police. Over time, the Supreme Court dialed back some applications of the rule, but in 2000 no less a conservative than Chief Justice William H. Rehnquist wrote that the* Miranda *warnings had become "part of our national culture" (*Dickerson v. United States). *Even so, the Roberts Court chipped away at the safeguard in a decision in 2010 that seemed to me to be ripped out of the television series "Law and Order."*

"Law-and-Order" Exception
(*Jost on Justice*, June 2, 2010)

"Law and Order" may have ended its 20-year run, but Briscoe, Curtis, and all the other cops and prosecutors on the compelling TV series can rest content after a Supreme Court decision on Tuesday [June 1] that eases the rule on police interrogation established in the landmark *Miranda* case. By a 5-4 vote, the justices gave the green light to the kind of subtle coercion that "Law and Order" detectives still practice in nightly reruns and that *Miranda* had sought to prevent.

Like many of the perps on "Law and Order," Van Chester Thompkins had nothing to say while two detectives from Southfield, Michigan, questioned him on Feb. 22, 2001, about a drive-by shooting outside a strip mall a year earlier. In Thompkin's case, he sat on a hard chair in an eight-foot by ten-foot interrogation room for three hours — long enough for three episodes — after refusing to sign a waiver of his *Miranda* right to remain silent.

For two hours and 45 minutes, Thompkins said nothing more substantial than to complain about the chair and to decline Detective Christopher Helgert's offer of a mint. In the real world, one would see that Thompkins did not want to talk. But, at the cop house, a different rule applies. Helgert kept up his monologue and finally figured out Thompkins' weak spot. "Do you believe in God?" he asked. Thompkins said yes. "Do you pray?" Again, Thompkins said yes. "Do you pray to God to forgive you for shooting that boy down?" Helgert asked. Tearing up, Thompkins answered in one word: "Yes."

As a district attorney in California in the 1930s, Earl Warren had experience with old-style police interrogations: slapping suspects around and the like. As chief justice, he learned that police had adopted other techniques. "The modern practice of in-custody interrogation is psychologically, rather than physically, oriented," Warren wrote in the 1966 *Miranda* decision. Police manuals, Warren explained, tell officers to isolate the suspect, display confidence, assume the suspect's guilt, and get him simply to elaborate on what the police pretend already to know.

The Supreme Court created the *Miranda* rule to combat what Warren aptly described as the inherently coercive nature of that kind of interrogation. Everyone is now familiar with the recitation of *Miranda* rights: the right to remain silent, the right to cut off questioning, the right to have a lawyer, and the right to have the lawyer present during interrogation. To safeguard those rights, the court said that police cannot use a suspect's statement unless they show that a suspect *knowingly* and *intelligently* waived those rights. And a valid waiver could *not* be shown, the court said, simply by the fact that a confession was in fact obtained.

In Thompkins' case, Michigan courts drove right by those waiver rules. Thompkins' statement was introduced and, in a close case, helped the prosecution get a conviction. On appeal, the Michigan courts said, counterintuitively, that Thompkins had to speak up in order to assert his right to remain silent. And, in seeming contradiction, the state courts said that Thompkins had waived that right with three one-word answers uttered after nearly three hours of interrogation.

The Supreme Court agreed. "The record in this case shows that Thompkins waived his right to remain silent," Justice Anthony M. Kennedy wrote for the Roberts Court's conservative majority in *Berghuis v. Thompkins*. The suspect's one-word answer about praying, Kennedy continued, "was sufficient to show a course of conduct indicating waiver." True, Kennedy conceded, Thompkins sat in a straight-backed chair for three hours, but — overlooking *Miranda* — the justice said there is "no authority" for the proposition that an interrogation under these circumstances is "inherently coercive."

For the four liberal dissenters, Justice Sonia Sotomayor, a former local prosecutor, labeled the decision "a substantial retreat from the protection against compelled self-incrimination" established by *Miranda*. That decision places a "heavy burden" on the prosecution to show that a suspect has waived the right to remain silent, she explained, and it was "objectively unreasonable" to conclude that the prosecution had shown a waiver in Thompkins' case on the basis of "three one-word answers, following 2 hours and 45 minutes of silence . . . ."

Sotomayor also criticized the court's new rule that a suspect must make a "clear statement" in order to assert a right to remain silent. "Advising a suspect that he has a 'right to remain silent' is unlikely to convey that he must speak (and must do so in some particular fashion) to ensure the right will be protected," she wrote.

For the majority, Kennedy suggested that the "clear statement" rule would not affect many cases. In a footnote, however, Sotomayor listed a raft of lower court decisions holding that suspects had not invoked a right to silence despite "an array of statements whose meaning might otherwise be thought plain." Like the suspect who said, "I just don't think I should say anything," but his later statements admitted anyway.

The new decision is not the first retreat from *Miranda*— and is unlikely to be the last. Yes, *Miranda* is still good law. But two decades of "Law and Order" show that fictional police know how to work around it. And the Roberts Court is OK with that in real life.

For all of its decisions favoring the rights of criminal defendants and suspects, the Warren Court also favored police in a decision, Terry v. Ohio *(1968), that allowed officers to "stop" an individual based on "reasonable suspicion" of criminal activity and to "frisk" the individual for weapons. Justice William O. Douglas, the lone dissenter, complained that the ruling amounted to "watering down" constitutional rights. In practice, police often stop individuals with little by way of "reasonable suspicion" of criminal activity. In many places, that meant stopping individuals largely based on their race or ethnicity – "walking while black (or brown)." Civil rights advocates mounted an ambitious legal challenge to the aggressive use of "stop and frisk" tactics by the New York City Police Department; the suit resulted in a dramatic ruling in August 2013 that found the department's practices unconstitutional and appointed a special monitor to work with the city to institute reforms.*

Policing Stop-and-Frisk
(*Jost on Justice*, Aug. 19, 2013)

A Cleveland police officer, patrolling his regular beat, observed two men walking up and down in front of a store window a dozen times, conferring with each other after each of the walk-bys. The officer, suspecting the two men were "casing the joint," stopped to question them and, after patting them down, discovered that both of the men, John Terry and Richard Chilton, were carrying weapons. Terry appealed his subsequent weapons conviction to the U.S. Supreme Court, which in *Terry v. Ohio* (1968) upheld the conviction after concluding that the officer had reasonable grounds for the initial "stop and frisk."

Thus was born the *Terry* stop: the Supreme Court-approved practice of stopping an individual if an officer has a reasonable suspicion of criminal activity and frisking the individual if the officer has a reasonable fear the individual could be armed.

Four decades later, three New York City police officers stopped David Floyd as he was walking from the subway toward home in the Bronx. The officers asked Floyd for identification and, fearful after he reached inside a pants pocket for his cell phone, patted him down for weapons. No weapon was found, and no charge was filed. Floyd asked for the officers' names and badge numbers, but they gave only their last names and badge numbers that did not match the names given.

Floyd's encounter with the NYPD in April 2007 was one of more than 4.4 million stops that New York City police officers conducted in an eight-year period under an aggressive policy initiated by Police Commissioner Raymond Kelly and supported and now vigorously defended by Mayor Michael Bloomberg. As in Floyd's case, the vast majority of the stops — almost 90 percent — resulted in no charges whatsoever. In about half of the stops, police also conducted a "frisk," but weapons were found in only 1.5 percent of the patdowns.

Those are the statistics that a federal judge, Shira Scheindlin, relied on last week [Aug. 12] in a 195-page ruling in a class action brought in Floyd's name, *Floyd v. New York*, that declared the NYPD's stop-and-frisk practices unconstitutional. The numbers speak for themselves. "How reasonable is it if 90 percent of the time you're wrong?" *Wall Street Journal* reporter Devlin Barrett asked rhetorically in an appearance on the public radio program *To the Point*.

The numbers are even more telling when broken down by race. More than half of the stops – 52 percent – involved African Americans, in a city where blacks make up about one-fourth of the total population. Hispanics were stopped in 31 percent of the encounters; they comprise about 29 percent of the city's population. As Scheindlin found, the statistics indicate a pattern of racial profiling by the police.

Bloomberg, in the final months of his 12-year tenure, has defended the police department's policies — what he calls "stop, question, and frisk" — as helping make New York the safest big city in the country. New York in fact has a low rate of homicides or other violent crimes compared with many big cities, but Bloomberg is taking credit for lowering the city's crime rate in a decade when the rate was declining nationwide. Moreover, Scheindlin found no reason to believe that the stop-and-frisk policies were responsible for reducing crime. Instead, she said the policies may be counterproductive by reducing citizen cooperation with police, especially in the minority neighborhoods singled out for the tactic.

Bloomberg also has defended the city's policies by stressing the supposedly detailed reports required for all stops — proof, he suggests, that the city has nothing to hide or be ashamed of. But Scheindlin was unimpressed after her examination of the reports: UF-250's, in police department parlance. First, as in Floyd's case, some number of stops are never documented at all. Moreover, the information in the UF-250's is often limited. Instead of providing a narrative, officers typically simply check off boxes to indicate the reason for the stop; "furtive movements" and "high crime areas" are the ones most frequently given. And even though *Terry* requires police have reason to suspect criminal activity, Scheindlin found that officers failed to specify any suspected crime in slightly over one-third of the reports.

Along with her ruling on the city's liability, Scheindlin issued a companion 39-page remedial order that designated Peter Zimroth, a private lawyer who was formerly the city's corporation counsel and a chief assistant district attorney, as a monitor to help institute and oversee reforms. She left most of the details to be worked out, but as one immediate step she ordered that officers in one precinct in each of New York's five boroughs to be equipped with body cameras to record all police encounters with civilians. Scheindlin said she will weigh later whether the benefits in reducing unconstitutional stops outweigh any financial or administrative hardships.

The city is vowing to appeal. Scheindlin is aptly described in her Wikipedia biography as an "aggressive" judge, and she has been reversed in several high-profile decisions. But several of the candidates vying to succeed Bloomberg responded last week by embracing the need to reform stop-and-frisk policies. Scheindlin stressed that she was not prohibiting stop-and-frisk, only insisting that the tactic be employed within constitutional limits. Bloomberg could serve his city better by cooperating toward that goal instead of defending a policy that, on close examination, seems to have gone beyond constitutional limits.

One month after taking office, New York City's new mayor Bill de Blasio dropped the city's appeal of Judge Scheindlin's ruling and agreed to put the ordered changes into effect. "We believe these steps will make everyone safer," de Blasio said.

#Prosecutors

Like all courthouse reporters, I relied on prosecutors in the local district attorney's office for much of my information about criminal cases when I worked the court beat for the Nashville Tennessean *in the 1970s. I thought all of them – well, almost all of them – were straight-shooters who followed Justice George Sutherland's famous admonition that prosecutors should strike "hard blows but fair ones." Some prosecutors, however, are – how shall I put it? – ethically challenged. A case before the Supreme Court in 2010 prompted me to examine the issue of prosecutorial misconduct.*

Blind Eye to Misconduct (I)
(*Jost on Justice*, Oct. 18, 2010)

Tea Party types who want to strike a blow against governmental abuse and constitutional violations need not travel to Washington, D.C., to find a target for their protests. They can go instead to the nearest state or federal courthouse, where prosecutors are quite likely to be committing negligent mistakes or willful misconduct far more often than commonly acknowledged.

The incidence of prosecutorial misconduct is unknown and unknowable. Even more than police, prosecutors commit their wrongdoing — most commonly, withholding evidence from defense lawyers — behind closed doors. This much is known: The few offending prosecutors who are caught are rarely punished in any meaningful way.

These conclusions reflect long-held beliefs among defense lawyers, civil libertarians and many criminal justice experts. They gain confirmation now from two critical studies: a six-month investigative project covering federal prosecutors by *USA Today* and a decade-long review of state cases in California by the Northern California Innocence Project at Santa Clara University Law School. Both find statistical evidence of prosecutorial wrongdoing, often linked to wrongful convictions, with hardly any of the errant D.A.'s suffering any form of punishment.

The two studies were published in September just as the U.S. Supreme Court was preparing to hear arguments in a notorious case of prosecutorial misconduct, *Connick v. Thompson.* John Thompson spent 14 years on death row in a Louisiana prison — and came within hours of execution — for a murder that he did not commit. He was convicted in part because a prosecutor knowingly withheld crucial evidence from the defense lawyer, evidence that the prosecutor was ethically and legally obliged to turn over.

Now freed from prison, Thompson wants some compensation for the years of freedom that the criminal justice system wrongfully took from him. But the Supreme Court has made it virtually impossible to sue an individual prosecutor. Prosecutors are immune for any official actions directly related to a criminal trial. In any event, the trial prosecutor, who surreptitiously removed forensic evidence from the storage room, died a few years back. He had confessed his misconduct to a colleague, but had taken no other action to right his wrong.

With personal liability foreclosed, Thompson instead is trying to hold the New Orleans district attorney's office itself responsible for failing to train assistant D.A.'s properly about the so-called *Brady* rule. The rule, established by the Supreme Court in *Brady v. Maryland* (1963), requires prosecutors to turn over any potentially exculpatory evidence to the defense.

Thompson's federal civil rights lawsuit runs into an obstacle. The Supreme Court's decision in another case, *Monell v. Dep't of Social Services of New York* (1978), allows a municipality to be held liable for a constitutional violation by one of its officials only if the plaintiff proves "deliberate indifference" on the municipality's part. In Supreme Court arguments on Oct. 6, the justices got tied up in knots over the question of whether a single egregious instance could show "deliberate indifference." They also pressed the former inmate's lawyer to specify exactly what training the district attorney's office should have been required to provide to new prosecutors.

Legally, it may be a close case. In real-world terms, it is not. New Orleans' longtime district attorney, Harry Connick Sr., appears to have fostered a lopsided attitude toward *Brady* in the office: Disclose nothing unless you absolutely have to; don't worry about being called on the carpet for withholding. The training manual for the office actually misstated the *Brady* rule.

Impunity for *Brady* violations and other prosecutorial misconduct appears to be the rule in other jurisdictions. In the *USA Today* story, reporters Brad Heath and Kevin McCoy documented 201 federal criminal cases since 1997 in which judges "blasted prosecutors for 'flagrant' or 'outrageous' misconduct" such as "hiding evidence," "lying to judges or juries," or breaking plea bargains. (Disclosure: Heath is a former student of mine at Georgetown Law Shool.)

The Justice Department's internal watchdog investigates such cases: 42 in 2001, 61 last year. But the department refuses, on privacy grounds, to say whether any of the prosecutors was punished. Using state bar records, however, Heath and McCoy found that since 2001 only one federal prosecutor has been suspended even temporarily from law practice because of misconduct. In the flagrant example they used to start the story, the federal prosecutor who concealed unfavorable information about the government's major witnesses got a slap on the wrist: a one-day training session on ethics.

In the California study, the Santa Clara law school project combed state appellate court decisions from 1997 through 2009 and identified 707 cases in which courts "explicitly found that prosecutors committed misconduct." The vast majority of convictions (548) were nevertheless upheld: no harm, no foul, apparently.

More troublingly, an examination of state bar records found public disciplinary actions against only 10 state prosecutors during the period, only six of them for trial-related violations. As Professor Kathleen Ridolfi and visiting journalist Maurice Possley conclude, judges, prosecutors, and the California State Bar are "casting a blind eye to prosecutors who place their thumbs on the scales of justice."

The Supreme Court could play a role in changing the lax attitude toward errant prosecutors, but the justices' questions in Thompson's case point in the opposite direction. One more sign of the justices' solicitude toward government attorneys came today (Oct. 18) when they agreed to hear former Attorney General John Ashcroft's appeal in a case, *Ashcroft v. Al-Kidd*, testing whether he can be held individually liable for alleged misuse of the federal material witness statute during the post-9/11 roundup of hundreds of wrongfully accused individuals.

My reading of the justices' questions in Thompson's case proved to be correct. The court's 5-4 decision threw out the jury award that Thompson had won. Despite the acknowledged violation of Thompson's rights, Connick's office was not liable because the majority found no proof of a "pattern or practice" of deliberate indifference to constitutional rights.

Blind Eye to Misconduct (II)
(*Jost on Justice*, April 4, 2011)

The government always wins when justice is done. That's what prosecutors often say when they lose a jury verdict. By that standard, the government lost big last week when the Supreme Court blinked at an evident injustice by giving the New Orleans district attorney's office a pass for constitutional violations that put an innocent man on the state's death row for 14 years.

John Thompson was, in fact, within hours of his scheduled execution in April 1999 before courts intervened to begin unwinding the tangle of belatedly acknowledged prosecutorial misconduct that led to tainted convictions for attempted armed robbery and capital murder in 1985.

Freed from prison in 2003, Thompson sued the Orleans Parish District Attorney's Office, including the former district attorney Harry Connick, for withholding the evidence that eventually cleared him. The withholding plainly violated a clear Supreme Court precedent, *Brady v. Maryland*, a 1963 decision as basic to prosecutors as *Miranda* is to police.

A federal court jury awarded Thompson $14 million. The district court judge and the Fifth U.S. Circuit Court of Appeals both found that Thompson had shown that Connick's office had been "deliberately indifferent" to defendants' rights. That is the strict standard the high court had previously established for holding local governments liable in federal civil rights suits.

In a 5-4 decision, the Supreme Court on March 29 threw out that verdict and ordered judgment in Connick's favor by focusing solely on the concealment of one piece of evidence in the robbery case against Thompson. A single *Brady* violation, Justice Clarence Thomas wrote for the majority in *Connick v. Thompson*, was not enough to show a "pattern or practice" of deliberate indifference.

Thomas and the other conservatives in the majority turned a blind eye to the evidence of other prosecutorial misconduct not only in Thompson's case but also in others. As Justice Ruth Bader Ginsburg explained in a bitter dissent, the "grave injustice" that Thompson suffered resulted from a "cavalier" attitude toward defendants' rights that appeared to be "standard operating procedure" in the prosecutor's office.

Similar violations are all the more likely, she suggested, because of the court's failure to require better training and monitoring of prosecutors in order for local governments to avoid liability for rights violations. And — although Ginsburg did not make the point — Thompson's wrongful convictions means that the actual killer in a high-profile murder has gone scot-free.

Thompson had initially been charged with the shooting death of the son of a prominent New Orleans businessman outside his home in December 1984. The case was weak from the outset. He had been implicated by a reward-seeking informant. When Thompson was arrested, prosecutors could plainly see that he did not match the description given by the sole eyewitness to the slaying.

Nevertheless, Connick, father of the same-named actor/singer, thought they had their man and clearly wanted a conviction. He appointed his third-in-command to head a team of three younger prosecutors to handle the case. They got a break of sorts when the victim of an unrelated robbery identified Thompson from his picture published in the newspaper. A swatch of cloth from the pants worn by one of the victims, stained with the perpetrator's blood, was sent to the New Orleans crime lab for analysis.

Prosecutors decided to try Thompson first in the robbery case, evidently hoping that a conviction would deter him from testifying in a later murder trial — as, in fact, actually occurred. In the robbery case,

Thompson's attorney asked for what *Brady* requires: disclosure of any exculpatory evidence. The prosecutors not only failed to mention the blood evidence, but actually removed the swatch from the evidence room before the defense attorney's inspection. Today, it is lost. But the lab report, found by investigators 14 years later, shows that the blood did not match Thompson's blood type.

After the attempted robbery conviction, prosecutors continued a policy of concealment in the murder trial. The informant's tape-recorded conversation was never disclosed, nor the eyewitness's unmatching description of the assailant. Without that information, Thompson's attorney was effectively prevented from impeaching their testimony.

In the later federal civil rights suit, Thompson introduced evidence from former prosecutors that the disregard for *Brady* in his case was — as Ginsburg put it — "neither isolated nor atypical." Indeed, state appellate courts had reversed four convictions from Connick's office for *Brady* violations in the decade before Thompson's trial. The former assistants testified to either minimal or non-existent training about *Brady*. Connick clearly signaled, they said, that when in doubt evidence should be withheld rather than disclosed.

The discovery of the *Brady* violation in the robbery case forced the reversal of that conviction. The state appellate court reversed the murder conviction as well, reasoning that the tainted robbery conviction had prevented him from testifying. In a retrial, he was acquitted.

In this sorry episode, the Supreme Court's majority discerns only a single injustice, not the "pervasive" disregard of prosecutors' obligations seen by Ginsburg and the other three liberal dissenters. The court has already given individual prosecutors virtually absolute immunity for rights violations during trials. With this ruling, those responsible for guarding against prosecutorial misconduct are largely protected from legal liability as well.

#Prisons

Prison reform was a popular cause when I was coming of age in the 1960s, but rehabilitation took a back seat to incarceration in the *law-and-order era of the late 20ᵗʰ century. By the turn of the century, prisons all around the country were busting at the seams thanks to tough – some would call them draconian – sentencing policies. Many states in the 1990s enacted so-called "three strikes" laws, which allowed sentences up to life imprisonment for third-time felony offenders. Ruling in a California case, the Supreme Court in 2003 found such laws did not amount to cruel and unusual punishment under the Eighth Amendment (*Ewing v. California*).*

Sentencing practices like those resulted in severe overcrowding in California's prisons, with more than 150,000 inmates housed in facilities designed to hold 80,000. The Supreme Court in 2011 ruled on a pair of cases brought on behalf of California inmates alleging that the overcrowding resulted in condition, including a lack of medical and mental health care, that amounted to cruel and unusual punishment. The court agreed in a 5-4 decision written by Kennedy that required the state to reduce the prison population to 137.5 percent of capacity. I wondered in my column how the four dissenters could have disagreed.

"Grim" Reality of California Prisons
(*Jost on Justice*, May 31, 2011)

The surprise in the Supreme Court's ruling in the California prison case is not the decision by five justices to uphold an order requiring the release of about 30,000 prisoners over the next five years. The surprise comes from the votes of the four dissenters to leave the appalling conditions in the state's prisons largely unaddressed.

The majority opinion in *Brown v. Plata* by Justice Anthony M. Kennedy, a Californian, paints a damning portrait of the consequences of the state's housing as many as 156,000 inmates in 33 facilities with a designed capacity of only 80,000. The crowding is not merely uncomfortable, but it is surely that: prisoners sleeping in triple bunk beds; 200 prisoners living in a converted gymnasium; 54 inmates sharing a single toilet.

More to the point, the overcrowding overwhelms the prison system's capacity to provide medical and mental health care to inmates with deadly consequences. Kennedy notes some of the victims of medical non-care. One inmate died of testicular cancer after doctors failed to diagnose the condition despite the inmate's complaining of testicular pain for 17 months. Another inmate, suffering from severe abdominal pain, died after a five-week delay in being referred to a specialist. Another prisoner, suffering from extreme chest pain, died after eight hours passed without an evaluation by a specialist. Another inmate died of renal failure after being given medications that actually exacerbated his condition.

The deaths are not merely anecdotal. Statistics for the two years before the trial of the case in 2008 showed that 66 inmates succumbed to "preventable deaths" in 2006, 68 in 2007 — one preventable death every five to six days in both years. The number was "extremely high," according to testimony by the former medical director for Illinois prisons.

The deaths included suicides at nearly double the average rate for prisons. The court-appointed special master concluded that nearly three-fourths of the suicides resulted from inadequate assessment, treatment or prevention — and, in that sense, were "most probably foreseeable and/or preventable." By 2010, there was no sign of improvement in suicide prevention.

The picture of mental health care was especially damning, with wait times for care ranging as high as 12 months. Suicidal inmates were sometimes held for prolonged periods in a telephone-booth sized cage without toilets. One inmate, unresponsive and nearly catatonic, was held in such a cage for 24 hours, standing in his own urine, because, according to prison officials, they "had no place to put him."

Routine medical care is routinely inadequate. Inmates with urgent care requests are seen only after a delay of two weeks or longer. When one prison was checked, only one-third of 300 inmates requesting urgent care had any appointment scheduled at all. Inadequate medical care in overcrowded facilities resulted, inevitably, in a high rate of infectious disease.

The inadequacies in medical care result from inadequate facilities and inadequate staffing. Medical staff work out of converted storage rooms, closets, and bathrooms. The state has not budgeted for sufficient medical staff, but fell short even of its budgeted understaffing: a 20 percent vacancy rate for surgeons, a 54 percent vacancy rate for psychiatrists.

"The medical and mental health care provided by California's prisons," Kennedy concluded, "falls below the standard of decency that inheres in the Eighth Amendment. The extensive and ongoing constitutional violation requires a remedy, and a remedy will not be achieved without a reduction in overcrowding."

The dissenting justices either minimize or wish away these problems. Instead of a prisoner-release order, Justice Samuel A. Alito Jr. says the prison system should hire more medical staff, get more supplies and equipment, keep better records, and improve sanitary procedures — as though the prison system had not tried. Chief Justice John G. Roberts Jr. joined Alito's opinion.

In his dissent, Justice Antonin Scalia, joined by Clarence Thomas, suggests that the only inmates entitled to be released are those shown to be currently suffering from inadequate medical care. The remedy overlooks the inevitable delay in documenting and adjudicating the level of undertreatment needed to be entitled to release. More broadly, as Kennedy notes, Scalia's solution overlooks the fact that healthy inmates are not "remote bystanders" in the overtaxed medical care system, but the system's "next potential victims."

The dissenting justices are willing to accept half measures because they fear the public safety consequences of moving 30,000 inmates out of the prison system. But they exaggerate the fears. First, many of the inmates will now be sent to county jails, not put out on the streets. Second, overcrowding can also be reduced by not returning parole violators to prisons. Third, expansion of good-time credits and diversion of low-risk offenders to community programs would have little if any impact on public safety.

Even under the terms of the lower court's order in the case, California prisons would still be housing 37.5 percent more inmates than they were designed to hold. The current overcrowding results from Californians' law-and-order binge — think of the state's "three strikes" law — combined with their refusal to pay for the facilities and services needed to provide inmates with medical and mental health care.

In his dissent, Alito said he feared a "grim" result from the prisoner-release order. The Supreme Court majority was right to be more concerned with doing something about the grim present.

Three years later, California had yet to reduce prison overcrowding to the level established by the three-judge court and upheld by the Supreme Court. In the meantime, Arizona's prison system had come under similar scrutiny — coincidentally at the same time that Arizona was ground zero in the nationwide controversy over inadequate medical care for military veterans.

Arizona's Prison Scandal
(*Jost on Justice*, June 8, 2014)

Military veterans in Arizona got the nation's undivided attention over the past few weeks after it was learned that hundreds of them had to wait for weeks or even months for appointments with doctors in the Veterans Administration's health care system. Now, let's see whether the 33,000 inmates in Arizona state prisons can get the same amount of attention over evidence that some of them have had to wait for months or even years for medical attention to severe, even life-threatening health conditions.

The allegations of inadequate health care come in a class action lawsuit that a federal appeals court cleared for trial last week [June 5]. The worst of the examples cited in the 63-page opinion from the Ninth U.S. Circuit Court of Appeals make the vets' complaints seem almost trivial by comparison. Consider these alleged incidents:

* A male inmate waited two years for a biopsy of a mass in his prostate because contracts with outside providers had been canceled. By the time of the biopsy, the cancer had advanced, resulting in more invasive surgery than would have been necessary with earlier care and after the surgery permanent catheterization.

* A female prisoner, four months pregnant, was referred to a medical unit after suffering bleeding and severe contractions, but was told the problems were all in her head. She was sent back to her cell, where she suffered a miscarriage less than two hours later.

* A mentally ill inmate bled to death in July 2010 after his second suicide attempt as correctional officers stood by and watched. In the ensuing investigation, one of the officers said he had called the inmate's name but elicited no reaction.

Along with specific examples such as those, the inmates' 74-page complaint filed in March 2012 included broad allegations that the prison system provided inadequate medical, mental health, and dental care and failed to provide timely emergency medical treatment or sufficient medications or medical supplies. Incontinent inmates, for example, were limited to one diaper per day.

Those are only allegations, but the complaint was sufficiently detailed and the allegations sufficiently serious to persuade U.S. District Court Judge Neil Wake to allow the 13 named plaintiffs to broaden the case to a class action on behalf of all Arizona prisoners. The allegations "are not merely isolated instances but, rather, examples of systemic deficiencies that expose all inmates to a substantial risk of serious harm," Wake wrote in his March 2013 ruling.

Wake, a Republican appointed to the bench in 2004 by President George W. Bush, said a broad ruling would be needed to raise the level of care and medical resources for all inmates, not just the individual plaintiffs who brought the suit. Wake also approved a class action on behalf of some 2,200 inmates contesting the state prison system's use of solitary confinement: isolating some prisoners for 22 hours a day over extended periods.

The allegations of inadequate medical care for inmates come as no surprise to state officials. The prison system's director of medical services was quoted in 2009 as telling a prison physician that the system was "probably" violating inmates' rights. "I do think that there would be numerous experts in the field that would opine that deliberate indifference has occurred," the director reportedly stated.

On appeal, the state did not contest the allegations, but attacked Wake's decision to certify the case as a class action on grounds the inmates' various allegations were not sufficiently similar to be tried together. In its decision, the Ninth Circuit panel found that Wake had properly identified 10 alleged practices or policies of the prison system that affected inmates generally, not just individual prisoners. Those policies, Judge Stephen Reinhardt wrote for the panel, are enough "glue" to hold a class action together. Reinhardt, a veteran liberal jurist, was joined in the opinion by Judges John Noonan, a conservative appointed by President Ronald Reagan, and Paul Watford, named by President Obama in 2012.

Arizona has the distinction of having the highest share of its population behind bars of any state in the West and one of the highest in the country, according to *The Arizona Republic*. The newspaper's ongoing coverage has documented a host of controversies over prison conditions, including the controversial use of private prisons. Murder and assault rates in the system are higher than the national average, the newspaper reported in July 2012. Officials responded to the newspaper by minimizing the statistics and in any event blaming the incidents on staffing cuts.

Trial of the case is now set for October, according to the American Civil Liberties Union's Prison Rights Project, which is coordinating the litigation. But the state could delay the trial by asking the U.S. Supreme Court to overturn the class certification order.

In a similar case, however, the court in 2011 allowed California inmates to proceed with companion class actions contesting overcrowding and inadequate health care in that state's prison system (*Brown v. Plata*). A three-judge court continues to supervise the state's compliance with orders to reduce the prison population and improve medical care.

Arizona faces the prospect of a similar court order, but the wheels of justice grind slowly: a final decision could still be years away. In an ideal world, perhaps public indignation would force changes in the meantime, but prisoners — unlike veterans — are easy for the public to put out of mind.

#CapitalPunishment

For a brief moment in the 1960s, a plurality of Americans opposed capital punishment, according to public opinion polls. The Supreme Court outlawed all existing death sentences by a 5-4 vote in 1972, only to uphold revised capital punishment statutes four years later. I wrote in a column in 1976 that the resumption of executions in the United States was likely to lead to a backlash against the death penalty: never have I been more wrong. Instead, public support for capital punishment remains strong despite the inconclusive debate over its deterrent effect and the strong evidence of arbitrariness and injustice in its actual practice. Over time, the Supreme Court has rejected broad challenges to capital punishment but limited its use in certain categories of cases. After he retired, Justice John Paul Stevens voiced regrets about his part in reinstituting the death penalty in 1976.

Stevens' Regrets on Death Penalty
(*Jost on Justice*, Dec. 1, 2010)

David Garland could hardly have wished for better luck than to have his new book on capital punishment favorably written up in the *New York Review of Books* by no less than a retired Supreme Court justice, John Paul Stevens. And for Stevens, the unsolicited assignment from the magazine's editors gave him the chance to elaborate on his reasoning in concluding two years ago that the death penalty as it operates in the United States today serves no good purpose and should be abolished.

Garland, a professor of law and sociology at New York University, is a little-known academic with a long list of titles on criminal law and sentencing. In *Peculiar Institution: America's Death Penalty in an Age of Abolition* (Harvard University Press, 2010), the transplanted Scotsman seeks in part to explain the persistence of capital punishment in the United States at a time when the practice has been abolished in form or in practice in the rest of the West.

From Stevens' account, Garland scrupulously avoids offering his own personal conclusion about the wisdom or morality of the death penalty. But Stevens says that Garland's account fortifies the justice's own view that the death penalty is "unwise and unjustified."

Garland's book may profitably be read in tandem with an earlier work, *The Death Penalty: An American History* (Harvard University Press, 2002), by Stuart Banner, who is now a professor at UCLA Law School. Both depict capital punishment in the United States as infected with racism, historically and today, and beset these days with delays that all but negate the death penalty's major stated purposes: deterrence and retribution.

Apparently more than Garland, however, Banner shows that along with the persistence of capital punishment, the United States has a long tradition of opposition to the death penalty. Even before independence, some Northern colonies had narrowed the list of capital offenses from those in England. Abolitionist sentiment also dates from colonial times and grew after independence.

Within the first years of the Republic, five states had abolished the death penalty for all crimes except murder. By the time of the Civil War, no Northern state provided capital punishment for any crime other than murder or treason. And Michigan in 1846 became the first state to abolish the death penalty altogether. Banner treats the decision as the start of a slowly emerging trend. Stevens faults Garland for treating it instead as idiosyncratic, the work of a few liberal reformers in the face of Michiganders' general views.

The death penalty continued to recede for a full century after the Civil War. New methods of execution were designed to be more humane: first, the electric chair; then, the gas chamber (and, now, lethal injection). Public executions disappeared. The number of executions fell over time. By the 1960s, abolitionists could see their goal within sight.

The Supreme Court's 1972 decision in *Furman v. Georgia* to invalidate all existing death sentences appeared to fulfill the abolitionists' goal. As Garland relates, however, the backlash was strong and swift. By 1976, in Stevens' first full year on the Supreme Court, two-thirds of the states had voted to reinstitute capital punishment.

Stevens provided the critical fifth vote to uphold state death penalty laws as long as death sentences were not mandatory and jurors (or judges) had full discretion to consider all aggravating and mitigating factors in imposing sentence. Stevens' hopeful expectation of a rational and equitable system of capital punishment was dashed by the Supreme Court itself. After the retirement of his fellow moderate Republican Potter Stewart in 1981, the court began to retreat from careful policing of capital cases.

As examples, Stevens points to the court's refusal in 1987 to act on the implications of a study showing death sentences imposed more often in cases with white victims than in those with victims of color. He faults the court for helping prosecutors block potential jurors with reservations about capital punishment. And he criticizes the court for reversing itself twice, in the span of only a few years, to allow the death penalty in felony-murder cases and to permit "victim impact" statements in capital sentencing hearings.

In 2008, Stevens went public with his frustrations in a separate opinion in the decision, *Baze v. Rees*, that upheld the current procedure for lethal injection executions. With no convincing evidence of deterrence, and no legitimate interest in retribution for its own sake, Stevens concluded that it was time for "a dispassionate, impartial comparison" of the "enormous" costs of the death penalty compared to its dubious benefits.

Garland casts doubt on the likelihood of such a debate. He views public support for the death penalty as a political and cultural phenomenon more than a considered legal policy choice — in effect, one battle in a broader culture war. Risk-averse politicians burnish their law-enforcement credentials by siding with public opinion.

The Supreme Court has nibbled at the edges over the past decade by prohibiting the death penalty for juveniles or offenders with intellectual disabilities and in non-homicide cases. The rulings, two of them written by the moderate conservative Anthony M. Kennedy, hark to the previous tradition of narrowing capital punishment. But barring a further shift by Kennedy, the Roberts Court's majority appears steadfast in giving states broad discretion to adopt what Garland provocatively calls this "peculiar institution."

The imperfect workings of the death penalty system can be seen in cases that reach the Supreme Court on other issues — in this instance, an Alabama death row inmate's Sixth Amendment claim of ineffective assistance of counsel.

Alabama's Backwater of Justice
(*Jost on Justice*, Jan. 23, 2012)

Some 80 years ago, a citizens' posse in Alabama hauled nine black teenagers off a railroad car and turned them over to authorities to be charged with raping two white girls. The Scottsboro Boys, as they came to be known, were convicted and all but one of them sentenced to death after a series of trials with inadequate legal representation and conducted in a mob atmosphere.

Well before the due process revolution, the Supreme Court could not countenance the product of Alabama's criminal injustice system — even with four doggedly conservative members. Twice, the court ordered new trials, first because of the lack of effective legal representation and then because of the systematic exclusion of African Americans from juries. Even after one of the accusers retracted the charges, four were convicted in a third trial. Alabama courts to the contrary notwithstanding, history now judges them to have been innocent.

Today, Alabama remains a backwater of justice in death penalty cases. But last week [Jan. 18], the Supreme Court — once again with four doggedly conservative justices – gave an Alabama death row inmate a limited reprieve. The court's 7-2 decision in *Maples v. Thomas* gives Cory Maples a second chance, despite Alabama's strenuous opposition, to show that he was convicted and sentenced to death only after being denied his Sixth Amendment right to effective assistance of counsel.

Maples' conviction and sentence are products of Alabama policies that give indigent defendants in capital cases only the bare rudiments of a legal defense. Court-appointed lawyers for indigent defendants need nothing more than five years' experience in criminal cases. They need not have handled a capital case before, and they do not have to undergo any training in the special procedural rules for capital cases.

Until 1999, court-appointed attorneys were paid only $40 an hour in the courtroom and $20 an hour out of court, with a $1,000 cap on out-of-court work. The cap was removed in 1999, and pay raised — but only to $70 an hour for work in or out of the courtroom.

With capital defense so constrained, Alabama unsurprisingly ranks high in the number of executions since capital punishment was restored in 1976: sixth among the states with 53 executions. And the state ranks fifth in the nation in the number of inmates currently facing death sentences, with 206 prisoners on death row. More than two-thirds of them were sentenced before the modest rise in indigent defense compensation in 1999.

Alabama is also one of the few states that does not guarantee representation to indigent capital defendants in postconviction proceedings. Death row inmates must look to volunteer lawyers for help, often to young lawyers performing pro bono service at big, out-of-state law firms.

Maples was charged with killing two friends in 1997 while out on the town with them. He was represented at trial by two court-appointed attorneys. Only one had ever tried a death penalty case, and he had not taken the prior case through a penalty phase hearing. Maples was convicted and sentenced to death, and his conviction and sentence were upheld on appeal.

Maples then filed a petition for postconviction relief in state court based on ineffective assistance at counsel, represented in the proceeding by two young lawyers from the New York firm of Sullivan & Cromwell: Jaasai Munanka and Clara Ingen-Housz. Predictably, an Alabama judge denied Maples' plea. The court clerk's office mailed notice of the decision to the two New York lawyers and to the Alabama lawyer who agreed to serve as local counsel as long as he did not have to actually work on the case.

Now, Maples fell victim to what Justice Samuel A. Alito Jr. called in a concurring opinion "a veritable perfect storm of misfortune" that caused him to miss the deadline for appealing the decision through no fault of his own. Munanka and Ingen-Housz had left Sullivan & Cromwell, but failed to notify Maples, the local lawyer, or the Alabama trial court of their move. The Sullivan & Cromwell mail room returned the notice to the court clerk, unopened. The local lawyer ignored it, assuming that the New York lawyers were still on the case. The court clerk did not attempt to find Munanka or Ingen-Housz.

With the deadline missed, the state appellate court dismissed Maples' appeal. In urging dismissal, the state's attorney said that Maples could still file a federal habeas corpus petition. But when he did, the state's lawyers said that federal courts should dismiss the petition because of his "procedural default." As Justice Ruth Bader Ginsburg noted in her majority opinion, there was "some tension" between the state's two positions.

Ginsburg led six other justices, including Alito and fellow conservative Chief Justice John G. Roberts Jr., in concluding that Maples was entitled to an appeal because he had been abandoned by his lawyers. "In these circumstances, no just system would lay the default at Maples' death-cell door," she wrote. Perhaps not, but Justices Antonin Scalia and Clarence Thomas would have. Alabama was entitled "to stand on its rights," Scalia wrote, "and enforce a habeas petitioner's procedural default even when counsel is to blame."

Maples now gets a chance to argue his Sixth Amendment claim before a federal judge, who will have no vested interest in excusing Alabama's record in indigent capital defense. As Ginsburg suggested, a just system — but not Alabama — would give Maples at least that much.

Alabama's death penalty system allows judges to override a jury's decision to impose life imprisonment instead of a death sentence, and judges often do. In a forceful dissent, Justice Sonia Sotomayor blamed the judges' penchant for imposing the death penalty on the state's system of partisan elections for judgeships.

Lightning-Strike Death Penalty
(*Jost on Justice*, Dec. 1, 2013)

When Justice Potter Stewart provided a critical vote in the Supreme Court's decision to strike down capital punishment in 1972, he wrote that the death penalty, as then administered, was "cruel and unusual in the same way that being struck by lightning is cruel and unusual." Four years later, Stewart provided a critical vote in reinstating capital punishment as long as courts held separate penalty hearings and defendants could present any possible evidence of "mitigating factors" for juries to consider.

Despite the implementation of those Supreme Court-ordered reforms, critics say the death penalty is still, 30 years later, as arbitrary as a lightning strike. But in one state, Alabama, one source of the arbitrariness is plainly visible: politically elected judges who condemn defendants to death after juries have recommended life prison sentences instead.

Only three states permit judges to override jury sentencing decisions not to impose the death penalty in capital cases at all — Delaware and Florida are the others — but only in Alabama are judges routinely exercising that power now. Of the 199 inmates now on Alabama's death row, 42 are there because judges imposed death sentences in the face of jurors' decisions to spare the defendants' lives. No judge in Delaware or Florida has done so since 1999; a fourth state that once permitted death sentences by judicial overrides, Indiana, changed its law and took that power away from judges.

The Supreme Court upheld Alabama's law in a 1995 decision, *Harris v. Alabama*. Justice Sonia Sotomayor drew attention to the practice last month [Nov. 18] in an opinion calling on the court to reconsider that decision. Along with Justice Stephen G. Breyer, Sotomayor dissented when the court declined to take up a new case, *Woodward v. Alabama*, challenging the practice.

As Sotomayor explained, Alabama is now "a clear outlier" among the 32 states that allow the death penalty. Juries have a role in 31 of the state death-penalty schemes (all but Montana), and they have a final say in all but three.

Florida had been the leader in judicial override death sentences in the 1980s with 89 in the decade, but the number dwindled to 26 in the 1990s until the practice disappeared after 1999. Indiana never had more than one such case per year; Delaware has had only such case ever, and that judicially imposed death sentence was eventually reduced to life imprisonment. But the practice continues in Alabama: 30 judicial override death sentences in the 1980s, 44 in the '90s, and 26 since 2000, an average of two a year.

Sotomayor believes the reason for Alabama judges' death-dealing inclinations is simple: politics. Judges are elected in partisan races in Alabama; Florida holds nonpartisan judicial elections, while judges are appointed by the governor in Delaware. Alabama judges, Sotomayor writes, "appear to have succumbed to electoral pressures." She noted that one Alabama judge, who has overridden jury verdicts to impose the death penalty six times, ran a campaign advertisement naming some of the defendants he had had sentenced to death; in at least one of the cases, the judge overrode the jury's contrary judgment.

Sotomayor relied heavily in her opinion on a report by the Equal Justice Initiative, the Montgomery, Ala.-based public interest law firm. Its 32-page report, "The Death Penalty in Alabama: Judge Override," made the point more forcefully, in part by citing statistics to indicate that death sentences by judicial overrides in Alabama peak in election years. "Because judicial candidates frequently campaign on their support and enthusiasm for capital punishment," the report states, "political pressure injects unfairness and arbitrariness into override decisions."

The report indicates that political pressure does not run the other way. In only nine cases have Alabama judges overridden jury recommendations to impose the death penalty in favor of a life sentence instead. And Alabama judges do not impose death sentences only after closely divided jury votes; in more than a dozen cases, judges sentenced defendants to death after jurors voted unanimously for life sentences.

In her opinion, Sotomayor also argued that the judicial override practice in Alabama runs afoul of the Supreme Court's line of precedents — the so-called *Apprendi* cases — requiring jury instead of judicial fact-finding to raise a defendant's sentence above the statutory minimum. (Breyer, a dissenter from those decisions, did not join that part of Sotomayor's opinion.) As Sotomayor detailed, the judge in the case under review sentenced Mario Woodward to death for the killing of a Montgomery police officer after rejecting the jury's 8-4 finding of mitigating factors based on Woodward's abused childhood and his good relationship with his five children. Under *Apprendi,* Sotomayor wrote, "a sentencing scheme that permits such a result is constitutionally suspect."

Justices use dissents from cert denials in part to highlight issues for possible later consideration. It takes only four votes to grant certiorari, so one question about Woodward's case is why the other liberal justices — Ruth Bader Ginsburg and Elena Kagan — failed to join Sotomayor's opinion. Perhaps they thought the case a poor vehicle to raise the issue: the mitigating factors in Woodward's favor do appear somewhat flimsy.

Or perhaps they feared that the liberal bloc could not persuade Justice Anthony M. Kennedy to provide a fifth vote against Alabama's judicial override practice, at least not now. Still, Sotomayor laid out a strong case that Alabama's lightning-strike death penalty system deserves "a fresh look."

Lethal injections became the nearly universal method of execution because it was seen to be simple, effective, and humane. "Botched" executions in 2014 suggested that assumption was not well founded, but the Roberts Court showed little interest in re-examining the practice.

Lethal Injections Challenged
(*Jost on Justice*, March 30, 2014)

Tommy Lynn Sells, a self-confessed serial killer on Texas's death row, wants the state to tell him about the drugs it plans to use to put him on death on Thursday [April 3]. Two lower courts moved to grant his request, but the Texas Supreme Court decided late last week [March 28] that Sells' interest in a humane execution may be outweighed by the state's interest in protecting the confidentiality and safety of the companies that supply lethal injection drugs.

Sells and a second Texas death row inmate, Ramiro Hernandez, are among condemned prisoners in several states waging uphill legal fights against state authorities over the drugs planned for use in lethal injection executions. Death penalty states are in a bind because one of the drugs formerly used in lethal injections, sodium pentothal, is no longer available.

States have scrambled for a substitute and, according to death penalty critics and lawyers for death row inmates, resorted to drugs of unproven efficacy and put up walls of secrecy to try to hide the problems. "The states are more secret than they've ever been," Deborah Denno, a law professor at Fordham University in New York and a leading authority on methods of execution, remarked to *The New York Times*'s Adam Liptak.

Many death penalty supporters may see the inmates' pleas for a "safe" method of execution as yet another tactic to delay or even avoid their death sentences —and an illogical argument at that. But lethal injection became the nearly universal method of execution in the United States over the past three decades because it came to be seen as the most humane of putting the condemned inmate to death.

Admittedly, murderers such as Sells show no such solicitude for their victims, but that failing is what distinguishes them from the rest of us. It is not too much to ask that courts make sure that lethal injections, as carried out, are the humane executions they are supposed to be.

Lethal injections typically proceed with administration of three drugs in sequence: sodium pentothal (also known as sodium thiopental) to render the inmate unconscious; pancuronium bromide, a neuromuscular paralyzing agent, to stop the inmate from breathing; and potassium chloride to induce cardiac arrest and thus death. But sodium pentothal is no longer available because the former U.S. supplier no longer makes it and European companies refuse to provide it for executions.

As Liptak related in his "Sidebar" column [March 11], reports of executions carried out in two states in January indicate that the substitute drugs used left the inmates conscious and in agonizing pain as the procedure continued. An Oklahoma inmate was heard to say, "I feel my whole body burning." An Ohio inmate was described by a reporter witness to have struggled, gasped for air, and choked for 10 minutes before succumbing.

Oklahoma is among the states refusing to tell inmates about the drugs now being used. A trial court judge ruled last week [March 26] that the law prohibiting release of that information violates inmates' due process rights. A judge in Tennessee, ruling in January in a similar suit, ordered the state to turn over the information requested; the ruling is on appeal. In Texas, Sells had won rulings from a lower court judge and an intermediate appellate court before the state supreme court intervened on Friday to block the release pending further consideration.

The issue reached the U.S. Supreme Court earlier this year in a plea by a Missouri death row inmate, Michael Taylor, seeking the identities of the physician, pharmacy, and laboratory who prescribed, compounded, and tested the drugs to be used for his execution. The Eighth U.S. Circuit Court of Appeals on Jan. 24 flatly rejected the plea in an en banc decision, *In re Lombardi*. Writing in *The Atlantic*, legal affairs commentator Andrew Cohen aptly called the ruling "terrible" from either a First Amendment or Eighth Amendment perspective. A month later, the Supreme Court refused on Feb. 25 to grant a stay of execution, but three justices —Ginsburg, Sotomayor, and Kagan — dissented, citing the dissenting Eighth Circuit judges. Taylor was executed later that day.

Among the issues confronting inmates in these cases is an earlier Supreme Court decision, *Baze v. Rees* (2008), that rejected a challenge to lethal injection protocols brought by Kentucky inmates. States are citing Chief Justice Roberts's plurality opinion in the case as requiring inmates that challenge an execution procedure to propose a valid procedure themselves. Lawyers for inmates argue that is an absurd requirement that would put them in an ethical conflict with their clients.

Two more cases raising these issues are already at the Supreme Court, as Liptak noted. In *Sepulvado v. Jindal*, 13-892, Louisiana death row inmate Christopher Sepulvado is claiming a due process right to "timely notice of the method by which he will be executed." Sepulvado's plea was to be conferenced by the justices on Friday; a decision whether to hear the case could come on Monday [March 31]. A second Missouri case, *Zink v. Lombardi*, 13-8435, is scheduled for conference this week.

For the most part, the Roberts Court majority has shown little sympathy for death penalty challenges. They may turn these pleas aside too, but at a cost to the public's seeming decision that executions be carried out according to modern views of common humanity.

The court declined to hear the Sepulvado and Zink cases, but the justices agreed in January 2015 to hear a similar case brought by Oklahoma death row inmates. The decision in Glossip v. Gross was expected by the end of June.

* * *

Remembering Trayvon Martin
(*Jost on Justice,* April 16, 2012)

Megan Kanka, seven years old, was raped and murdered on July 29, 1994, by a next-door neighbor, who unbeknownst to anyone in her suburban New Jersey neighborhood had two previous convictions for sexually assaulting young girls. Just one month later, the New Jersey legislature passed a law requiring convicted sex offenders to register with a state database and making that information available to the public.

Washington State had passed the first such law four years earlier, but the measures are now universally known as "Megan's Laws" and have been enacted in various forms by Congress and by legislatures in every state. One can question the wisdom or the effectiveness of the laws, but they are firmly established as a lasting legacy to an innocent victim of a senseless crime — an attempt to show that Megan Kanka did not die in vain.

Trayvon Martin, who prosecutors say was an innocent victim of a senseless crime, deserves no less. Even as state attorney Angela Corey and her team of prosecutors prepare to try George Zimmerman on a charge of second-degree murder, legislators in the 20 or more states that passed so-called "Stand Your Ground Laws" in the past seven years should begin the task of rewriting or repealing those measures — so that Trayvon Martin, in some sense, not have died in vain.

Florida has the dubious honor of having passed the first of these laws expanding the right of self-defense to include the use of deadly force in public settings under specified circumstances and eliminating any duty to retreat if possible to avoid doing so. The Florida legislature approved the measure in April 2005 at the strong urging of the National Rifle Association (NRA) and in the face of opposition from law enforcement in the state. Miami Police Chief John Timoney called the bill unnecessary and dangerous and presciently warned — according to the *New York Times*'s account— that "many people, *including children, could become innocent victims*" (emphasis added).

With the NRA driving them, similar laws were passed in more than a dozen other states by the end of the 2006 legislative season even as Florida prosecutors were finding the state's version to be an impediment to convictions in killings of dubious self-defense. Today, the Association of Prosecuting Attorneys counts 30 states in all that have liberalized the rules of self-defense since 2005. Some, but not all, of those laws have been enacted after full public debate. As one example, Wisconsin's measure was enacted with little public attention after a stealth letter-writing campaign by the state's NRA affiliate, according to a recent account in the *New York Times*.

The prosecutors' group points to data from the FBI that suggest the laws may have contributed to a sharp increase in the number of homicides by private citizens deemed to be "justified," not only in Florida but also nationwide. The FBI counted 192 "justifiable" private citizen homicides in 2005 and 278 in 2010 — a 45 percent increase in just five years. In Florida itself, the number has tripled, according to the state's Department of Law Enforcement, from an average of 12 per year before 2005 to 36 per year since.

Florida's law may or may not prove determinative in the case against Zimmerman, the hyperactive neighborhood watch coordinator now in custody after being charged with second-degree murder on April 11, nearly seven weeks after the Feb. 26 killing. Zimmerman shot and killed Martin after he pursued the African American teenager on the unfounded suspicion that Martin was "up to no good" in the gated community that Zimmerman had undertaken to patrol. But the law at least played a part in the decision by Sanford authorities not to arrest Zimmerman that night even though the chief investigator said Zimmerman's claim of self-defense was not to be believed.

From all that appears, the case is now in good hands in Florida's justice system. Corey was brought in from Jacksonville as special prosecutor after state's attorney Norm Wolfinger recused himself. Corey made an impressive appearance in the nationally televised announcement of the charges against Zimmerman. The affidavit backing up the charge, released the next day, provides a succinct statement of the evidence supporting the accusation. The defendant himself is now being represented, pro bono, by a well regarded Florida attorney, Mark O'Mara. Trayvon's parents and many of those who have clamored for an arrest are now satisfied that the case is in the courts.

The groundswell of indignation at the killing could now be turned to the broader purpose of restoring the law of self-defense to the sensible balance that had obtained for most of U.S. history until the NRA-led drive of the past decade. Anglo-American law had long recognized the so-called "Castle Doctrine" that permits the use of force, even deadly force, in self-defense within one's home. Expanding that doctrine to public settings has made the streets not safer, but less safe, according to law enforcement officials.

The NRA has been lying low since the Martin killing, but former NRA president Marion Hammer, a Floridian who played a key role in enactment of the "Stand Your Ground Law," insists there is no need to change it. If Trayvon Martin were alive today, he might have a different opinion.

Zimmerman was tried and acquitted. The verdict, I wrote afterward, was unsatisfying but not unexpected.

No Answers From Verdict
(*Jost on Justice*, July 14, 2013)

The not-guilty verdict in the George Zimmerman case came as no surprise to those who had carefully followed the three-week trial. Nor to those who had predicted from the first that no Florida jury would convict the white/Hispanic wannabe-cop in the shooting death of the unarmed black teenager Trayvon Martin in a gated community in Sanford, Florida. Nor to the criminal justice experts who explained, also from the start, that a self-defense defense is hard for the prosecution to rebut, especially if the victim is dead.

The six jurors — all women, none of them African American — surprised some observers by deliberating for 16 hours and 20 minutes before returning their verdict late Saturday night [July 13]. With so much attention to the prosecution's shortcomings and the defense team's skillful playing of the reasonable-doubt card, some expected a verdict within a couple of hours.

The anonymous jurors have exercised their right to confidentiality, so the course of their deliberations remains for now unknown. Suffice it to say that the reports that the jury "believed" Zimmerman's claim of self-defense may be an overstatement. It was enough for an acquittal that none of them found him "guilty" beyond a reasonable doubt of either second-degree murder or manslaughter.

The televised trial tested the patience of some observers, who thought Americans should be paying more attention to events in Egypt or the debate over electronic surveillance. But the Zimmerman case raised profound issues: race, crime, guns. The availability of gavel-to-gavel coverage prepared Americans for a verdict that might otherwise have been a jarring and disorder-producing shock.

Despite their importance, those issues were not argued in the courtroom. Judge Debra Nelson prohibited the prosecution from saying that Zimmerman had "racially": profiled Martin on that rainy night in February 2012. Florida's "Stand Your Ground" law — so much the focus in the weeks after the killing — was in the background but not front and center: Zimmerman declined the chance to use the law to get the case dismissed without a full trial.

Instead, the trial turned into, of all things, a trial: with testimony from eyewitnesses, earwitnesses, investigators, experts, and friends and family of victim and defendant. Those who hoped for a conviction began complaining about the prosecution's case by the time the trial reached the halfway point. They saw miscues, mistakes, and missed opportunities that doomed the case.

The judgment is too harsh. For one thing, the defense often has the advantage in a high-profile trial. The prosecutors are typically career civil servants: underpaid, overworked, underresourced. The defense lawyers — whether paid or pro bono — are often in a better position to pull out all stops for this one case, with a payoff in the form of national publicity and a possible book deal. The O.J. Simpson trial is an example, and not an isolated one.

In any event, the Zimmerman prosecution team had to play the hand it was dealt — and it was not a good one. Martin was not alive to give his version of the fight that ensued after Zimmerman exited his car and the two of them — a burly adult and a wiry teen — struggled on the ground. Rachel Jeantel, the cellphone friend speaking with Martin in the moments before his death, was a witness with an unhelpful attitude. And the police investigators, including lead detective Chris Serino, very unhelpfully said they believed Zimmerman's version, his inconsistencies notwithstanding.

Prosecutors perhaps could have done more with those inconsistencies and more with the logical inferences from some of the uncontradicted evidence. In the end, however, the trial came down to two highly disputed questions of fact: who was on top on the struggle and who was heard to scream in the final moments. The eyewitnesses from the neighborhood supported the defense version that it was Zimmerman on the ground, pummeled by Martin atop him. And the earwitnesses too — except for Martin's mother — indicated it was Zimmerman, not Martin, heard to scream on the 911 tape.

The prosecution team responded to the verdict with as much dignity as they could muster. "I am disappointed with the verdict," said chief prosecutor Bernie de la Rionda. "We accept it." Co-counsel John Guy commended the Martin family. "They've been dignified, they've shown class," he said.

The same cannot be said for Zimmerman's family or his chief counsel, Mark O'Mara. Zimmerman's brother, Robert Zimmerman, said on CNN that the family fears people "that would want to take the law into their own hands" — apparently unaware of the irony. And O'Mara went so far as to say that if Zimmerman had been black, he would never have been charged. As refutation, bloggers dug up a 2007 case from

New York in which a black homeowner was convicted of manslaughter for the shooting death of a white punk making trouble in his front yard.

Was justice done? The Martin family had their day in court, however unsatisfying. Zimmerman goes free, not guilty but also not innocent. But true justice would require that Martin have found his way home that night, unimpeded. Do we know the truth of what happened that night? No. A nation still divided by race and ideology has to live with two versions of truth, never to meet.

9

#CivilJustice

The civil justice system has been the subject of fierce attack over the past several decades. The critics – business interests and political conservatives – contend that the legal system tilts too far in favor of plaintiffs and that trial lawyers exploit those advantages for their benefit more than for the sake of injured victims. The tort reform movement has succeeded in enacting any number of laws at the state level to make it harder for plaintiffs to recover and in any event to limit the size of potential damage awards.

The Roberts Court has proved to be sympathetic to those arguments, most dramatically perhaps when it gutted a major class action charging the giant discount retailer Walmart with discriminating against female employees. I discussed the case in a column after oral arguments in May 2011 and then again, along with other decisions, after the term had ended.

The Women of Wal-Mart
(*Jost on Justice*, April 24, 2011)

One year after the Deepwater Horizon explosion and oil spill, the job of cleaning up the Gulf coast still faces daunting challenges. So too the job of compensating the victims of this environmental disaster: tens of thousands of people whose lives and livelihoods have been damaged by the oil that has fouled beaches and spoiled valuable fisheries.

Despite the challenges, the victims of the Gulf oil spill have one thing going for them: public and political pressure on BP, operator of the doomed rig, to make the victims whole as best it can. Under pressure from politicians from President Obama down, BP pledged $20 billion to a victim compensation fund to be administered by a respected lawyer, Kenneth Feinberg. The process has been controversial, but in advance of the one-year anniversary [April 20] Feinberg was making a maximum media effort last week to answer criticisms and to renew the commitment on BP's behalf to do the right thing.

A month earlier, another corporate giant, Wal-Mart Stores, faced a critical Supreme Court showdown in a lawsuit brought on behalf of women employees who claim they are victims of a long-standing "pattern and practice" of illegal sex discrimination in regard to pay and promotions. Wal-Mart's purported victims got some support from civil rights and women's rights groups, but the company has been spared the kind of public and political pressure that BP is experiencing.

Instead, Wal-Mart, the nation's largest private employer, has managed to depict itself in court and in the public mind as a victim itself. In legal filings, and in arguments at the high court (March 29), Wal-Mart's lawyers maintained that a company with $419 billion in sales last year faces the risk of "devastating" financial liability from what they and an array of business groups supporting the company insist on calling a "gargantuan" class-action lawsuit.

Ten years after the lawsuit was filed, the plaintiffs' allegations and Wal-Mart's substantive defense have yet to be fully aired in a courtroom. Instead, lawyers on both sides have spent a staggering number of hours on a preliminary but crucial issue: whether to certify the suit to be tried as a class action on behalf of as many as 500,000 women currently working for Wal-Mart. (Wal-Mart's lawyers refer to 1.5 million potential class members, but that figure includes former employees, who have been cut out of the case for now.)

The rule authorizing class actions in federal court, Rule 23 of the Federal Rules of Civil Procedure, is forbiddingly wordy. Court decisions interpreting and applying it are similarly complex. Over the past two decades, both Congress and the Supreme Court have been making it harder for plaintiffs to bring and win these cases. Even skeptics and opponents, however, acknowledge that class actions can sometimes be the only viable legal remedy for wronged investors, consumers, or workers. And plaintiffs' attorneys note that in some circumstances companies benefit from resolving a multitude of potential legal claims in one big proceeding instead of countless small cases.

The case that began as *Dukes v. Wal-Mart* takes its name from lead plaintiff Betty Dukes, who was hired in 1994 as a $5 per hour part-time cashier at the Wal-Mart in Pittsburg, Calif. By her account, she was unfairly passed over, disciplined, and demoted at various points because of the company's ingrained mistreatment of female employees. Dukes' case was taken on by the Impact Fund, an Oakland-based public interest law firm, and its senior counsel, Brad Seligman.

So far, Dukes' legal team has persuaded a federal district court judge and a 6-5 majority on the Ninth U.S. Circuit Court of Appeals to allow the case to go forward as a class action. To get to that point, they presented evidence, both statistical and anecdotal, of sex discrimination in Wal-Mart's employment practices. The statistics are stark. As of the first court ruling, in 2004, two-thirds of Wal-Mart workers were women, but women comprised only about one-third of management-level employees. A statistician found a 5 percent to 15 percent gender gap in pay for women in all 41 of Wal-Mart's regions.

Starker still were affidavits submitted by 120 current or former employees altogether. Under oath, women from all over the country described a climate of sexism and gender stereotyping that demeaned them day by day and limited their pay and advancement. Some described being told that they were being paid less than male workers because men needed extra money to support families. One woman who complained about sex discrimination said she was fired after contacting the lawyers in the suit.

Whether or not the case proceeds as a class action, the affidavits lay out tenable individual cases of illegal sex discrimination. Years later, however, the women are still waiting their day in court. And it is not yet clear when, where, or whether that day will come. Supreme Court justices appeared dubious during oral arguments about whether the case satisfies Rule 23's somewhat rigorous requirements. If no class action is allowed, the claims may be too insubstantial, or too old, to succeed as individual cases.

As BP's experience illustrates, mass justice is difficult and contentious under even the best of circumstances. But, as legal expert Geoffrey Hazard remarked during the early days of class actions, "mass-produced wrongs" sometimes call for a mass-produced legal remedy. The women of Wal-Mart are waiting to see whether the judicial system will be up to that challenge in their case.

The court ruled against the plaintiffs in a 5-4 decision; the majority said the plaintiffs had failed to show a companywide policy of sex discrimination as required to pursue the case as a class action. The decision was one of several that term that made it harder for plaintiffs to pursue claims of wrongdoing in court.

Closing Courthouse Doors
(*Jost on Justice*, Aug. 15, 2011)

When the Supreme Court adjourned for its summer recess last year, the court's conservative majority was under fire for having opened the floodgates to unlimited political spending by corporations. The ruling in the Citizens United case seemed to many emblematic of the Roberts Court's undue solicitude for the rights and interests of corporations.

This year, the justices left Washington with the court's conservative majority under fire again for rulings that benefited business interests. The Roberts Court was seen by many as having closed the courthouse doors to ordinary Americans seeking justice for wrongs done to them in the workplace or marketplace.

"We take so seriously in this country the notion that any person with a claim should have his or her day in court," said Erwin Chemerinsky, the liberal dean of the University of California-Irvine Law School. "But a majority of the Supreme Court doesn't seem to believe it."

Far from denying the accusation, many of the court's admirers acknowledge that the conservative majority is deeply skeptical of litigation. The Roberts Court "sees the court system as being overused and misused by whoever's invoking it," says Tom Goldstein, Supreme Court advocate and founder of SCOTUSBlog.

"The Supreme Court is not going to expand existing precedents to allow more litigation," says Jonathan Adler, a conservative constitutional law expert at Case Western Reserve University School of Law. "You see that across a wide range of areas."

As prime examples, the court's critics cite the two headline-making decisions that will make it harder for plaintiffs to mount broad legal attacks against discrimination in the workplace or corporate fraud in the marketplace. Both decisions — gutting the big sex discrimination suit against Wal-Mart and barring a class action by cell phone customers against AT&T — came on 5-4 votes that pitted the court's conservative majority against the liberal bloc.

A review of the full term confirms Adler's point that the court's aversion to litigation runs across many areas. The victims of the court's attitude come from all walks of life. A blue-collar worker in New Jersey injured on the job by an allegedly defective machine is told he must sue the manufacturer in England. Women in Louisiana and Minnesota suffering from a debilitating side effect of a prescription medication are blocked from suing the drug makers. A Louisiana man wrongfully convicted of murder because of prosecutorial misconduct loses his bid to hold the district attorney's office liable

Prison inmates will not be allowed to recover damages for violations of their religious rights. Anyone detained by the government using the material witness statute as a pretext cannot recover for loss of liberty. Taxpayers will find it harder to challenge government tax policies that breach the separation of church and state.

The cases that reach the Supreme Court are rarely open and shut, so there are two sides to each of these cases. Some turn on dissection of federal statutes, others on application of Supreme Court precedents. Some are by 5-4 votes, others by a broader majority. But they share a common theme. The Roberts Court sees no need to read laws and interpret past decisions when possible to open the courthouse door and assure plaintiffs a viable path to legal remedy.

The ruling in *Wal-Mart Stores, Inc. v. Dukes* raises the burden on plaintiffs in a job discrimination case to produce evidence of a company's wrongdoing at a preliminary stage or pursue the suit through individual complaints instead of a class action. The decision in *AT&T v. Concepcion* gives businesses a roadmap to enforce arbitration clauses in preprinted consumer contracts that consign a defrauded customer to individual instead of classwide arbitration. The majority in each case was indifferent to the likelihood that many workers or consumers would never be able to take their claims to court.

The injured worker in *J. McIntyre Machinery, Ltd. v. Nicastro* was blocked from suing in New Jersey by a 6-3 majority blind to the English manufacturer's business-seeking in the United States. The 5-4 majority in *PLIVA, Inc. v. Mensing* read federal drug regulations so woodenly as to exempt a generic drug manufacturer from any ongoing duty to warn users of side effects. The 5-4 majority in *Connick v. Thompson* rejected evidence from the wrongfully convicted plaintiff that disregard of an important constitutional rule was standard practice in the Orleans Parish district attorney's office.

In *Sossamon v. Texas*, the 6-2 majority held that a federal law providing state prisoners "appropriate relief" against state governments for violations of their religious rights does not allow monetary damages as one of the possible remedies. A five-justice majority in *Ashcroft v. Al-Kidd* gave the government carte blanche to use the material witness statute to jail someone when there is not enough evidence for an arrest. In *Arizona Christian School Tuition Organization v. Winn*, the 5-4 majority repudiated a line of decisions allowing taxpayers legal standing to challenge tax policies as violations of the Establishment Clause.

The court's admirers find these rulings sound examples of judicial restraint. But the court-made rules created in these decisions also reflect a conscious policy preference that is at tension with the inscription above the Supreme Court's doors: Equal Justice Under Law.

Two years later, there was more of the same from the Roberts Court.

Cutting Back Civil Litigation
(*Jost on Justice*, June 23, 2013)

The Supreme Court's conservatives — Roberts, Scalia, Kennedy, Thomas, and Alito — are not the monolithic bloc often depicted. Roberts and Kennedy sometimes line up with the liberal justices on First Amendment issues. Scalia often breaks from the conservatives on Fourth Amendment issues. But the five are quite consistently together in voting to cut back legal remedies in civil litigation.

Five of the five-vote decisions so far this term have pitted the conservatives against the four liberal justices in rulings that limited civil lawsuits – by consumers, workers, opponents of government wiretapping, and victims of atrocities committed abroad. In the most recent, the court last week [June 20] torpedoed a federal antitrust complaint against American Express for allegedly using its monopoly position in corporate credit cards to force merchants to pay the high fees charged for its mass-market consumer cards.

The Court's 5-3 decision in *American Express v. Italian Colors Restaurant* held the plaintiff, a small Italian restaurant in Oakland, California, to a one-sided arbitration agreement that blocked it from joining with other merchants to press the case. The three liberal dissenters – with Sotomayor recused – rightly said the ruling made it impossible as a practical matter to pursue the complaint.

With the court's biggest cases still pending — gay marriage, affirmative action, voting rights — the decision was a distraction for most court watchers and the general public. But corporate lawyers took note. They hailed the decision as a victory against run-amok litigation even as public interest groups blasted the ruling — in the words of the group Public Justice — as "the worst Supreme Court arbitration decision ever."

The case represents the latest setback for merchants in a long fight against American Express's "Honor All Cards" policy. American Express has an effective monopoly on corporate credit cards. As a result, businesses that serve corporate customers are effectively forced to honor American Express's consumer credit cards too even though the service charges are 30 percent higher than those for competing cards.

In antitrust terms, American Express's policy is a "tying arrangement" – conditioning the use or purchase of one product or service on the use or purchase of another. Tying arrangements can be legal or not depending on the company's market power for the particular good or service and the effect of the arrangement on competition.

Those are issues for a court to sort out and rule on, but the evidence needed costs real money. An expert report in this case was likely to cost between several hundred thousand and one million dollars. Italian Colors' potential recovery was nowhere near that much: around $38,000. No economically rational plaintiff would bring that case.

A class action on behalf of all similarly situated plaintiffs — either in court or in arbitration — solves the financing problem by allowing costs to be shared and by offering the prospect of a big recovery. But American Express made sure that was not going to happen. American Express's agreement with merchants requires all disputes to be resolved in arbitration and on an individual rather than classwide basis. The agreement goes even further, as Justice Elena Kagan pointed out in her dissent. A confidentiality agreement prevented any informal cooperation with other merchants; and a merchant could not recover expenses from American Express even if successful.

The Supreme Court conservatives enforce arbitration agreements, even with onerous terms like those, on the ground that that is what Congress intended when it passed the Federal Arbitration Act back in 1923. The justices apparently indulge the fiction that these fine-print agreements are voluntary contracts. The federal appeals court in New York City looked at these terms and said, in short, no way. It relied on a doctrine in Supreme Court precedents that allow agreements to be invalidated if they prevent the "effective vindication" of a federal statutory right.

For the Supreme Court majority, however, Justice Antonin Scalia was not buying it. "[T]he fact that it is not worth the expense involved in *proving* a statutory remedy does not constitute the elimination of the *right to pursue* that remedy," Scalia wrote in the key passage.

Kagan accurately summed up the result. "The monopolist gets to use its monopoly power to insist on a contract effectively depriving its victims of all legal recourse," she wrote. The message from the Court, she added, is quite simple: "Too darn bad."

Two business lawyers briefing reporters at a U.S. Chamber of Commerce-sponsored event the next day applauded the ruling and disputed Kagan's dire assessment. Theodore Boutrous, victorious lawyer two terms ago in defanging the big sex discrimination case against Wal-Mart, insisted that the Justice Department and the Federal Trade Commission could bear the load on antitrust cases. "The notion that we need private lawyers to bring these cases is wrong," he said. Kannon Shanmugam joined in debunking class action litigation in general. "What Justice Kagan doesn't appreciate is that these cases are lawyer-driven," he said.

Perhaps, but Congress approved Rule 23, the class action rule in the Federal Rules of Civil Procedure, to allow some forms of mass litigation to ensure effective vindication of legal rights. Brian Fitzpatrick, a civil litigation expert at Vanderbilt Law School, said the latest decision continued a series of Roberts Court rulings that allow companies to use arbitration to protect themselves from class actions. "There is little future" for class actions, he warned.

Medical malpractice suits have been one of the major targets of the litigation critics. In this column, I tried to debunk the scary picture of an "explosion" in malpractice suits and to refocus the discussion on the real issue: the rising number of preventable medical errors.

Malpractice Blame Game

(*CQ Weekly*, March 28, 2005)

Gresham's law, the 16th century dictum that "bad money drives out good," applies to political discourse as well. Bad politics, we often find, drives out good policy. The "crisis" in Social Security provides one current example, but a more protracted illustration is the 30-year-old war over medical malpractice.

As in the past, today's debate over whether and how to compensate victims of medical injury consists largely of exaggeration, distortion and obstruction by all concerned: doctors, lawyers and insurers.

From the doctors' point of view, there is nothing wrong with the health care system except the need, as Shakespeare put it, to first kill all the lawyers. Lawyers talk about doctors as uncaring, incompetent, or too gullible to realize they're being gouged by insurance companies. For their part, insurers see no need to strengthen the states' notoriously lax regulation of the insurance industry.

Obscured by the demonizing and dissembling are some plausible proposals to address the issues of medical injuries and patient compensation. These include health care system changes to guard against medical mistakes, insurance regulation changes to require more transparent rate-setting, and no-fault compensation or legal changes to reduce the cost and expense of litigation.

Simply capping damages in medical malpractice cases, as President Bush and congressional Republicans are urging, is just that: simplistic. But as long as Bush and others insist on treating greedy trial lawyers as the only problem — with the plaintiffs' bar responding in kind — any other proposal will get too little attention and too little traction to win adoption.

First, a primer on some undisputed facts. Preventable medical errors are a leading cause of death in the United States, according to the Institute of Medicine, which in 1999 estimated the toll at 44,000 to 98,000 deaths per year. And most victims of medical injury do not file malpractice claims. That was documented by an influential Harvard study more than a decade ago and is certainly even truer today.

So, whatever the reasons for rising insurance premiums, the health care system has a real problem in terms of patient safety that the medical profession largely disregards. In the same vein, trial lawyers see no need to tinker with the fault-based jury system for medical injury cases, even though they turn away many serious cases because of the time and expense in bringing such suits.

The best evidence also contradicts Bush's claims about "skyrocketing" jury awards. Malpractice payouts reported to the National Practitioner Data Bank increased to $4.3 billion in 2004 from $3.0 billion in 1991. That's far from an explosion — and not enough to justify the double-digit increases in malpractice insurance premiums faced by some (not all) doctors in some (not all) states.

As for the "junk" or "frivolous" medical liability suits that the president denounces, no less an authority than Victor Schwartz, a Washington lawyer and leading "tort reform" advocate, says there aren't any. Medical malpractice cases are too expensive to bring, he says, unless the lawyer sees some prospect of recovery at the end. The real impact of caps on jury awards is murky at best, but one recent peer-reviewed study by Columbia law professor Catherine Sharkey raises doubts that they even accomplish the intended goal of reducing payouts. Instead, Sharkey concludes, capping non-economic damages (for pain and suffering) merely tends to boost awards for economic damages.

So, instead of the name-calling debate between doctors and lawyers over damage caps, imagine a discussion over potentially less-polarizing proposals. For the health care system, one could start with mandatory reporting of medical errors and disclosure of now-confidential sanctions against doctors. As it stands, doctors shield information about the bad apples in the profession. In addition, some non-controversial changes could reduce medical errors, such as computerized entry of doctors' medication orders.

For the insurance industry, greater scrutiny of state-level rate filings could shed light on the disputed causes of rising malpractice rates: lawsuits, as doctors and insurers say, or poor returns on investments, as lawyers insist. In addition, state-administered insurance pools can cushion the impact on high-risk specialties such as neurosurgery and obstetrics. In Maryland, the legislature decided to tax HMOs to give doctors rate relief — in effect, industry-wide risk-spreading.

As for the legal system, the non-governmental Joint Commission on Health Care Accreditation added its voice in February to proposals for alternative mechanisms for compensating injured patients, including mediation or no-fault administrative systems. While none is a silver bullet, individually or collectively these ideas may offer a greater prospect for improving patient safety and compensation, and controlling insurance costs than Bush's damage caps and other liability limits. But don't expect to hear much about them as long as doctors and lawyers keep up the mutual recriminations that are more likely to produce gridlock than meaningful reform.

The litigation system critics also contend that punitive damage awards are exploding out of control. Again, the evidence shows otherwise. But in successive cases the Roberts Court stepped in to reduce punitive damage awards against one of the nation's largest tobacco companies and the giant oil company responsible for what was then the worst oil spill in American history.

Just Deserts
(*CQ Weekly*, Oct. 23, 2006)

Jesse Williams rationalized about the dangers of smoking cigarettes for more than 40 years. In part, he trusted the tobacco companies when they said that the link between smoking and lung cancer had not been proved. But when Williams was diagnosed with inoperable lung cancer in 1996, he told his wife Mayola, "Those darn cigarette people finally did it. They were lying all the time."

In 1999, two years after his death, an Oregon jury ordered the Philip Morris Co. — the maker of Williams' favorite brand, Marlboro — to pay Mayola $820,000 in compensatory damages and another $79.7 million in punitive damages. Oregon courts have twice upheld the punitive damage award, satisfied that the jury had reason to find that Philip Morris had perpetrated a fraud on Williams and other smokers in the state and that the company's conduct was both profitable and reprehensible in the extreme.

Next week, Philip Morris, the nation's biggest tobacco company, will ask the Supreme Court to throw out the punitive damage award. The company hopes to use the case to persuade the justices to set stricter rules for the federal courts to follow in an area traditionally left to the states.

The war over punitive damages has now been raging for more than three decades. Business lobbies and other "tort reform" groups have planted in people's minds the image of an out-of-control civil justice system that frequently imposes outlandish punitive damage awards on companies based mostly on knee-jerk hostility to big corporations.

Any number of research reports and academic studies have shown that image to be essentially false. One report in the late 1990s by the

Rand Corp. Institute for Civil Justice concluded that punitive damages are seldom sought and even more rarely awarded. A more recent study by University of Georgia professors Susette Talarico and Thomas Eaton found that out of 25,000 state civil lawsuits studied, punitive damages were sought in only about 3,700 cases and awarded in only 15.

As Talarico laments, such research gets far less attention from the public than the occasional spectacular case with a multimillion- dollar punitive damage award. "These become the basis for most people's generalizations about the tort system," she says.

A few of those spectacular cases have reached the Supreme Court and drawn the justices, very tentatively, into setting due process limits on punitive damages. A decade ago, the court threw out a $4 million punitive damage award against the German automaker BMW in a lawsuit stemming from a a flawed automobile paint job. Three years ago, the court threw out a $145 million punitive damage award against State Farm Mutual Automobile Insurance for mishandling a claim that cost the policyholder a $185,000 court judgment.

In both cases, plaintiffs presented strong evidence that the companies were guilty of patterns of fraudulent behavior toward customers. Juries may consider the companies' reprehensibility in awarding punitive damages, the justices said, but the disparity between compensatory and punitive damages was too high in both cases. In its State Farm ruling, the court suggested that rarely should punitive damages be more than 10 times actual compensation.

By that standard, the Philip Morris case — with its 97-to-1 ratio — seems ripe for reversal. Yet, as pointed out by Mark Tushnet, a plaintiff-oriented professor at Georgetown University Law Center, Oregon courts tried to apply the Supreme Court precedents in upholding the award to Williams. The Oregon judges understood that the 10-to-1 formula was only a guide — and only one of several factors to be considered. And, unlike the other Supreme Court cases that have set precedent in this area, Philip Morris was found to have extremely reprehensible conduct over an extended period of time that did more than financial harm to the customer. It killed him.

Philip Morris contends that, historically, punitive damages have not been used to punish defendants for harm to anyone other than the individual plaintiff. It also warns that the next Oregon jury could hit the company with another, duplicative punitive damage award for the same conduct. And it notes that it was among the tobacco companies that in 1998 agreed to pay states more than $40 billion to settle smokers' health-related claims.

Williams' attorneys have rebuttals for each of those points. In particular, they note that Oregon law guards against repetitive punitive damage awards by providing that juries in subsequent cases would be told to take any prior awards into account. In any event, Philip Morris cites no actual case in which a corporate defendant has been hit with one after another punitive damage award.

Hard cases, it is said, make bad law. The justices may see *Philip Morris v. Williams* as an example of a civil justice system that runs roughshod over defendants in open defiance of the high court's own rulings. Both premises are at least somewhat misleading. Even if the court overturns the award, as many experts expect, the justices should leave juries and judges in state court systems a wide degree of discretion in meting out civil justice system as they — rather than corporate wrongdoers — think best.

The court's eventual decision in February 2007 threw out the punitive damage award after accepting Philip Morris's argument that punitive damages cannot be imposed for harms suffered by nonparties. Oregon courts, however, reaffirmed the award and the Supreme Court eventually acquiesced.

Damage Controlled
(*CQ Weekly*, July 23, 2008)

The American justice system is not beset by "runaway" punitive damage awards. In fact, punitive damages are "infrequent," and there has been no "marked increase" in the number of awards or their typical size. Those assertions don't come from the trial lawyers lobby; they are the conclusions of the Supreme Court. Indeed, they appear in a 5-3 opinion joined by four of the most conservative justices — and would undoubtedly be endorsed by the trio of liberal dissenters.

The court's assessment of the state of punitive damages in this country was buried, however, under a dramatic headline: "Justices Cut Damages for Exxon Valdez Spill." The court decided last month that instead of the $5 billion award voted by a federal trial court jury in Alaska, or the $2.5 billion penalty approved by a federal appeals court, Exxon deserved only a little over $500 million in punishment for its corporate recklessness in causing the worst oil spill in American history.

The court's solicitude for the company stemmed from what Justice David H. Souter, writing for the majority, called "the stark unpredictability" of punitive damage awards. In the 1990s, he was the most liberal of the justices joining a series of decisions that set some quite-loose due process limits on such awards in state courts. The Exxon case — brought under federal maritime law — gave the court a clear opening to regulate punitive damages under its common-law authority over the field.

Souter took the task seriously, carefully surveying a range of recent studies. "It's the most empirically informed opinion the Supreme Court has written on civil litigation in a long time," commented Richard Nagareda, a tort expert at Vanderbilt Law School. And the research, Souter concluded, "tends to undercut" much of the "audible criticism" of punitive damages. That criticism has come loud and long from the business community, which for more than two decades has depicted class actions and other civil suits as part of a run-amok system that imperils corporate America and the U.S. economy.

Instead, what Souter found was no problem with "mass-produced runaway awards" and "no marked increase" in the percentage of cases that ended with the defendant having to pay money to the plaintiffs as punishment for the behavior that led to the lawsuit. The median ratio of punitive to compensatory damages may have increased but remains below 1-to-1, he said. In sum, he concluded, the research revealed "an overall restraint" in the awarding of punitive damages by both juries and judges.

The Exxon Valdez case, of course, was no run-of-the-mill suit. In March 1989, the 1,000-foot supertanker spilled 11 million gallons of oil in Prince William Sound after a relapsed alcoholic skipper turned the helm over to a third mate, who ran the ship aground on a reef. Although

Exxon knew the captain, Joseph Hazelwood, often drank with crew members, the company left him in command.

The spill devastated the region's fishing economy. Five years later, a federal court jury found Exxon's conduct reckless, awarding $287 million in compensatory damages and adding a $5 billion punishment. The trial judge and the 9th U.S. Circuit Court of Appeals tried to heed the Supreme Court's punitive damages decisions, one of which suggested a 9-to-1 punishment-to-compensatory ratio as the outer limit. After calculating the economic harm at about $500 million, Judge Russel Holland set punitive damages at $4.5 billion. The appeals court lowered the amount to $2.5 billion on the ground that Exxon's lapses had not been intentional or aimed at increasing profits.

The lower courts' efforts were lost on a Supreme Court majority consisting of Chief Justice John G. Roberts Jr. and Justices Souter, Antonin Scalia, Anthony M. Kennedy and Clarence Thomas. They were instead concerned about "the spread" in punitive damages generally — in statistical parlance, the "standard deviation" was too high. "Outlier cases," Souter wrote, "subject defendants to punitive damages that dwarf the corresponding compensatories."

As a clear alternative, Souter proposed a 1-to-1 ratio as the limit for punitive damages in maritime cases, at least if the conduct was neither malicious nor profit-seeking. (He rounded up from the ratio of 0.65 to 1 that the research found in recent jury awards.) Souter labored to explain away alternatives: more explicit jury instructions, or the 2-to-1 or 3-to-1 ratios of many states. "Some will murmur," he acknowledged, "that this smacks too much of policy and too little of principle."

Many longtime tort reform advocates hailed the decision, though without mentioning the underlying refutation of their arguments. In *The Wall Street Journal*, former publisher L. Gordon Crovitz said the case would be an antidote to "out-of-control jury awards" that "sometimes bankrupt companies and industries." The U.S. Chamber of Commerce saw the decision as a signal to state and federal judges to rein in punitive damages across the board.

Exxon was not and is not near bankruptcy, but the Alaskan fishermen whose lives have never been the same reacted with disillusionment. Their lawyer, Brian O'Neill of Minneapolis, could offer no solace when he met with some of them five days later. "We got screwed," he said, according to the *Anchorage Daily News.* "I'm ashamed and embarrassed about what the court system did."

Federal law allows courts to award attorney's fees for successful plaintiffs in federal civil rights suits. Fees are based primarily on hours worked, but judges can award bonuses for exceptional work in difficult cases. The fee awards are important to the public interest law firms that take on institutional reform cases, but the Roberts Court decided the judge who oversaw a major reform of Georgia's foster care system had been too generous to the lawyers responsible for the changes.

"Bonus" Fee Awards Trimmed
(*Jost on Justice*, April 26, 2010)

In the world of high finance, top executives can walk away with seven- and eight-figure bonuses even after flushing their firms down the toilet. (Think, Bear Stearns; Lehman) But under a new Supreme Court decision, public interest lawyers who succeed in hard-fought federal civil rights suits are exceedingly unlikely to see any bonuses in the fee awards permitted under the law.

The Supreme Court's 5-4 decision last week in *Perdue v. Kenny A.* [April 21] threw out a $10.5 million fee award for a group of public interest and private attorneys for work over an eight-year period in a suit that succeeded in overhauling Georgia's dangerous and dysfunctional foster care system. Lawyers in the case still stand to get at least $6 million for the nearly 30,000 hours spent investigating and litigating the suit. But the ruling represents a setback for lawyers who take on difficult institutional reform litigation with no assurance of eventual reimbursement and ultimately prevail, but only in the face of years of dogged resistance from government lawyers.

In *Kenny A.*, lawyers from the New York City-based group Children's Rights teamed with attorneys from the Atlanta firm Bondurant, Mixson & Elmore in filing suit in 2002 on behalf of a class of 3,000 abused or neglected children in Georgia's foster care system. Three years later, the suit resulted in a mediated consent decree requiring extensive reforms in foster care in two metropolitan Atlanta counties, Fulton and DeKalb. With the decree signed, the plaintiffs' lawyers applied for attorneys' fees, as permitted under federal civil rights laws. They asked for $14 million. Half of the amount was based on hours billed at prevailing rates in the Atlanta area. The other half was an enhancement based on superior work and results.

Lawyers for the state, who had fought the case with every possible pretrial motion and dilatory tactic, objected to the proposed fee. After scrutinizing the fee application, Senior U.S. District Court Judge Marvin Shoob trimmed the basic amount to $6 million, but added a 75 percent enhancement based on, among other factors, the "extraordinary results" achieved. Shoob added that the lawyers had shown "a higher degree of skill commitment, dedication, and professionalism" than he had seen in attorneys in any previous case in his 27 years on the bench.

That was not enough for the Supreme Court's conservatives, who decided that Shoob had gone overboard in approving a 75 percent enhancement. For the majority, Justice Samuel A. Alito Jr. sneered at the fee award as a "windfall" for the lawyers.

The decision marked the court's most extended discussion of when, if ever, a fee award can be increased because of exceptional performance or difficulties. In 2002, the court endorsed an approach to fee awards developed in lower federal courts known as the "lodestar method." That approach calls on federal judges to apply the prevailing rates for legal services in the area — the "lodestar" — to the billable hours documented by the successful lawyers. In passing, the court indicated that enhancements might be permitted in extraordinary circumstances.

The good news for public interest lawyers in the new case is that the court reaffirmed its in-passing comment. The bad news is that the five-justice majority declared "a strong presumption" that the lodestar amount is sufficient. Lawyers seeking an enhancement, Alito explained, must identify and prove with specificity the factors showing the lodestar fee to be inadequate. Justices Anthony M. Kennedy and Clarence Thomas added brief concurrences to underscore that enhancements would be permitted — in Kennedy's words — "only in the rarest circumstances."

Writing for the four liberal dissenters, Justice Stephen G. Breyer detailed both the difficulties in the case and the importance of the result in arguing for upholding the fee award. Evidence in the case filled 20 large boxes, Breyer said, and the record covered 18,000 pages. The suit documented unsanitary and unsafe conditions in foster care shelters and inadequate medical and mental health services. Children were at risk of assault or sexual abuse by other children or even by staff.

The state's Office of the Child Advocate had complained about the problems, but to no avail until the civil rights suit, Breyer noted. "If this is not an exceptional case," he concluded, "what is?"

In his opinion, Alito noted that attorneys' fees in civil rights cases against government agencies are often paid for, in effect, by state and local taxpayers. The money used to pay the fees, he complained, "is money that cannot be used for programs that provide vital public services." Tellingly, Alito expressed no concern about the money that the state spent litigating the case, including $2.4 million on outside counsel.

Marcia Robinson Lowry, executive director of Children's Rights, voiced confidence afterward that the lawyers will be able to justify an enhanced fee when the case returns to lower federal courts. Perhaps. But Carl Tobias, a professor at the University of Richmond Law School, aptly observed that the ruling makes any bonuses in civil rights cases far less likely in the future. "The whole mood and tone of the opinion," Tobias told the *Atlanta Journal-Constitution*, "is that it's going to have to be an extraordinary situation."

10

#BusinessLaw

"The business of America is business," President Calvin Coolidge famously remarked, a few years before the Great Depression shattered confidence in U.S. entrepreneurs and financiers. Today, the people who run businesses, large and small, are routinely exalted as "job creators" even as some of these companies engage in financial shenanigans, mistreat workers, trick consumers, or pollute the environment. The law seeks to regulate businesses in the public interest, but the degree of regulation is a subject of fierce debate both in politics and in the law.

#BizCourt

My debut column with CQ Weekly *examined the Rehnquist Court's record on business-related cases. With Rehnquist suffering from thyroid cancer, I also anticipated the likely importance of business issues in the confirmation of his eventual successor.*

Rehnquist Court and Business
(*CQ* Weekly, Jan. 31, 2005)

William H. Rehnquist came to the Supreme Court in 1972 as the most conservative member of a still somewhat liberal bench. When he leaves the court as its chief justice some time in the seemingly near future, his tenure will be remembered for its shift to the right, especially on many social issues that have cleaved the court — and the nation — for the past 30-plus years.

The Rehnquist Era also has had mixed results on less emotional, but equally divisive, issues that affect business and industry. Civil lawsuits, land use limitations and environmental regulations have received steady attention from the Rehnquist Court — although not always consistent treatment. Like social conservatives unhappy with the court's reaffirmation of abortion rights and affirmative action, business interests count disappointments along with their gains despite seven Republican-nominated justices in the past 10 years.

The mixed voting patterns make it hard to handicap the likely effect on business when President Bush gets his opportunity to fill seats on the court. Business lobbies are already mobilizing to help make sure their issues — like "tort reform," or putting limitations on lawsuits and punitive damage awards — are part of the debate in the next big confirmation fights.

For economic conservatives, the Rehnquist record starts with a line of positive decisions that gradually imposed constitutional limits on punitive damages awarded without regard to the proven economic losses. In *State Farm Mutual Automobile Insurance Co. v. Campbell* (2003), the court held that punitive damages would be constitutionally suspect if they exceeded the amount of a "substantial" compensatory damage award — which covers financial losses — and hardly ever upheld if more than 10 times the amount.

In another line of decisions stretching over several years, the court has also given property owners some protections from the adverse effects of land use or environmental regulations. In 1992, the court ruled that landowners are entitled to compensation if a regulation destroys all economically viable use of their property. Two years later, the court limited zoning authorities' ability to require landowners to set aside part of their property for public use as a condition of development.

And in other business-oriented areas, the court has expanded First Amendment protections for advertising — a.k.a. "commercial speech." It issued a series of decisions somewhat narrowing employers' obligations under the Americans with Disabilities Act. And it has taken a more skeptical attitude toward antitrust law and federal regulation generally than did the Warren or even the Burger court.

Still, business interests have ended up with less than they asked for. The limits on punitive damages are loose, land-use regulations are still generally upheld, and commercial speech remains relegated to second-class status under the First Amendment. "The business community has done well but not exceptionally well under the Rehnquist court," says Mark Levy, a corporate lawyer in Washington who follows the court closely. Most recently, the court rejected business groups' efforts to strike down the McCain-Feingold limits on election-related "issue advertising" and partly salvaged the federal sentencing guidelines that have led to increased prison time for many white-collar convicts.

Ironically, Rehnquist has not been a leader in some of the pro-business decisions. He dissented in the court's early commercial speech cases and remains more willing to uphold government regulation than, say, fellow conservative Clarence Thomas. Rehnquist was also a late convert to limiting punitive damage awards. And the court under Rehnquist has sharply reduced the number of cases it decides — leaving many business-related issues without an authoritative, national resolution.

Business cases often cut across the court's customary conservative-liberal lines. Justices Thomas and Antonin Scalia, for example, have dissented from the punitive damage rulings because they take a narrow view of the scope of the Constitution's due process protections. They also cast pivotal votes in an unexpected 2003 decision, *Norfolk & Western Railway Co. v. Ayers*, favoring plaintiffs in asbestos litigation.

On the other hand, the court's senior liberal, John Paul Stevens, was an early proponent of limiting punitive damages, but he generally favors regulators on environmental and consumer protection issues. And liberal Stephen G. Breyer often sides with business on antitrust and regulatory issues, though not on commercial speech or civil rights.

Business groups have generally applauded Bush's choices for lower courts. And the National Association of Manufacturers is preparing to put its muscle and millions of dollars behind efforts to win Senate confirmation of Bush's second-term nominees, including for the

Supreme Court. "We're going to be very active," says John Engler, NAM's president and a former Republican governor of Michigan.

Liberal groups likewise are lining up for that debate. Nan Aron, president of the Alliance for Justice, says the Rehnquist court has hurt the environment, consumers and workers and accuses Bush of favoring the interests of "big business" in his judicial nominations so far.

So, issues such as abortion and affirmative action may be only part of the volatile mix in the looming battle over the Supreme Court.

Senate Democrats and liberal advocacy groups did criticize both of President Bush's Supreme Court nominees: Roberts and Alito, for their records on business issues. Roberts won confirmation by a vote of 78-22, Alito by a vote of 58-42. On Jost for Justice, *I marked Roberts' fifth anniversary as chief justice by assessing the court's record on business issues. A leading corporate lawyer summed it up well: "The Rehnquist Court was quite a good forum for business. The Roberts Court is even better."*

Wide Strike Zone for Business
(*Jost on Justice*, Sept. 27, 2010)

Chief Justice John G. Roberts Jr., former Reagan and Bush I administration lawyer and former corporate attorney, won Senate confirmation in 2005 after promising that he had no "agenda" for the Supreme Court. But five years later, no one should be surprised that Roberts and the court he leads have regularly favored business interests in the legal issues that business counts as high priorities.

Numbers help tell the story. Among 53 cases over the past five years where the U.S. Chamber of Commerce has participated, Roberts voted for the Chamber's position 70 percent of the time, according to an analysis by the consumer-oriented Constitutional Accountability Center. In the 17 closely divided cases, Roberts batted 90 percent for business. By way of comparison, the four liberal justices (Stevens, Souter, Ginsburg, and Breyer) voted for the Chamber in the mid-30 to mid-40 percent range; Sotomayor was slightly lower, but with a small sample in her single term.

Roberts' votes have helped give business victories in such areas as preemption, arbitration, securities fraud, and civil litigation. Business interests use preemption to rein in states that have more consumer-friendly state law or regulations than the federal government. They want courts to enforce take-it-or-leave-it arbitration contracts to force workers or consumers into a stacked dispute-resolution system and shut them out of courts. And business has worked tirelessly for decades to try to limit the ability of investors to recover for losses due to securities fraud or for consumers to be fully compensated for injuries from unsafe products.

In contrast to the overturned precedents discussed here last week ["Judging Roberts: Riding Roughshod Over Precedent"], Roberts and fellow Bush appointee Samuel A. Alito Jr. have not changed, but only fortified, the court's orientation on these issues. "The Rehnquist Court was quite a good forum for business," Maureen Mahoney, a corporate lawyer and former clerk to Chief Justice William H. Rehnquist, remarked at the end of Roberts' second year as chief justice. "The Roberts Court is even better."

Preemption cases remain somewhat hard to predict. Truckers and medical device manufacturers won preemption cases, but the court in 2008 rejected efforts by drug makers and tobacco companies to escape state court suits for inadequate warnings about their products. Roberts, however, has been consistent. With one exception in his first term, Roberts has always backed federal preemption, whether in the majority or in dissent.

On arbitration, the Roberts Court has continued the general pattern of rejecting efforts by workers or consumers to escape arbitration clauses in employment or purchase contracts. Some rulings have been by lopsided margins, but two significant decisions in 2010 came on 5-4 votes that pitted the Roberts-led conservatives against the liberal bloc.

The Rehnquist Court dealt investors a blow in 1994 by rejecting any "aiding and abetting" liability for securities fraud; the 5-4 ruling blocked a suit against a bank that had, unknowingly, helped further the fraudulent conduct. The Roberts Court took that ruling one step further in 2008 by freeing a company from securities fraud liability even if it had *knowingly* participated in the misconduct. The 5-3 vote was mostly along ideological lines; Alito was recused.

The Roberts Court has been somewhat more generous in interpreting federal job discrimination laws. In particular, it has actually widened protection for employees claiming retaliation for complaining about alleged discrimination. But one major ruling in 2009 made age-discrimination suits much more difficult to win. And the famous *Ledbetter* ruling in 2007 would have narrowed employers' liability for pay discrimination but for the law Congress passed to overturn it.

Roberts pledged in the confirmation hearing that he would just call balls and strikes and let the political branches decide the rules of the game. But he dissented in 2007 when the liberals plus Kennedy read the Clean Air Act to require the Environmental Protection Agency to regulate "greenhouse gases." And when Congress required the EPA to use the "best technology" available to "minimize" fish kills at electric power plants, Roberts joined the majority decision in 2009 to allow the agency to retreat from that standard by adopting a cost-benefit analysis. The decision could have saved electric utilities billions but for the Obama administration's reversal of the Bush administration rule.

One big company that did save billions thanks to a Roberts Court decision is Exxon, which won a 5-3 decision in 2008 cutting a $2.5 billion punitive damage award for the Exxon Valdez oil spill by more than 80 percent to $500 million. Here, the Roberts Court itself defined the strike zone by using its power over federal maritime law to impose a 1-to-1 ratio of punitive to compensatory damages. True, the liberal Souter wrote the decision, but Roberts and three fellow conservatives provided the other votes.

The Chamber of Commerce prevailed in 64 percent of the cases counted by the Constitutional Accountability Center: not a bad batting average. That number includes the business community's biggest win: the *Citizens United* decision in January freeing corporations to spend unlimited sums in political campaigns. After five Roberts Court years, Mahoney remains a fan. The Supreme Court, she told the Chamber of Commerce-sponsored preview of the coming term, is "the best court" in the country for getting what she called "a fair hearing" on business-related issues.

Why did business groups do so well at the Supreme Court, first under Rehnquist and then in particular under Roberts? One explanation from a leading Supreme Court watcher: better lawyering in getting their cases heard and in winning the justices' votes.

Friends in High Places
(*CQ Weekly*, Nov. 19, 2007)

"Equal Justice Under Law" is carved in big letters over the Corinthian columns framing the main entrance to the Supreme Court. While the goal has always been more aspirational than actual, a leading expert says the gap between the hope and the reality is widening.

The reason: the emergence of an elite corps of Supreme Court advocates, most of them with big corporate law firms in Washington, who appear to be having outsized influence in shaping the court's docket and its decisions to advance the interests of well-heeled business clients. The lawyers in what might be called this legal-commercial complex are well known in legal circles — and hardly at all otherwise. But their influence has been surging in the past two decades, according to Richard Lazarus of Georgetown University.

Today, according to Lazarus' exhaustive compilation for a forthcoming article in the *Georgetown Law Journal*, "expert" Supreme Court advocates — those with at least five appearances before the court — are behind nearly half the cases the court agrees to consider. Non-government lawyers who have made 10 or more arguments at the court used to be a rarity; in the last term, they filled nearly one-fourth of the argument slots. The trend is more than a legal business story, according to Lazarus, a left-leaning environmental law expert who is well regarded for running Georgetown's Supreme Court Institute on a nonpartisan basis. (Update: Lazarus is now at Harvard.) He sees "preliminary indications" that this newly emerged Supreme Court bar is having "a significant, long-term substantive impact" — specifically, helping business get more cases on the court's shrinking docket and winning favorable rulings in cases that pit big business against workers, consumers, small businesses and government regulators.

In fact, the business community's success was one of the big stories as the second year of the Roberts Court ended in June. The U.S. Chamber of Commerce's National Legal Center claimed its most successful year at the high court since the chamber established a full-time litigating arm 30 years ago.

As Lazarus tells it, the rise of the Supreme Court bar began when Rex Lee chose not to return to Brigham Young law school in 1985 after stepping down as the solicitor general, or chief Supreme Court advocate, for the Reagan administration. Instead, Lee joined the Washington law firm of Sidley Austin to head a specialized Supreme Court practice. The firm's subsequent success spurred other big firms to follow suit. And other solicitors general have now also followed the path to the private sector, including Democrats Walter Dellinger and Seth Waxman. So, too, did a deputy solicitor general in the first Bush administration: John G. Roberts Jr., who gained pre-eminence as a Supreme Court advocate representing for the most part business clients with the Washington firm of Hogan & Hartson [update: now Hogan Lovells].

Litigators such as Roberts can do disproportionately well at the court, Lazarus says, because justices rely on lawyers to help do their jobs, especially in screening cases. With 9,000 petitions for review in the most recent term, the justices cannot read even most of them. Law clerks acknowledge they look more closely at petitions filed by experienced Supreme Court practitioners. And business groups also file friend-of-the-court briefs to red-flag cases raising important issues for the business community.

Once the court agrees to hear a case, the elite advocates know best how to fashion an argument either to win, or at least minimize the impact of a loss. This "advocacy gap" matters more in business cases than in higher-profile cases, Lazarus says, because the justices are less familiar with many of the topics themselves.

Lazarus sees the Supreme Court bar's impact in three areas in particular: antitrust, punitive damages and (oddly) railway law, where business interests have been winning consistently in recent years. He could also have listed employment discrimination and securities law, where plaintiffs have also recently been taking it on the chin. In those and other areas, interest groups opposing the business community are typically under-resourced and overmatched.

The lawyers responsible for those business successes minimize their role. Maureen Mahoney of Latham & Watkins stressed to *Legal Times'* Tony Mauro that the pro-business trend has been developing for a while and that the court now includes seven Republican-appointed justices likely to look well on business interests for the most part. Lazarus acknowledges that political reality — but suggests the lawyers sing a different tune in persuading business clients to pay six-figure retainers for working on a Supreme Court case.

What could be wrong with better legal advocacy, some might ask, especially at the nation's highest court? "Better decisions require better advocacy on all sides," Lazarus replies, "not just on behalf of some sides." He offers some suggestions for righting the balance, such as support for the Supreme Court clinics sprouting at several top law schools. As a first step, perhaps law students can help close the gap, but the bar — and the court itself — may need to do more to move toward what is now the receding goal of equal justice for all.

Here are my columns on three cases that illustrate the Roberts Court's tilt toward business interests.

Antitrust Precedent Test
(*CQ Weekly*, April 16, 2007)

Nearly a century ago, the Supreme Court interpreted the still-new Sherman Antitrust Act to prohibit a manufacturer from requiring a retailer to set a minimum price for its product. Congress could have overturned the rule against "resale price maintenance," but it never has. A few years ago, lawmakers even went so far as to prohibit the Justice Department from arguing in court to scrap the rule.

Last month, however, the Bush administration joined a variety of business groups in urging the Supreme Court to do just that. And the court's conservatives, including possibly Chief Justice John G. Roberts Jr., seem determined to do so — or at least open to the argument. For Roberts, the case, *Leegin Creative Leather Products Inc. v. PSKS Inc.,* may be the most clear-cut test so far of his commitment to the role of precedent in Supreme Court decision-making. Repeatedly during his confirmation hearings in September 2005, Roberts deflected fears from Democratic senators that he would bring a conservative agenda to the court by stressing his respect for the principle of *stare decisis* — Latin for "let the decision stand."

Roberts sent mixed signals, however, during the March 26 argument in the case. So did Justice Anthony M. Kennedy, the swing vote between the court's conservative and liberal blocs. With the four liberal justices seemingly strongly inclined to preserve the existing rule, business groups need both Roberts and Kennedy to overturn the prior decision.

Antitrust law can be complex, but the rule against minimum retail pricing is a straightforward application of the Sherman Act's basic prohibition against price-fixing — either by competitors or, in this instance, by a manufacturer and its dealers. This rule has readily observable real-world consequences, too, although consumer groups and business lobbies disagree about the impact.

Consumer groups say the rule against resale price maintenance has been the basis for the growth of discounters such as Wal-Mart, and the resulting lower retail prices. Business groups, however, say manufacturers have a legitimate interest in requiring their dealers not to set prices too low, for fear that they will skimp on customer service and shortchange manufacturers on product promotion.

Those supposed benefits of resale price maintenance did not figure in the court's 1911 decision declaring the practice a "per se" violation of antitrust law — that is, virtually always illegal. Writing for the court in *Dr. Miles Medical Co. v. John D. Park & Sons Co.*, Justice Charles Evans Hughes said such restrictions were "injurious to the public interest and void." Seven years later, however, the court gave manufacturers a different way to control their dealers. In the so-called *Colgate* case, it said manufacturers could recommend a uniform price for their products and then refuse to provide their wares to dealers that did not agree to abide by that figure.

That seemingly artificial distinction has helped drive arguments by academic economists in recent years against preserving the rule. More broadly, though, the antitrust skeptics who seem to dominate academia strongly argue for a manufacturer's right to control its product distribution. They want resale price maintenance agreements to be judged under a "rule of reason" — weighing the costs to competition against the benefits in consumer service.

The issue reached the high court in an antitrust suit brought by Kay's Kloset, a women's clothing store in Texas, after Leegin, a Los Angeles-based manufacturer of women's accessories, cut the store off for selling its trademarked goods at a discount. The store won at trial, and Leegin was ordered to pay $3.6 million in damages.

Representing Leegin, attorney Theodore Olson told the justices that the 1911 rule against resale price maintenance is "widely recognized as outdated, misguided and anti-competitive." For Kay's Kloset, attorney Robert Coykendall countered that discouraging price cuts is "bad antitrust policy."

Liberals Stephen G. Breyer and David H. Souter were most forceful in defending the existing rule. They asked Olson and deputy solicitor general Thomas Hungar why the court should change the rule on the basis of economists' views when Congress has left it standing. Conservatives Antonin Scalia and Samuel A. Alito Jr. made clear their views on the opposite side. What's wrong with allowing some companies to make money out of service instead of cheap prices, Alito asked.

In his questions, Roberts focused on the *Colgate* case. Why change the rule if manufacturers can use that 1918 decision to get around it, he asked. But later Roberts turned that point around and asked, why preserve the rule if it can be so readily circumvented?

Precedent figures strongly in some higher-profile cases before the court this term — notably, the challenge to the federal ban on "partial birth" abortions and cases from Seattle and Louisville on race-based pupil assignments in public schools. By the time they are all decided, probably in late June, the Roberts Court will have given liberals and conservatives alike some telling clues about how far it will use its power to rethink or even reverse prior decisions.

The court in fact used the Leegin case to overrule the previous ban on price resale maintenance in a 5-4 decision written by Kennedy;

Breyer emphasized his dissent for the liberal bloc by reading portions from the bench.

Levels of Deception
(*CQ Weekly*, Sept. 24, 2007)

When Enron was front-page news back in 2002, George W. Bush was out front promising to crack down on corporate crime and fraud. "No boardroom in America is above or beyond the law," the president told a Justice Department conference that September.

The department's corporate-crime task force deserves credit for winning guilty pleas or convictions against many of the Enron malefactors, including former Chairman Ken Lay and ex-CEO Jeffrey Skilling. With the public furor subsided, however, the Bush administration is now asking the Supreme Court to adopt a narrow view of federal securities law that may prevent investors from going after some of Enron's enablers — the banks and brokerages that helped the company get away with cooking its books for so long.

The government's position is made clear in *Stoneridge Investment Partners v. Scientific-Atlanta,* which the court will hear Oct. 9. It involves an instance of accounting fraud much smaller than Enron's, but the case already is being described as one of the most important matters of business law coming before the justices in their new term.

Charter Communications, a big cable television operator based in St. Louis, came up with this plan in the face of a below-expectations earnings report in 2000: It would buy cable TV boxes from Motorola and Scientific-Atlanta for $17 million more than the normal price in return for those companies agreeing to buy $17 million in advertising on Charter's cable systems. For those vendors the transactions were a wash — with free advertising thrown in. But Charter improved its apparent cash-flow performance, and bolstered its stock price, by treating the revenues as current earnings and the cable-box purchases as a capital expense. Two years later, when this arrangement hit the financial press, Charter's stock plummeted to 78 cents a share from $26. In response, Stoneridge Investment Partners filed a class action lawsuit blaming the stock's collapse on fraudulent transactions that violated federal law and Securities and Exchange Commission rules.

Corporate America hates such suits. But for more than 60 years, federal courts have recognized claims by aggrieved investors as an aid to SEC enforcement of laws essential to guaranteeing the integrity of financial markets. The Supreme Court gave its own blessing to such suits in 1971, although ever since it has found ways to narrow their reach. In one 1994 decision, *Central Bank of Denver v. First Interstate Bank of Denver*, the court ruled that a plaintiff may not recover damages from someone who aids or abets someone else's securities fraud.

Charter settled with Stoneridge, but the cable-box companies persuaded two lower federal courts to dismiss the cases against them. They argued that their role was, at worst, aiding and abetting. Now, Stoneridge wants the Supreme Court to set aside the Central Bank precedent and recognize "scheme liability" for the two vendors' active and knowing participation in the purported fraud.

The SEC voted to side with the investment group. Treasury came down on the other side, arguing that tougher private securities litigation rules would imperil the competitive standing of U.S. financial markets vis-à-vis other countries. After consulting the White House, Solicitor General Paul D. Clement lined up with Treasury, Motorola and Scientific-Atlanta.

The government's brief gives the investors half a loaf by agreeing that the companies' alleged conduct amounted to "a deceptive device or contrivance" in violation of securities law. But it gives those companies the bigger half by arguing that the investors had to prove — and did not — that they relied on the two companies' deception in buying or holding Charter's overvalued stock.

Donald Langevoort, a securities expert at Georgetown University, calls the government's reliance theory "curious." But he's downright dismissive of the "Chicken Little" briefs filed by business groups warning that the sky will fall if the administration's side loses and the court takes a more investor-friendly approach. In fact, Langevoort says, the SEC's anti-fraud language, known as Rule 10b-5, is plenty broad enough to justify Stoneridge's suit. It prohibits "any person, directly or indirectly" from employing "any device, scheme or artifice to defraud . . . in connection with the purchase or sale of any security."

The University of California, the lead plaintiff in the Enron fraud litigation, warns that a ruling for the cable-box companies could cripple its claims against the secondary actors in that financial scandal. Merrill Lynch, the lead Enron defendant, says the argument is neither proper nor correct. How much impact the issue might have on the justices is anyone's guess.

Given how favorable the last Supreme Court term was to business interests, most handicappers predict the companies will win. But it could be close. Justice Stephen G. Breyer has recused himself, and six other justices split in the Denver banks case. That seems to put the two Bush nominees, Chief Justice John G. Roberts Jr. and Samuel A. Alito Jr., in the pivotal role. Both were reliable votes for business interests last year. A decision is due by next June.

Roberts and Alito provided the decisive votes in the eventual 5-3 ruling that gave what amounts to a get-out-of-court free card to many of the lawyers, accountants, or other secondary actors in securities fraud suits.

Free Pass for Multinationals?
(*Jost on Justice*, March 4, 2012)

In John Le Carre's *The Constant Gardener*, an ethically challenged multinational drug company colludes with a fictitious Kenyan government in lethal testing of an experimental drug on unwitting TB patients. The company covers up its activities with a campaign of intimidation that includes the murders of a human rights activist and eventually her husband, the novel's title character.

Le Carre's story is fiction, of course. But the former British intelligence agent built his reputation as a novelist on intricate plots constructed with enough factual knowledge and research to be plausible. And the history of U.S. and multinational corporations in Third World countries gives credence to the idea that big companies at times might either participate in or turn a blind eye to human rights abuses committed for the benefit of their exploitative operations.

The Movement for the Survival of the Ogoni People thinks that corporate conduct of this sort not only can happen, but did — in the oil-rich Niger delta region of Nigeria in the early 1990s. Ogoni activists waged a campaign against the environmental and financial rape of their homeland by the British- and Dutch-based Royal Dutch Shell. To counter the campaign, Shell called on the military dictatorship of Gen. Sani Abacha, which responded with a brutal crackdown reported to have claimed 2,000 lives and displaced 80,000 people.

The victims included Dr. Barinem Kiobel, who was arrested in 1994 along with other leaders of the movement. The so-called Ogoni 9 were allegedly held incommunicado, tortured, and tried by a kangaroo court before they were executed only 10 days after their convictions.

Today, Kiobel's widow, Esther, is seeking justice in U.S. courts under a federal law enacted at the nation's founding to create a legal remedy for violations of international law. But if Supreme Court justices' questions during arguments last week (Feb. 29) are any indication — and they often are — Kiobel and the other plaintiffs are likely to be have the courthouse door shut in their faces with a decision shielding foreign corporations from responsibility for human rights abuses in foreign countries, at least in U.S. courts.

Kiobel is the first of 12 named plaintiffs in suit filed in federal court in New York City in 2002 against Royal Dutch Shell under the Alien Tort Statute. The law, passed by the First Congress in 1789, gives federal courts jurisdiction over "any civil action by an alien, for a tort only, committed in violation of the law of nations or of a treaty of the United States," 28 U.S.C. § 1350. In their complaint, the plaintiffs alleged that Shell participated with the Abacha dictatorship in torture, extra-judicial executions, and crimes against humanity directed against the Ogoni activists.

The Alien Tort Statute had gone all but unnoticed for most of U.S. history until human rights lawyers used it in the late 1970s to bring a suit in behalf of a Paraguayan asylee, Dolly Filártiga, whose teenage brother Joelito was killed at the direction of a Paraguayan police inspector, Americo Norberto Peña-Irala. Both Filártiga and Peña-Irala were in the

United States: Filártiga as an asylee, Peña-Irala on an expired visitor's visa. In a decision now viewed as established precedent, the Second U.S. Circuit Court of Appeals said the 1789 law gave federal courts jurisdiction over the case (*Filártiga v. Peña-Irala*, 630 F.2d 876 (2d Cir. 1980)). The Filártigas eventually won a $10 million judgment, never collected.

Since 1980, human rights lawyers have filed similar suits in U.S. courts, with only limited success, against individuals as well as corporations. In 2004, the Supreme Court officially ratified such causes of action but only for clearly recognized violations of international law (*Sosa v. Alvarez-Machain*). And in an unelaborated footnote, the court raised without resolving the question whether international law would recognize holding a corporation liable for violations.

In the Ogonis' case, a sharply divided Second Circuit panel seized on that footnote to dismiss the suit even though Shell's high-priced legal team had never raised the issue. In dissent, Judge Pierre Leval insisted that corporate liability for torts was recognized in 1789 and is well established today. The pivotal vote was cast by Chief Judge Dennis Jacobs, who explained in the later decision to deny a rehearing that he saw little need to hold corporations responsible. "Examples of corporations in the atrocity business are few in history," Jacobs wrote.

The Roberts Court's conservative majority made clear in last week's arguments in *Kiobel v. Royal Dutch Petroleum Co.* they have little use for the suit either. "What business does a case like that have in the courts of the United States?" Justice Samuel A. Alito Jr. asked the plaintiffs' attorney, Paul Hoffman, a longtime civil liberties lawyer from California.

Earlier, Chief Justice John G. Roberts Jr. and Justice Anthony M. Kennedy both signaled unmistakably that they saw no basis in international law for haling a foreign company into U.S. courts even for egregious human rights violations. Liberal justices made no headway in shoring up the case, even when Justice Ruth Bader Ginsburg noted the post-World War II precedent of holding I.G. Farben responsible for the German chemical firm's role in the Holocaust.

Shell denies responsibility for the Abacha regime's abuses — and *perhaps* the company was only a passive observer. U.S. courts could provide a forum for resolving that issue, but not if the Supreme Court gives foreign corporations a free pass as it appears inclined to do.

The court unanimously ruled that the suit against Shell did not belong in federal court. A five-justice majority led by Roberts appeared to all but eliminate federal jurisdiction over suits for human rights violations abroad; four liberal justice led by Breyer said they would allow some such suits if the conduct "adversely affects an important American national interest."

#CorporateMisconduct

"A man with a briefcase can steal more than any man with a gun." The quote is attributed on the Internet to the Eagles' founding drummer Don Henley, but the same thought about corporate predations dates back at least as far the Populist and Progressive movements of late 19th and early 20th century America. I vented in columns about some of the 21st century's business-world malefactors.

Levels of Deception
(*CQ Weekly*, Feb. 18, 2005)

When little Tommy takes the witness stand in *The Miracle on 34th Street*, the judge asks whether the boy knows the difference between telling the truth and telling a lie. "Oh, sure," Tommy replies. "Everybody knows it's wrong to tell a lie."

Some corporate executives appear to have missed that most obvious lesson. Just look at the criminal trials of two one-time chief executives now under way in federal courts.

Bernard Ebbers, the former chairman of the now former WorldCom, is being tried in New York City for securities fraud and other charges in connection with the $11 billion accounting scandal that led to the telecommunication company's demise. Meanwhile, Richard Scrushy, the ousted founder of HealthSouth Corp., is on trial in the company's hometown of Birmingham, Ala., on fraud and various other charges in an alleged scheme to overstate the hospital chain's earnings by $2.7 billion.

In both cases, federal prosecutors say the accounting shenanigans were aimed at deceiving investors about a company's financial performance in order to maintain stock prices — and thus the value of both men's substantial holdings. Both men have proclaimed their innocence, blaming the frauds on underlings.

Whatever verdicts are eventually returned, the evidence already shows that Ebbers and Scrushy had no qualms about publicly lying about their companies. These and other accounting scandals in recent years show that market forces alone — Adam Smith's famous invisible hand — are not enough to keep companies honest. The government has had to step in to ensure that investors don't get burned by fictitious financial information.

As a result, the courts, state attorneys general, the executive branch and even a supposedly "business friendly" Congress are tightening the screws on corporate executives' ability to dissemble the facts of their business and financial operations. The charges against Scrushy, for example, include the first prosecution for false corporate reporting under the Sarbanes-Oxley Act, the law enacted in 2002 in the wake of the Enron scandal. The act requires that chief executive officers personally sign and attest to the truth of financial statements.

Jurors in Scrushy's trial heard the company's chief financial officer, William T. Owens, in a secretly taped conversation, worrying about his own legal exposure from the company's use of "phony financial statements." Scrushy had no reaction, Owens said.

Jurors in Ebbers' case recently watched a tape of Ebbers telling CNBC in early 2002 that the company was ahead of projections based on "very conservative" accounting. In fact, the company's chief financial officer, Scott Sullivan, had been repeatedly warning Ebbers about aggressive accounting — as recently as two weeks earlier in a handwritten memo contradicting the rosy scenario.

Ebbers' alleged crimes occurred before Sarbanes-Oxley became law. But both his and Scrushy's cases show exactly what kinds of legal defenses the law seeks to preclude. "It would no longer be possible for a CEO to say, 'Gee, I was out of the loop,' " says Elliot Schwartz of the Council of Institutional Investors in Washington.

In the meantime, though, corporate America is dealing with the consequences of all this lying. Big companies are paying more eight- and nine-figure settlements in shareholder class action litigation to try to compensate investors for their losses, according to a report this month by NERA, the economic consulting firm. Among the payouts last year: $2.6 billion by WorldCom, $460 million by Raytheon, $300 million by Bristol-Myers Squibb.

Has corporate America learned the lesson? "Only time will tell," says Schwartz. But he stresses that the government has to supplement market forces to try to protect investors — and that government policies are more likely to have a lasting effect. "You'd have to pass new laws or new regulations, whereas in the market it's easier to have backsliding," Schwartz says.

This new emphasis on government regulation suggests another venue to watch: shareholder suits. Congress has just passed and President Bush just signed a law shifting many consumer class actions from state to federal courts. Supporters say the law will control "lawsuit abuse" by making it harder for plaintiffs' lawyers to engage in "forum shopping." Critics fear the law may prevent disclosure or punishment of corporate misdeeds.

But shareholder litigation, almost always filed in federal courts, has played a key role in trying to recover the moneys that investors lost because of corporate scandals. Many of the recent settlements also include corporate reforms aimed at preventing future abuses.

Despite abuses, consumer class actions also can sometimes correct corporate misbehavior. The accounting scandals suggest that courts have a vital role to play in trying to make sure that companies are operating within the law.

The Deepwater Horizon, *a nine-year-old floating oil rig in the Gulf of Mexico chartered to BP (formerly, British Petroleum), exploded on the morning of April 20, 2010. The explosion claimed 11 lives; oil flowed out of control for nearly two months in the largest oil spill in U.S. history. BP sought to deflect blame for the disaster to the rig operator,*

Transocean, and the contractor, Halliburton. But BP had a record of safety violations. I contrasted the slap-on-the-wrist treatment of BP with the draconian prison sentence imposed on a teenaged juvenile offender in Florida.

Giving BP a Pass
(Jost on Justice, June 9, 2010)

Terrance Graham was a two-time juvenile offender, barely past his 19th birthday in 2006, when Judge Lance Day in Jacksonville, Fla., decided to send him to prison for the rest of his life "to protect the community." Imagine what harms might have been prevented if the repeat corporate offender BP had come up before a likeminded judge sometime in the past.

* * *

The cause of the April 20 blowout of BP's Deepwater Horizon well in the Gulf of Mexico remains to be determined. So, too, the full extent of the economic, environmental, legal, and social costs of what is already the worst oil spill in U.S. history, a spill unlikely to be contained for at least two months, if then.

Seven weeks later, however, this much is known: BP has a long history of safety and environmental violations that can be blamed for the deaths of 15 refinery workers in Texas, the spoilage of Alaska's North Shore, and lesser injuries to workers and environments at other sites.

The company has twice pleaded guilty to federal criminal charges. It was put on probation after the Texas refinery explosion in March 2005. Four years later, the Occupational Safety and Health Administration (OSHA) hit the company with a record $87 million fine for failing to correct the problems.

In all, BP has paid or has pending over $730 million in fines, penalties, or settlements to federal, state, or local governments in recent years for environmental, worker safety, or price manipulation violations, according to a report by the consumer protection group Public Citizen.

BP's record of lawbreaking was no secret, but it was not well known. The March 2005 explosion at BP's 1,200-acre oil refinery in Texas City, just outside Houston, killed 15 workers and injured some 170 others. But the accident was not front-page news outside Texas. Nor were the later investigations that found "significant process issues" at all five of BP's refineries in the United States.

In like vein, the 200,000-gallon oil spill from a BP pipeline on Alaska's North Slope in March 2006 made front-page news in Alaska, but not the rest of the country. The spill, the largest ever on the North Slope, was linked to corrosion in the pipeline. BP had known about the problem at least since 2004, according to later investigations.

In October 2007, the company pleaded guilty to federal crimes for both incidents: a felony violation of the Clean Air Act for the refinery accident, with a $50 million fine; a misdemeanor violation of the Clean Water Act for the oil spill, with $4 million in restitution to the state of Alaska and a $4 million payment to the National Fish and Wildlife Foundation. On the same day, the company agreed to pay $303 million to settle civil charges that it unlawfully manipulated prices in the market for propane. The guilty pleas were seen as an effort at good corporate citizenship by BP's then-new CEO: Tony Hayward.

* * *

After his first arrest — for a botched restaurant robbery — Terrance Graham negotiated a favorable plea agreement and vowed to do better. "I've decided to turn my life around," Graham promised. After the second offense — a home-invasion robbery — an exasperated Judge Day scolded Graham for blowing his second chance. "If I can't do anything to get you back on the right path," the judge said, "then I have to start focusing on the community and trying to protect the community from your actions."

* * *

Four and a half years after the Texas City refinery explosion, OSHA concluded last October that BP had failed to make the safety improvements at the facility as promised. The agency proposed fines totaling $87 million. BP said it would contest the penalties. In March, the agency proposed a separate $3 million fine for safety violations at BP's refinery in Oregon, Ohio, near Toledo.

An analysis of OSHA's data base by the Center for Public Integrity, the Washington-based journalistic watchdog group, found BP far and away the worst safety offender among U.S. refineries. BP was responsible for 829 "willful" violations from the period June 2007-February 2010, the center said; the total for all other refineries: 22.

Now, internal documents obtained by Pro Publica, the nonprofit investigative journalism group, purportedly detail the company's disregard of safety and environmental problems in the past. The documents — leaked by someone "close to the company" but critical of its performance — depict a corporate environment in which employees were pressured to cut corners and to keep any safety concerns to themselves.

* * *

Terrance Graham will get a new sentence after the U.S. Supreme Court ruled on May 17 that life without parole is cruel and unusual punishment for a juvenile offender. But Florida Attorney General Bill McCollum is promising that Graham will still serve "a very long term in prison." Meanwhile, U.S. Attorney General Eric Holder says the Justice Department has opened a criminal investigation of BP in the wake of the Gulf spill. "We will prosecute to the fullest extent of the law anyone who has violated the law," Holder said.

[Postscript: The Justice Department filed a civil suit against BP on August 31, 2012, blaming the spill on the company's "gross negligence and willful misconduct." BP agreed in November 2012 to plead guilty to manslaughter for the deaths and to pay $4.5 billion in fines and other payments, reportedly the largest penalty of its kind in U.S. history. In a civil trial, however, BP now faces a possible penalty of $18 billion after a federal judge's ruling on Sept. 3, 2014, that the company was "grossly negligent" and must bear two-thirds of the responsibility for the spill.

[As for Graham, he was resentenced in February 2012 to 25 years in prison. His lawyer had urged a 15-year sentence, according to the account in The Florida Times Union.*]*

* * *

The financial crisis of 2007-2008 had more bad actors than all the prosecutors and regulators could shake a stick at. I opined on one of them: the credit rating agency Standard & Poors, which gave triple A ratings to junk packages of subprime mortgages put together by its fee-paying clients. Conflict of interest much?

Subprime Performance
(Jost on Justice, Feb. 27, 2013)

The unnamed senior analyst was new to the credit rating agency Standard & Poor's in July 2007 when he told an investment banker client by e-mail that the job was "going great." Except, the analyst added sardonically, that the world of mortgage-backed securities that accounted for much of the company's business was "crashing," investors and the media "hate us," and "we're all running around to save face."

Continuing the e-mail string two days later, the analyst acknowledged that there had been "internal pressure" for S&P to lower its all-important investment ratings on many deals. But the pressure apparently came to naught. Why? Because "the leadership was concerned of p*ssing off too many clients" and "jumping the gun ahead of" S&P's lesser rivals in the credit-rating business, Fitch and Moody's.

The newbie analyst's unguarded admission of S&P's conflict of interest between satisfying clients and providing objective financial advice was one of many revealing e-mails cited in the government's massive suit filed last week [Feb. 4] charging S&P with fraud. The 119-page complaint depicts S&P as giving its coveted investment-grade triple-A rating to packages of subprime mortgages even as S&P analysts and executives were well aware of the record level of delinquencies in the mortgage marketplace.

The suit, *United States v. McGrawHill*, filed in federal court in Los Angeles, represents the government's most ambitious effort to date to go after one of the financial companies that played a part in the great financial crisis of 2007-2008. (McGraw Hill is S&P's parent company.) The government is asking for up to $5 billion in civil penalties under a 1989 law, the Financial Institutions Reform, Recovery and Enforcement Act, which Congress passed after the savings & loan crisis of the 1980s. The law allows the government to recoup fraud-related losses suffered by federally insured banks and credit unions.

In announcing the lawsuit, Attorney General Eric Holder said S&P's "egregious" conduct went "to the very heart of the recent financial crisis." S&P analysts were aware as early as 2003 of doubts about the accuracy of its ratings for financial packages made of up residential mortgages, Holder said. But S&P executives allegedly ignored the warnings, concealed facts, made false representations to investors and financial institutions, and took "other steps" to manipulate the ratings, all for the purpose of increasing S&P's revenue and market share.

Prepared for the filing — S&P was reported to have turned down a proposed settlement — the company sent the high-powered Wall Street attorney Floyd Abrams out to answer the charges. In a succession of TV interviews, Abrams tut-tutted the seemingly damning e-mails cited in the government's complaint.

The government had picked a few "angry" or "embarrassing" e-mails out of 20 million pages of documents, Abrams said. Overall, he insisted, the evidence would show that S&P was doing its best in difficult times to make good judgments about what was going to happen in the future. And if S&P got it wrong, Abrams said, so did everybody else: the other credit rating companies and the top government leaders, including the Bush administration's secretary of the treasury, Henry Paulson.

The government's complaint, however, charges that the company was not merely wrong, but knowingly and intentionally wrong. In the government's telling, the company stood to gain more from pleasing the clients who paid six-figure fees to have their investment packages favorably rated than it stood to lose from misleading investors about the risks of billion-dollar bundles of subprime residential mortgages.

One analyst complained in a 2004 e-mail about losing a deal to Moody's because S&P was requiring higher credit support for a favorable rating. Over time, the government alleges, S&P stopped being so demanding. By 2006, one analyst was asking rhetorically: "Does company care about deal volume or sound credit standards?" Despite the unprecedented level of mortgage delinquencies, S&P failed to downgrade any of the mortgage-backed securities even when they consisted primarily of subprime mortgages.

Experts handicapping the suit disagree on its prospects. Writing in the *New York Times'* blog *Dealbook*, law professors Peter Henning and Steven Davidoff argue the government faces an "uphill battle" despite "the colorful e-mails." A few complaints by low-level employees will not be enough to prove intentional fraud, Henning and Davidoff suggest. In addition, the government will have trouble showing that investors relied on the ratings since prospectuses typically include boilerplate advice not to rely on them.

Disagreeing, former financial executive Richard Eskow argues in an op-ed in *Huffington Post* that the government makes out a "strong" case that S&P intentionally misled investors about its internal controls, methodology, and objectivity. Eskow, now a senior fellow with the liberal group Campaign for America's Future, also notes the irony that S&P, accustomed to bragging about the quality of its services, will be defending in part by saying, "We weren't crooked, just incompetent."

Whatever the outcome of the suit, Eskow argues that the credit rating agency system remains "broken" despite efforts by Congress to fix it. An amendment sponsored by Sen. Al Franken, the Minnesota Democrat, sought to eliminate the conflict of interest inherent in the system of issuer-paid ratings by having an independent board pick the agency to rate structured deals. The Securities and Exchange Commission, however, has failed to act on the issue. Despite its subprime performance in the past, the credit rating industry apparently has enough clout in Washington to bottle up any reforms that threaten its lucrative business.

S&P agreed in February 2015 to pay a $1.37 billion penalty to settle the government's suit. Two weeks earlier, the company agreed to pay $77 million to the Securities and Exchange Commission and two *states, Massachusetts and New York, to settle charges tied to its ratings of mortgage-backed securities.*

* * *

Insider trading has been illegal under federal law for 80 years, but the practice is hard to detect and, disturbingly, accepted by too many in the world of finance. I explored the issue when the government charged the multibillionaire Steven A. Cohen and his wildly successful hedge fund SAC Capital Advisors with using insider trading as the very heart of its investing strategies.

Rotting From the Top?

(Jost on Justice, July 29, 2013)

Nearly one-fourth of 250 finance industry professionals surveyed by a New York City law firm recently said they would likely engage in illegal insider trading to make $10 million if they could get away with it. It is not known whether billionaire hedge fund owner Steven A. Cohen was one of those questioned, but if he was — and if he answered honestly — then surely he was one of those willing to break the law for a good-sized profit.

Not only would Cohen trade on illegal inside information, but he actually did — often and at a substantial profit, according to the criminal indictment unsealed in federal court in Manhattan on Thursday [July 25] against his hedge fund, SAC Capital Advisors. The 41-page indictment depicts SAC Capital as an insider trading machine, whose outsize profits depended on "widespread solicitation and use of illegal inside information" and "an institutional indifference" to violations "on a scale without known precedent in the hedge fund industry."

Cohen himself was not indicted — he was identified only as "SAC Owner" — but the indictment puts him and his $15 billion fund in the government's crosshairs for the second time in a little over a week. The Securities and Exchange Commission (SEC) filed an administrative proceeding against Cohen on July 19, charging him with failing to investigate suspicious trading activity at SAC or to take steps to prevent illegal conduct.

Together, the government actions, if successful, could bar Cohen from managing investor funds and force SAC Capital to disgorge profits linked to illegal insider trading. SAC pleaded not guilty to the indictment on Friday; Cohen's attorneys have vowed to contest the administrative proceeding. In the meantime, however, some investors are reportedly voting with their wallets by withdrawing money from the fund.

Far from being the clueless head of a company rotting from the bottom, Cohen is depicted in the indictment as the rot at the very top. SAC Capital's hiring policies, trading operations, compliance systems, and compensation practices combined to make insider trading a way of life at the fund, according to the indictment.

To start, SAC sought to hire portfolio managers and research analysts "with proven access to public company contacts likely to possess inside information." One new hire came with the recommendation that he had a house share with the chief financial officer of a Fortune 500 company and was "tight with management." Richard Lee was hired at Cohen's insistence in April 2009, over the objections of SAC's legal department, despite information that he had been part of an "insider trading group" at the hedge fund where he had been working. Lee pleaded guilty to federal conspiracy and securities fraud earlier last week [July 23].

Employees were "financially incentivized," according to the indictment, to recommend to Cohen "high conviction" trading ideas in which SAC would have an "edge" over other investors. As one example, research analyst Jon Horvath recommended selling Dell stock on Aug. 26, 2008, because of a "second hand read" from contacts inside the company about an upcoming unfavorable earnings report. Cohen liquidated his $12 million holding within 10 minutes after receiving the recommendation. Horvath pleaded guilty to conspiracy and securities fraud in connection with Dell trades in September.

In another example, Cohen liquidated $700 million in holdings in two drug companies, Elan and Wyeth, on July 20, 2008, after health care analyst Matthew Martoma passed along inside information about the soon-to-be-announced negative results of clinical trials of a new drug. By selling and shorting the stock, Cohen realized $276 million in profits or avoided losses. Martoma was indicted in December in connection with the trades. Cohen allegedly knew Martoma was paying a doctor involved in the drug trials for the tips.

SAC's compliance systems reflected what the indictment calls "a lack of commitment" to address the insider trading issues. The indictment notes that up until 2009 the compliance department did not do keyword searches of employees' e-mails for terms suggestive of insider trading. In the only insider trading violation uncovered internally, two portfolio managers were found to have used inside information to trade on a health company stock in July 2009. They were fined, but allowed to keep their jobs; no report was made to regulatory authorities.

Cohen and SAC Capital are Exhibit Number One of the ethics gap in the financial services industry identified by the survey released in mid-July by the law firm of Labaton Sucharow, which specializes in representing plaintiffs and whistleblowers in securities fraud litigation. More than half of the financial industry professionals surveyed — 52 percent — thought their competitors probably engaged in unethical or illegal behavior. Nearly one-fourth — 24 percent — thought some of their co-workers had done so. Substantial numbers viewed compensation systems as encouraging unethical conduct (26 percent) and top officials as likely to turn a blind eye to improper conduct by a "top performer" (17 percent).

Back in baseball's steroid era, true fans knew the home run records were too good to be true. Financial experts know that some of the returns posted by hedge funds and individual investors are similarly too good to be true. Baseball can at least claim to be trying to clean house; the government's moves against SAC are one step in cleaning up the ethical rot on Wall Street.

SAC Capital pleaded guilty in November 2013 to criminal fraud charges for allowing, if not encouraging, insider trading; the fund was required to pay a record $1.8 billion fine. Eight of the hedge fund's employees were convicted of insider trading; some received prison sentences. Cohen has not been charged criminally; he faces civil charges for allegedly failing to prevent insider trading, but denies the allegations.

#Epilogue

Having come of age in the South during the civil rights revolution, I had a natural interest in the analogous struggle for racial equality in South Africa during the apartheid era. As editor of The Los Angeles Daily Journal, *I created an assignment for myself: three weeks in South Africa in January 1986 to report on the country's legal system and the anti-apartheid challenges to it. In my final column after the visit, I noted that the law can be used either to protect liberty, as in the United States, or to extinguish it, as in South Africa. I rejoiced when Nelson Mandela was released from prison and was privileged to watch from the House of Representatives press gallery when he addressed the United States Congress in October 1994 as president of the Republic of South Africa. When Mandela died in December 2013, I reflected on his legacy: the rule of law as an instrument of freedom and equality.* Nkosi Sikelel' iAfrica.

The Liberating Rule of Law
(*Jost on Justice*, Dec. 8, 2013)

Nelson Mandela, who died last week [Dec. 5] at age 95, transformed not only the political landscape of his beloved country, but also its legal system. Under apartheid, law was an instrument of racist, rights-denying repression. Today, thanks in part to the law-trained Mandela, South Africa's constitution and its court system showcase the powerful role that law can play in protecting liberty and justice for all.

The system of racial separation and oppression known to the world by the Afrikaans term apartheid was erected only in mid-20th century.

Racial segregation and discrimination date from Dutch colonial times, yes, and were tightened piece by piece by the Union of South Africa in the first half of the 20th century. But the white supremacist National Party used law to erect a more thoroughgoing system after it came to power in 1948.

Over the next five years, South Africa's Parliament enacted piece by piece the legal pillars of "grand apartheid." The Population Registration Act of 1950 formalized racial classification and required race-designating identity cards for all adults. The Group Areas Act of 1950 allotted living areas by race. The Bantu Authorities Act of 1951 set the stage for the creation of the "bantustans" as phony homelands for black South Africans. Two years later, the Bantu Education Act established an unequal education system that aimed to consign blacks to lifetimes as laborers.

Along the way, Parliament forbade interracial marriages (1949) and interracial sexual relations (1950). And the Suppression of Communism Act of 1950 banned any political party that subscribed to communism, which was defined so broadly as to gag opposition to apartheid as disruptive to racial harmony.

Apartheid might have been turned back in infancy but for the National Party's success in disenfranchising multiracial "colored" voters, a foul deed accomplished despite the resistance of the country's highest court. (Blacks and Asians had no voting rights.) The Separate Representation of Voters Act of 1951 removed coloreds from the common voters roll in Cape Province, but four voters backed by the United Party challenged it in court.

The Appeal Court ruled the law invalid because Parliament had enacted it without the two-thirds majority required to change so-called "entrenched" clauses in the constitution. Parliament responded by enacting a law allowing it to overrule decisions of the Appeal Court. The Appeal Court ruled that measure invalid as well, but the National Party countered by increasing the court from five to 11 members and then packing it with pro-Nationalist judges. A temporarily enlarged Parliament re-enacted the law in 1956. Originally, coloreds were at least allotted four seats in Parliament, but those were abolished in 1969.

The courts were obliging instruments of repression for the next four decades — as exemplified by the famous Rivonia trial, where Mandela received his life prison sentence in 1965. Mandela's release in 1990 set the stage for his election four years later as the first president of the multiracial, democratic Republic of South Africa.

With the help of a panel of professional judges, Mandela chose the 11 members of the newly established Constitutional Court of South Africa. The court was predominantly white but with three blacks and one Asian, and the white judges included Arthur Chaskalson, Mandela's former lawyer, and other human rights veterans. As presiding judge, Chaskalson proclaimed the court's obedience not to Parliament but to the constitution. "For the first time, the constitution trumps Parliament," Chaskalson declared, according to the *Washington Post*'s account.

Not quite four months later, the Constitutional Court abolished the death penalty. The court declared in the ruling that capital punishment was inconsistent with the rights to life and dignity enshrined in the nation's new constitution, given the arbitrariness of its imposition and the risk of error and the lack of any proven deterrence.

Since that time, the Constitutional Court has continued to issue landmark, rights-expanding decisions. The court followed its capital punishment decision with a ruling in 2001 that barred extradition of suspects from South Africa to a country where they might be subject to the death penalty.

The court in 2000 ruled that the government must provide housing relief to people living in intolerable or crisis situations. Three years later, it ruled that rights to land under customary law must be recognized and that communities dispossessed of land owned under customary law are entitled to restitution.

Along with other protections in its Bill of Rights, South Africa's new constitution represented an important milestone for LGBT rights as the first national charter to prohibit discrimination on the basis of sexual orientation. The Constitutional Court gave that provision substance with its ruling in 2005 by recognizing marriage rights for same-sex couples; the court gave Parliament 12 months to enact legislation, stipulating that any law be "truly and manifestly respectful of the dignity of same-sex couples." Parliament passed conforming legislation in November 2006.

South Africa faces immense problems as it enters its third decade as a multiracial democracy: poverty, crime, and growing impatience among the black majority about persistent economic inequality. Yet Mandela's insistence on the rule of law appears to have survived more than a decade after he relinquished office, according to John Campbell, a senior fellow for Africa policy studies at the Council on Foreign Relations. Human rights are protected, he writes in a blog post, freedom of speech absolute — at least for now. "These are major democratic achievements," Campbell concludes, "and they owe much to Nelson Mandela's vision for his beloved country."

About the Author

Kenneth Jost has covered legal affairs as a reporter, editor, and columnist for more than 40 years. He is the author of the annual series *Supreme Court Yearbook*, the one-volume encyclopedia *Supreme Court A to Z*; and *The New York Times on the Supreme Court*, all published by CQ Press. He has been staff writer, associate editor, and contributor for *CQ Researcher*, CQ Press's award-winning weekly backgrounder on public policy issues. He was a member of the *CQ Researcher* team of writers that won the American Bar Association's Silver Gavel Award for reports on legal affairs.

Jost is a Phi Beta Kappa graduate of Harvard College, where he was news director of WHRB-FM, the student-operated radio station. He was principal anchor of WHRB's coverage of the student strike in 1969 and co-author of *The Harvard Strike*, published by Houghton-Mifflin. After college, he was a reporter and courts columnist for *The Nashville Tennessean*. He took a sabbatical from journalism to serve as chief legislative assistant to then-Rep. Al Gore, a college classmate and newsroom colleague from *The Tennessean*. While working on Capitol Hill, he attended Georgetown Law School and was elected editor in chief of the *Georgetown Law Journal*. He graduated summa cum laude in 1981 and now teaches media law at the school as an adjunct professor.

Jost served six years as editor of the *Los Angeles Daily* Journal, the nation's largest daily law newspaper, and returned to Washington in 1987. He first wrote for *CQ Researcher* in 1988 and has written more than 170 reports for *CQ Researcher* on various topics, including legal affairs, social policy, and international human rights. He is a member of the Society of Professional Journalists and the National Lesbian and Gay Journalists Association and a former president of NLGJA's Washington, D.C., chapter. His articles have appeared in *The New York Times* and *The Washington Post* and in the *ABA Journal* and other legal publications. He has appeared as an analyst on CNN, C-SPAN, Fox News, MSNBC, and various local radio and TV channels. He began writing the blog *Jost on Justice* in 2009. He posts on Facebook (KenJost) and Twitter (@jostonjustice). On Facebook, he lists his religion as "Baseball" and his political views as "Liberty and Justice for All." He lives in Washington, as do his two children: Nicole and Andrew (AJ).